1 & 2 SAMUEL

BELIEF

A Theological Commentary
on the Bible

GENERAL EDITORS

Amy Plantinga Pauw
William C. Placher[†]

1 & 2 SAMUEL

DAVID H. JENSEN

WJK WESTMINSTER
JOHN KNOX PRESS
LOUISVILLE · KENTUCKY

Book design by Drew Stevens
Cover design by Lisa Buckley
Cover illustration: © David Chapman/Design Pics/Corbis

Library of Congress Cataloging-in-Publication Data

Jensen, David Hadley, 1968-
  1 & 2 Samuel : a theological commentary on the Bible / David H. Jensen. -- 1st edition.
    pages cm. -- (Belief: a theological commentary on the Bible)
Includes bibliographical references and index.
ISBN 978-0-664-23249-8 (alk. paper)
1. Bible. Samuel--Commentaries. I. Title.
BS1325.53.J46 2015
222'.407--dc23

                                                                          2014049524

For Erik, Kirsten,
and their families

Contents

Publisher's Note

William C. Placher worked with Amy Plantinga Pauw as a general editor for this series until his untimely death in November 2008. Bill brought great energy and vision to the series, and was instrumental in defining and articulating its distinctive approach and in securing theologians to write for it. Bill's own commentary for the series was the last thing he wrote, and Westminster John Knox Press dedicates the entire series to his memory with affection and gratitude.

William C. Placher, LaFollette Distinguished Professor in Humanities at Wabash College, spent thirty-four years as one of Wabash College's most popular teachers. A summa cum laude graduate of Wabash in 1970, he earned his master's degree in philosophy in 1974 and his PhD in 1975, both from Yale University. In 2002 the American Academy of Religion honored him with the Excellence in Teaching Award. Placher was also the author of thirteen books, including *A History of Christian Theology, The Triune God, The Domestication of Transcendence, Jesus the Savior, Narratives of a Vulnerable God,* and *Unapologetic Theology.* He also edited the volume *Essentials of Christian Theology,* which was named as one of 2004's most outstanding books by both *The Christian Century* and *Christianity Today* magazines.

Series Introduction

Belief: A Theological Commentary on the Bible is a series from Westminster John Knox Press featuring biblical commentaries written by theologians. The writers of this series share Karl Barth's concern that, insofar as their usefulness to pastors goes, most modern commentaries are "no commentary at all, but merely the first step toward a commentary." Historical-critical approaches to Scripture rule out some readings and commend others, but such methods only begin to help theological reflection and the preaching of the Word. By themselves, they do not convey the powerful sense of God's merciful presence that calls Christians to repentance and praise; they do not bring the church fully forward in the life of discipleship. It is to such tasks that theologians are called.

For several generations, however, professional theologians in North America and Europe have not been writing commentaries on the Christian Scriptures. The specialization of professional disciplines and the expectations of theological academies about the kind of writing that theologians should do, as well as many of the directions in which contemporary theology itself has gone, have contributed to this dearth of theological commentaries. This is a relatively new phenomenon; until the last century or two, the church's great theologians also routinely saw themselves as biblical interpreters. The gap between the fields is a loss for both the church and the discipline of theology itself. By inviting forty contemporary theologians to wrestle deeply with particular texts of Scripture, the editors of this series hope not only to provide new theological resources for the church but also to encourage all theologians to pay more attention to Scripture and the life of the church in their writings.

We are grateful to the Louisville Institute, which provided funding for a consultation in June 2007. We invited theologians, pastors, and biblical scholars to join us in a conversation about what this series could contribute to the life of the church. The time was provocative and the results were rich. Much of the series' shape owes to the insights of these skilled and faithful interpreters, who sought to describe a way to write a commentary that served the theological needs of the church and its pastors with relevance, historical accuracy, and theological depth. The passion of these participants guided us in creating this series and lives on in the volumes.

As theologians, the authors will be interested much less in the matters of form, authorship, historical setting, social context, and philology—the very issues that are often of primary concern to critical biblical scholars. Instead, this series' authors will seek to explain the theological importance of the texts for the church today, using biblical scholarship as needed for such explication but without any attempt to cover all the topics of the usual modern biblical commentary. This thirty-six-volume series will provide passage-by-passage commentary on all the books of the Protestant biblical canon, with more extensive attention given to passages of particular theological significance.

The authors' chief dialogue will be with the church's creeds, practices, and hymns; with the history of faithful interpretation and use of the Scriptures; with the categories and concepts of theology; and with contemporary culture in both "high" and popular forms. Each volume will begin with a discussion of *why* the church needs this book and why we need it *now*, in order to ground all of the commentary in contemporary relevance. Throughout each volume, text boxes will highlight the voices of ancient and modern interpreters from the global communities of faith, and occasional essays will allow deeper reflection on the key theological concepts of these biblical books.

The authors of this commentary series are theologians of the church who embrace a variety of confessional and theological perspectives. The group of authors assembled for this series represents

more diversity of race, ethnicity, and gender than any other commentary series. They approach the larger Christian tradition with a
critical respect, seeking to reclaim its riches and at the same time to
acknowledge its shortcomings. The authors also aim to make available to readers a wide range of contemporary theological voices
from many parts of the world. While it does recover an older genre
of writing, this series is not an attempt to retrieve some idealized
past. These commentaries have learned from tradition, but they are
most importantly commentaries for today. The authors share the
conviction that their work will be more contemporary, more faithful, and more radical, to the extent that it is more biblical, honestly
wrestling with the texts of the Scriptures.

William C. Placher
Amy Plantinga Pauw

Acknowledgments

The stories of 1 and 2 Samuel are filled with unforgettable characters. I cannot write about them without remembering and giving
thanks to the many people who have made my work on this commentary possible. My colleagues at Austin Presbyterian Theological
Seminary and the board of trustees have consistently supported my
research and approved the sabbatical leave that made this book finally
come to light. Friends in the Workgroup on Constructive Christian
Theology provide thoughtful theological conversation every year
in the spring. Members of First Presbyterian Church, Georgetown,
Texas, offered lively questions as I presented some of the material
contained in these pages. Alison Riemersma provided superb proof-
reading and helped me with many technical issues. Because many
of the stories in 1 and 2 Samuel focus on family dynamics, I have
continually had in mind the family members that nurture me: Molly,
Grace, and Finn Jensen, who share their daily lives with me; my parents, John and Gretchen Jensen (though Dad's life was ending as this
book was being completed, our family feels his presence even now);
and my siblings, Erik Jensen and Kirsten Bassion and their growing
families. As of this date, they include Megan, Emma, Jakob, Todd,
Siri, and Emily. But above all, I owe thanks to Molly. She makes
being a part of this family a joy.

Introduction:
Why Samuel? Why Now?

First and Second Samuel describe the emergence of monarchy in ancient Israel by focusing on three human characters: the transitional figure of Samuel, a prophet and priest who is Israel's last judge; Saul, Israel's first king, who is beset by tragedy; and David, who succeeds Saul as God's anointed. These books form part of a larger body of literature, often referred to as the Deuteronomistic History, which portrays the corporate life of Israel from the settlement of Canaan to the Babylonian exile. The episodes in 1 and 2 Samuel are striking in their depiction of human characters—priests, soldiers, kings, prophets, and royal advisors—but also significant in how they narrate the central character of this history, the God of Israel. History, in these books, is not simply an accounting of royal intrigue, military battles, and socioeconomic struggle, but also the stage on which God reveals God's very self. First and Second Samuel relay some of the most memorable vignettes in all of Scripture—the call of Samuel, David's battle with Goliath, and David's seizure of Bathsheba as his wife—and discover in them the hand of God.

Why read these stories? A casual glance at them indicates that they are not "objective" history (if there ever has been such a thing), since they clearly favor David. If history is simply the witness of the victors, perhaps these volumes contain royal propaganda burnished by David's partisans. Furthermore, many—if not most—of the events that Samuel narrates probably did not happen in the way that the authors describe, and some events may have not occurred at all. Bias toward David and exaggeration of historical detail, no doubt, saturate these pages. If we read 1 and 2 Samuel chiefly as textbooks of ancient history, we will emerge disappointed.

Another way of considering these stories is that they relate legends distant from our own time and somewhat irrelevant to modern concerns: kingship is hardly a model of government for the twenty-first century; patriarchy pervades many of these stories; and abhorrent violence occurs over and again. These stories, on first glance, may seem to perpetuate many of the old oppressions that most modern readers long to overcome.

Yet as we read them, even these aeons hence, these stories captivate, entice, and challenge us. Many of the stories are unforgettable; many are exquisitely crafted in terms of plot and narrative suspense. The characters that populate the drama of Samuel's pages have become characters not only of Western culture, but throughout the world. King David has entered our collective lives all these centuries subsequent to his reign. Simply put, these are stories that have grabbed us and will not let us go. Why read Samuel? At the risk of oversimplifying, I would suggest that we ought to read Samuel for at least three reasons: Samuel narrates (1) the complexities of the human person, (2) the ambiguities of our social arrangements as nations, and (3) God's agency in a conflicted world. *Personhood, politics,* and *theology* occupy much of Samuel's time, and they ought to occupy ours as well.

Personhood

What does it mean to be human? To whom do we owe allegiance? Where do we belong? How do we account for the beauty and the tragedy, the healing and violence, the good and the ill, of human life? These are questions that human beings have been asking for millennia and Samuel asks them as well. Our technological age has several ways of addressing these questions. Thanks to scientific advances, we have uncovered the biological rhythms of human life, the deep-seeded drives that make our species survive. Psychological research, moreover, has revealed that the human person is not always a rational creature, but possessed by passions that express our longing for belonging and acceptance by others. There are also economic accounts of the human person that stress production and possession. The natural sciences teach us that we are what we eat; the psychological, that we are what we desire; the economic, that we are what we produce and consume. But beneath all of these explanations of the person, we also remain a mystery: full of contradiction, surprising in our capacity to forgive and hold grudges, crafters of beauty and ugliness in the world; capable of agency but also beset and moved by forces larger than ourselves. Samuel is aware of all of this and is quite attentive to the mystery of the human person. In an era that is sometimes prone to reducing the person to specific features—economic, sexual, biological, social—Samuel's voice is sorely needed. Through a remarkable series of characters, readers glimpse the broad range of the promise and peril of what it means to be human in light of God.

Samuel talks about the human person formed by family. On one level the chapters in these books are a series of family stories. Ours is an age that recognizes some of the importance of family, with "family values" heralded on the right and the left. But one tendency in North America is to romanticize family ties, to construe the bonds of hearth and home as a refuge and a place of nurture in a hostile world. By contrast, Samuel's depiction of family is devoid of sentimentality or romanticism. No model family exists in its pages. Instead, what readers find are rivalry, betrayal, and jealousy, as well as fidelity and loyalty within multiple families. Samuel recognizes that families form us, for good *and* for ill. In these pages are arguments between husband and wife, disagreements and rebellion between parent and child, as well as parental longings for children that are ultimately fulfilled. The families of 1 and 2 Samuel are marked by bonds of fidelity and scarred by the deepest betrayals. They are families that are very much like our own. Even when these families seem unfamiliar, we read their stories to gain a better understanding of what it means to be formed by family. But perhaps most significantly in our time, Samuel's vision of family is more expansive than the vision of many proponents of family values in our time. Unlike the relatively contained nuclear families of modern postindustrial societies, Samuel's family embraces multiple generations, related by blood and friendship, and reflects larger orderings of kin and tribe. Family, for Samuel, makes sense not in isolation from other societal groupings but in relation to them.

Samuel also considers the person to be formed by bonds of friendship and loyalty. Throughout these books, people make pledges to one another: to be with, to remember, to love. For Samuel, the promises we establish make us the persons we are. In these promises readers glimpse both the height of human character and the depth of misery. For these promises are sites of betrayal *and* beauty. Perhaps the most vivid example of a promise in these books is the covenant between David and Jonathan. The bonds of their particular friendship sink deeper than the ties of family. Theirs is a striking friendship, pledged in secret but resulting in distinctly public actions: Jonathan's eventual rejection of his father's kingship and David's subsequent protection of Jonathan's family. To be a person, in this vision, is to be bound up with others. In an age such as ours that often celebrates autonomy and freeing ourselves from ties, the person in Samuel's vision is marked by the claims of others and the claims that one makes for others.

Much in these pages celebrates the wonders and accomplishments of its human characters: military triumph, courageous acts of leadership, pledges of faithfulness, keen prophetic insight, a reverence for ancient traditions. But Samuel's read of the person is hardly an unvarnished celebration of the human. His vision is also attuned to the tragedy of humanity, a tragedy that we often bring on ourselves. The human person, in these pages, is capable of tremendous beauty but just as often is the agent of harm, violence, and evil. We see humanity at its best and at its worst on these pages. Samuel does not explain evil away by resorting to a formulaic theodicy (an account of evil in light of God's goodness); Samuel tells stories of horror and betrayal and lets the narration do the talking. Samuel, in other words, considers the person as an agent of sin, beset by sin. Even the person who is God's chosen, David, is not exempt from this disturbing pattern. Indeed, in some regards, he is the prime exemplar of it. For David commits the most infamous sin in the entire trajectory of events: his seizure of Bathsheba that leads to the murder of her innocent husband, Uriah. Samuel narrates the depths of human nefariousness as part of the human experience and suggests in the telling of these stories that there is another way, a way of faithfulness and keeping the commandments. To live as one bound by the commandments of God, yet prone to breaking them, is part of what it means to be human in Samuel's world.

Politics

Those of us who live in the United States inhabit a world where nation claims ultimate loyalty and the defense of the nation claims an ultimate priority. These are the days of the Patriot Act, wiretapping for the sake of safety, border fences for the sake of protection, drone attacks for the sake of combatting terrorism. These are also the days of multiple wars and an all-encompassing war on terror that seems to have no end. These are the days of a strong nation, despite recent economic turmoil, that is forceful in its displays of power. It is illustrative in our day to read Samuel since it narrates Israel as it grows in power. On these pages, Israel transitions from a somewhat loose gathering of tribes routinely routed by other nations (such as the Philistines) into a more centralized nation headed by a king who expands the nation's territory and deals with its external threats. Though this change can be easily exaggerated, Israel's status as a nation in relation to its neighbors does shift in these pages: it appears to grow richer and more powerful and bears the consequences—for good and for ill—of those changes. Israel longs for a king on these pages and eventually gets one. But in its desire to be "like the nations" Israel also succumbs to pitfalls that come as a result of its increasing power. If Israel becomes a nation to be reckoned with, it must also reckon with itself and the tragedies that its own national aspirations gestate.

One of the ways Samuel attends to the ambiguity of the nation is by calling attention to the violence of the state. Battles permeate these pages: some of them necessary, some of them defensive, others aggressive and seemingly unnecessary. The nation, or the emerging nation and its leadership, is involved in all of these acts of violence. The king that Israel longs for has to resort to slaughter, propping himself up by violence. In the power struggles that Samuel narrates, we catch glimpses of a *Realpolitik* designed by cold and often calculating men. We see the state sacrificing people in the name of national interest and sometimes incurring divine judgment as a result. If the means of violence have changed dramatically since Samuel's time (with chemical and nuclear weaponry replacing shields, swords, and spears), then the temptations to violence and the use of violence by the state have changed rather little. Because Samuel describes this violence so realistically, his words might enable us to understand (and even resist) violence in our time, especially when the state tells us that violence is good.

Samuel narrates intrigues among the powerful: kings and would-be kings, military commanders and insurrectionist leaders, wealthy landowners and powerful priests. Much of the Israelites' lives can be understood as we consider their struggles, as Samuel—like many other writers of history—devotes ample words to the affairs of the powerful. Yet amid palace intrigue and military tactics emerges another way of telling the story: from the perspective of the outsider. Samuel attends, from time to time, to those who bear the consequences of state violence and the shenanigans of the powerful. In Samuel's narrative, the outsider often introduces a critical shift in events. For example, David begins as an outsider, overlooked by everyone except God. But as David grows to "insider" status, we meet others outside the corridors of power who change the course of history. In the midst of all these stories about the mighty, readers sense God's preference for those on the margins: those without land, those without reins of authority. Most readers discern in these books a skeptical stance toward stately power, particularly regarding the monarchy. If kingship is a boon to Israel's aspirations to become "like the nations," it also results in inattention to its covenant with God and to those on the margins of society. Persons in the United States have to read stories like this. In a day that celebrates the triumphs of the nation and our increasing wealth, we have become increasingly ill-equipped to address those who have fallen through prosperity's cracks. Disparity between the wealthiest and the poorest in American society now rivals the disparities of the robber-baron era of the 1920s.

While the wealthiest are able to command the best medical care in the world, one-third of children in the state of Texas do not have health insurance and often do not receive basic preventative care. The values of a nation—in Samuel's time as well as ours—are often revealed in the faces of those on the margins, far from the palace in Jerusalem or 1600 Pennsylvania Avenue.

In light of political struggle, military violence, and the status of insider and outsider, Samuel also asks questions about the nature of leadership. In some respects, the books are fixated on leadership. The entire trajectory of the two books concerns the quest for an appropriate leader: emerging first in Samuel's combination of priestly and prophetic gifts, succeeded by Saul's military prowess, and eventually consolidated in David's charisma, statesmanship, and valor. Ours is also an era that is fascinated and in some ways obsessed by leaders: we want to know about their personal lives; when they fail to conform to our expectations, they fall rapidly from grace. We rally around leaders who profess to have the elixir for what ails us. Sometimes they make good on promises, but other times they let us down. Leadership furthermore seems as much about personal ambition as it is about national good.

What makes a good leader? Samuel does not offer an easy answer to that question but instead shows us a spectrum of different leaders. No ideal leader exists on these pages; rather, Israel lives and learns from the experience of its various leaders and experiences good and ill from God's chosen leader, David. The character of leadership on these pages is somewhat of a mystery, for some of the leaders with nobly good intentions fail, while others whose personal failings are great retain God's anointing and blessing despite their foibles. One mark of good leadership, however, is the ability of leaders to look beyond themselves: to the well-being of others and to the claims of God on them. In an age where leaders often seem preoccupied with personal ambition and reelection and where many of us fall captive to sound bites from would-be leaders, these are words that our society desperately needs to hear. Samuel lays bare the struggles of a nation, its leaders, and how those struggles affect the life of peoples—insiders and outsiders—who are bound by God's claim on them.

Theology

The human characters in Samuel are unforgettable. But the character who is most central to its narrative cadence is YHWH, the God of Israel. As battles rage on, as kings jockey for power, as prophets speak God's word, it is YHWH who gives armies their power (or not), who anoints leaders (or takes away God's blessing), and who inspires prophets. The God of Israel is the agent of history, and God is intimately involved with the affairs of God's people. This is not a God who sets the wheels of history in motion and lets go, but a God who immerses God's self in history, for the sake of God's people.

It has become somewhat problematic in our time to talk about God's agency in history. Massive horrors of the twentieth and twenty-first centuries make God's goodness and power somewhat questionable, to say the least. (How is God present—or not—in the midst of Auschwitz, Hiroshima, and Darfur?) Many of us operate with a God-of-the-gaps understanding of divine presence in history. Most things can be described by natural laws, human agency, and otherwise predictable patterns. Human beings caused Darfur and Auschwitz; military planners orchestrated Hiroshima; natural forces spawned the Asian tsunami. Invoking God's presence in these catastrophes can seem problematic or even blasphemous. The massive suffering of the last century makes talk of God's agency problematic, while scientific investigation can render divine presence irrelevant.

Our problem when we read Samuel is that many of us construe divine agency and human agency in inverse proportion: the more God is the agent or cause of something, the less we human beings are responsible for it. Some of the more extreme interpretations of God's sovereignty during the history of the church have suggested this: God is "in charge," and it is our responsibility to "let go." More God, less me. We are merely puppets on divine strings, carrying out what has already been determined in the divine mind. Thus, while many in our society struggle with the very notion of divine agency, others of a more "religious" bent discern God's hand everywhere as one that controls our every action.

Samuel suggests something different from a modern scientism that has little room for divine agency and an all-controlling religious sensibility that leaves no room for human freedom. For Samuel, it is not a matter of "all God" and "no us." Rather, God's agency animates and sustains human freedom. In Samuel, God works *through* people: fragile, fallible, and misguided people who are also capable of initiating healing, hope, and transformation. God chooses what is fragile and imperfect to accomplish God's purposes in history. In other words, God chooses us. This God does not so much act on the affairs of the world as much as in and through those affairs. This is why, in Samuel, God rarely acts *directly* in the course of human events. Instead, God inspires, moves, and blesses people who in turn act, bless, and move in the world. If God is the chief actor in history, this does not deprecate our role in it. Indeed, God's action is often hidden in 1 and 2 Samuel: far more attention is devoted to human affairs than the direct hand of God. In Samuel, God acts in history while humans are also responsible for their own actions in history.

Samuel often expresses this confluence of divine and human agency in spirit-language. God sends God's spirit to leaders and prophets, sometimes in unpredictable and unexpected ways. This spirit even terrifies and torments, as we learn from the example of Saul. On the pages of Samuel's narrative, readers catch glimpses of a divine spirit that moves and sustains the human spirit but also shakes and confounds persons to their core. However, wherever spirit hovers, it operates not by coercion but through inspiration and disruption. Israel's God, who is spirit, enters into human history and assumes all the risks that relationships with a particular people entail. The God who inspires is a God who will not let go of those God has chosen, even when those people become oblivious to the spirit's action among them.

This is why Samuel is also occupied with themes of fidelity: God's call on people and claim of them and the obligations this call entails. The God who enters into history and is the driving force of history is a God who makes promises to ordinary people, promises that make ordinary affairs and people extraordinary. God calls a child, Samuel, to be prophet to a nation. God chooses a somewhat ragtag tribe, Israel, to be a light to the nations. God chooses a shepherd, David, to become the king of a nation. In calling and choosing, God makes special pledges to a people, some of them rather remarkable.

One of these is the stunning claim that God will establish the throne of David's kingdom "forever" (2 Sam. 7:13). The God of history is a promise maker who will not forsake promises and people, even when the people fail. But perhaps most importantly, the God who emerges on these pages is also a God of mystery, not subject to human manipulation, whose ways are not always abundantly clear or discernible but whose presence in the midst of history is assured as promises are made and renewed.

Authorship

The broad consensus of most biblical scholars is that 1 and 2 Samuel come to us in their present form by the editorial hand of the Deuteronomist, often referred to as "D." This author/editor (or school of author/editors) composed and edited the span of Old Testament books from Deuteronomy through 2 Kings, which took its final form after Israel's return from the Babylonian exile (sixth century B.C.E.). The period of time surveyed in this history is substantial, from the journey into the promised land to exile in Babylon. The sheer span of this history means that D's editorial hand plays a significant role in the biblical interpretation of Israel's history. Because many of the narratives in 1 and 2 Samuel antedate D by centuries, most scholars assume that D combined several earlier traditions into their present form. The result is a combination of early traditions under the guidance of a masterful editor.

The Deuteronomistic view of history and Israel's destiny might best be captured in these words: "See, I am setting before you today a blessing and a curse: the blessing, if you obey the commandments of the LORD your God that I am commanding you today; and the curse, if you do not obey the commandments of the LORD your God, but turn from the way I am commanding you today, to follow other gods that you have not known" (Deut. 11:26–28). God sets before Israel a promise to be with God's people. Israel will flourish if the people keep the commandments and heed God's promises; if Israel refuses to keep the commandments and forsakes God's promises, it will experience desolation. Thus, the events of Israel's history make sense in light of its own faithfulness and failure in relation to the commandments and divine promise.

Sometimes this view of history is caricatured, then as well as now, as if every blessing is the result of personal faithfulness, as if all favor is somehow "earned" and every calamity the result of sin. Our time is full of proclamations such as this, such as Pat Robertson's claim that the 2010 Haitian earthquake was the result of a "pact with the devil" sealed long ago by the nation's founders and Jerry Falwell's remark in the midst of the U.S. AIDS epidemic that the disease was a "gay plague." But glib claims such as this actually bear little resemblance to Samuel's view of history. Samuel's narration of history does not establish every single event as the result of a particular action (or inaction) of human beings—which inevitably places us at the center of history—but senses God's guidance as the Lord of history. Samuel takes a "big picture" view of God's involvement in the affairs of humanity, where even small events are mysteriously related to God's purposes. But as the Deuteronomist proclaims God as Lord of history, the pages of 1 and 2 Samuel also reveal struggles and tensions in this interpretation of history, provoking our own questions. As Marti Steussy asks, "If you interpret everything that happens as a direct reflection of divine will, what kind of God will you end up with? A God who is not particularly loving or lovable and who is not a champion of the oppressed."[1]

These pages do not promise unambiguous rewards for all who are faithful or unmitigated suffering for those who are unfaithful. In these pages noble intent is sometimes met with ignominy. History does not proceed on these pages via preset formulas. History is complex and conflicted; God's involvement in history is often hidden from view. But at all times Israel is called to the God who establishes a people with a promise. If the consequences of that promise are sometimes elusive, the promise abides throughout history. This promise and God's presence within it call modern readers to be participants in the making of history as well. For that reason, and many more, we ought to read Samuel again and again.

1. Marti J. Steussy, *Samuel and His God* (Columbia, SC: The University of South Carolina Press, 2010), 101.

1 SAMUEL

1 Samuel 1:1–7:17

Great Expectations: Samuel and the Ark

The stories begin with a series of expectations: for a child, for a great nation, for God's blessing. They begin with one of the most common desires of people across cultures and times—longings for a child to call one's own. Hannah's prayer is as old as the human race, uttered countless times each year: "Please, O God, send me a child." A child's birth, whether experienced as an answer to a prayer or as a surprise, often signals hope. In 1 and 2 Samuel children sometimes appear in pivotal roles or as agents who shift the course of the story. First Samuel begins with a seemingly personal story that has vast national implications: one woman's longing for a child results in the upending of history and status, clarifying what it means to be a nation in covenant with God. The beginnings of this story combine the personal, the political, and the theological, themes that are echoed throughout the episodes that follow.

These opening chapters also focus on the question of what it means to hear the command and call of God. How does one discern God's call amid the surrounding din? In these first pages a boy named Samuel hears a call that is not immediately discernible. His call, like Hannah's hope, is not focused chiefly on himself. Most visions of calling these days tend to focus on the individual: "Am *I* really hearing God?" "What am *I* to do with my life?" Though such questions of individual agency are not foreign to the Deuteronomist, they represent a truncated version of Samuel's call, a call that also concerns the life of Israel. The nation, in this sense, is also a response to God's call.

These stories also deal with piety and religiosity. In them we find people at prayer and in praise, trusting in God and relying on God's favor. Readers glimpse some of the religious practices of ancient Israel, particularly in relation to the ark. The narratives surrounding the ark are perhaps the most difficult for contemporary readers to understand. At first glance, these narratives evoke a primitive religion that has little in common with more "advanced" societies. They seem primitive because they give so much credence to holy objects: the ark is a holy thing that may not be touched or handled indiscriminately. Israel reveres the ark because of its power, a power that stems from the living God of Israel. To lose the ark is to risk courting with disaster, a fate that Israel experiences when the Philistines capture the ark in battle. But these narratives reveal more than primitive fetishism; they vividly express how the living God comes near to humanity. They express how the God of Israel, the God of the universe, makes a home among mortals and sinks an anchor amid human things. These stories demonstrate how a people at prayer, in lament, and in praise come into contact with the living God through ordinary, tangible things. This is not religious primitivism but the heart of an incarnational faith.

1:1–8

Haves and Have-nots

Monarchy emerges in Israel with a seemingly personal story, as the Deuteronomist introduces readers to a family and rivals within it. Elkanah is the patriarch, the one who in ancient society exercises the most power, but in this story Hannah exhibits the greatest agency. The one who ought to be content with her lot decides that she is not. Her story, in many respects, is a story between haves and have-nots: between a wife who has children and a wife who does not, between a man with patriarchal authority and women with none, between the mighty and the lowly. As the story progresses, however, the orders between the haves and have-nots get overturned.

The personal story that begins here soon becomes more than personal, as the birth of this long-awaited child, Samuel, catalyzes the longings of a nation.

The family is in many ways somewhat ordinary yet in other ways set apart. Elkanah has two wives, Peninnah (who has given birth to children) and Hannah (who has not). Bigamy, of course, was common during this period of Israel's history. Because he was able to support more than one wife, Elkanah's economic status was higher than abject poverty but probably lower than ostentatious wealth. His lineage, which stretches back to his great-grandfather, is a "sign of a noble and well-known family."[1] He comes, in other words, from a family with a name (vv. 1–2). The Deuteronomist suggests that he is from Ramathaim (referred to in the New Testament as Arimathea, cf. Mark 15:43). The Chronicler, however, lists him as a Levite (1 Chr. 6:26), the tribe that bears responsibility for the ark. This connection is important, because it situates Elkanah's acts of piety in a long line of actions related to Israel's central religious practice. The story begins with a somewhat ordinary family whose religious actions set them apart.

> The poor person is the one who has been converted to God and puts all his faith in him, and the rich person is one who has not been converted to God and puts his confidence in idols: money, power, material things.
>
> Oscar Romero, *A Shepherd's Diary*, trans. Irene Hodgson (Cincinnati: St. Anthony Messenger, 1996), 125.

Elkanah's family journeys to Shiloh to worship and make sacrifice. These are the days before there is a temple in Israel, before Jerusalem is claimed as an Israelite city. At this time, the sanctuary in Shiloh, according to most biblical scholars, was the most significant one for Israel's cultic practice. The family journeys to Shiloh, the highest holy place in the land, and performs their religious duty. The sacrificial portions, however, are a bit out of the norm. Elkanah gives portions to Peninnah and all her sons and daughters (vv. 3–4), but to Hannah he offers more. Is this favoritism? Compensation, perhaps, for Hannah's lack of children? The Deuteronomist's reason for this double portion is succinct: "because he loved her, though the LORD had closed her womb" (v. 5). The juxtaposition between a husband's love and God's action of closing a womb here is striking. On the one hand it is a direct expression of affection and a pledge

---

1. Hans Wilhelm Hertzberg, *I & II Samuel: A Commentary*, trans J. S. Bowden. (Philadelphia: Westminster Press, 1964), 22.

of faithfulness. Elkanah does not love Hannah because she supplies him with offspring but because Hannah is Hannah. This steadfast love, shown with a seemingly excessive portion, at first seems to contrast with God's closing of Hannah's womb. Whereas Elkanah loves Hannah and gives her more than enough, God withholds something from Hannah and closes her off.

The phrase "the LORD had closed her womb" raises a host of questions. For the Deuteronomist, God's activity is primary: beneath, behind, above, and beyond all human action. God is the source and author of events that unfold on the pages of history. But is God the author of *every* event and circumstance in the lives of people? All the tragedies and joys? Every birth and every death? Each instance of suffering and each occasion for celebration? The language in this passage is strong. God is the direct cause of Hannah's infertility. The vision of God's sovereignty is quite comprehensive: even the reproductive lives of Hannah and Elkanah are governed by God's action and rule. John Calvin, in an analogous manner, has a strong version of God's providence: "There is no erratic power, or action, or motion in creatures, but that they are governed by God's secret plan in such a way that nothing happens except what is knowingly and willingly decreed by him."[2] Sometimes in the wake of Calvin, well-meaning theologians have claimed that because God is sovereign, we must acquiesce to whatever hand we're dealt: sickness or health; wealth or poverty; suffering or happiness.

> **Nothing takes place without [God's] deliberation.**
>
> John Calvin, *Institutes* 1.16.3; ed. John T. McNeill, trans. Ford Lewis Battles (Philadelphia: Westminster, 1960), 1:200.

Because matters are out of our hands, we might as well resign ourselves to our lot and trust that God has the best intentions for us. There is, to be sure, much comfort in this sentiment, that "in life and in death we belong to God,"[3] that our lives are entrusted to the creator and ruler of the universe and that we are cared for by God and matter to God. But Hannah does not resign

---

2. John Calvin, *Institutes of the Christian Religion* 1.16.3, 1:201.
3. A Brief Statement of Faith—Presbyterian Church (U.S.A.), in *The Constitution of the Presbyterian Church (U.S.A.)*, Part I, *Book of Confessions* (Louisville, KY: Office of the General Assembly, Presbyterian Church (U.S.A.), 1996), 10.1.

herself to her lot; her sense of God's sovereignty involves a struggle, as she prays earnestly for a change in her life: the birth of a child. Trusting in God's sovereignty need not lead to resignation over the present; it may lead to actions that fervently attempt to change the course of history. People of faith are not remarkable for their acceptance of the status quo. That is the mark of a cynic. People of faith are remarkable for how they envision a different world, despite the signs and events of the times. Just like Hannah did.

The difference in status between Hannah and Peninnah reveals rivalry in the family. Hannah's barrenness causes her rival to provoke her. The one with much denigrates the one who has little. In a patriarchal world, a woman has status on the basis of her offspring, the legacy that she provides for her husband. Here is a glimpse of some of the insidious sides of oppression and imbalance of power: those who experience oppression can become agents of oppression themselves or hold within themselves festering wounds of the effects of sin. Many Korean American theologians have dubbed this dynamic "han," a Korean word that speaks to the experience of sin from the "underside." In Andrew Sung Park's words, *han* is *"frustrated hope, the collapsed feeling of pain, letting go, resentful bitterness,* and *the wounded heart."*[4] Sin has many faces and is experienced in many ways, both in those who commit actions that oppress others and those who internalize the effects of oppression.

But no one is immune from sin's grip. On these pages, we see rivalries for power and favor that lead to further denigration of the one who has little. In response to Peninnah's words, Hannah weeps and refuses to eat (vv. 6–7).

Elkanah's response to Hannah's predicament is both compassionate and obtuse. The one who gives Hannah a double portion also says to her that he is to be more to her than ten sons (v. 8). In effect, Elkanah disregards the typical

> Sin causes *han* and *han* procreates sin. Sin is of sinners; *han* is of the sinned-against. The sin of sinners may cause a chain reaction via the *han* of the sinned-against.
>
> Andrew Sung Park, "Sin," in Miguel A. De La Torre, ed., *Handbook of U.S. Theologies of Liberation* (St. Louis: Chalice, 2004), 115.

---

4. Andrew Sung Park, *The Wounded Heart of God: The Asian Concept of Han and the Christian Doctrine of Sin* (Nashville: Abingdon Press, 1993), 31, italics in original.

ways in which husbands of his time value their wives. He is bound to Hannah not on the basis of offspring but because of a promise he has made to her. By saying that he is more than ten sons to her, Elkanah seems also to be saying that Hannah is more than ten sons to him. Yet at the same time these words demonstrate a failure to understand the depth of Hannah's pain. As Johanna van Wijk-Bos notes, "They must have been the final straw for Hannah, for in the next breath she appeals for help to an authority higher than Elkanah or the local priests."[5]

1:9–18

A Prayer

Hannah regards the hand she is dealt and considers the words of her rival and her husband: Peninnah's words cause tears while Elkanah's words are intended to comfort. But Hannah takes their words and charts her own course, "gets on her feet and makes a move toward her liberation from the oppressive forces of culture and family."[6] No one encourages her to seek a change, but change is precisely what Hannah implores. She heeds the words of her husband by eating and drinking, but then she rises and presents herself "before the LORD" (v. 9) and prays with all her might. Many of the words of her prayer are not recorded, but at the prayer's core is a vow: that if God will "not forget" Hannah and give her a son, then she will set him before God as a servant, a nazirite, one set apart from society for a cultic purpose.

There are hundreds of prayers offered in Scripture: some in thanksgiving, others in confession, others in lament. Hannah's prayer, like some others, is a prayer of petition. What is the purpose of petitionary prayer? The great nineteenth-century Reformed theologian Friedrich Schleiermacher claimed that petitionary prayer is not a bargain we strike with God, asking God for something in exchange for something else. Such understandings are problematic

---

5. Johanna W. H. van Wijk-Bos, *Reading Samuel: A Literary and Theological Commentary* (Macon, GA: Smyth & Helwys Publishing, Inc., 2011), 27.
6. Ibid.

since they render God a cosmic ATM who bestows us with things if we only will ask for them (and if there are enough cash reserves!). We petition God not in order to get what we want but in order to make our petition more in line with God's will for our lives. The chief model for petitionary prayer, in Schleiermacher's reading, is Jesus' prayer in Gethsemane, as recorded in Matthew: "My Father, if it is possible, let this cup pass from me; yet not what I want but what you want" (26:39). As Jesus is facing impending death, he asks God initially for his life to be spared. In Schleiermacher's words, "He began with the definite wish that his sufferings might pass away from him; but as soon as he fixed his thought on his father in heaven to whom he prayed, this wish was at once qualified by the humble, 'if it be possible.'"[7] Jesus desires to live but places desire in the context of God's wider intent for Jesus' life. Jesus' posture in this earnest request is the model for our posture whenever we ask God something: "If our prayer has not the effect of moderating the wish that it expressed, of replacing the eager desire with quiet submission, the anxious expectation with devout calmness; then it was no true prayer, and gives sure proof that we are not yet at all capable of this real kind of prayer."[8] Petitionary prayer, in this view, does not change *God's* action toward us but changes *our* posture in relation to God. We ask for something, but in the asking we find that what we ask is changed. There is much wisdom in Schleiermacher's sermon, particularly when we recognize that we often ask for the wrong things. In a consumer age where persons pray for victory on the football field, for financial success,[9] and for new cars, Schleiermacher's view of petitionary prayer is sorely needed. If our petitions are simply expressions of any and all desires, then prayer seems little more than selfish clamoring. Often our desires need to be modified to bring us into greater conformity with the way of Jesus.

But is this the case with *every* prayer of petition? Hannah's prayer

7. Friedrich Schleiermacher, "The Power of Prayer in Relation to Outward Circumstances," in Keith Clements, ed., *Friedrich Schleiermacher: Pioneer of Modern Theology* (Minneapolis: Fortress Press, 1991), 189.
8. Ibid., 192.
9. Rev. Dr. Leroy Thompson is renowned for his "Money Cometh to You" conferences, which promise that God can solve all financial difficulties for the faithful. At a recent conference, participants prayed with open hands: "Money! Cometh to me now!" See Michael Brendan Dougherty, "Man of the (Fine) Cloth," *New York Times Magazine*, July 31, 2011, 14.

does not modify its desire but increases the intensity of her desire. She prays fervently and silently, with lips moving. The priest Eli thinks that she is drunk, and embarrassed for her, tells her to quit making a spectacle of herself (vv. 12–14). In her defense, Hannah clarifies that she has been praying the entire time, speaking out of "great anxiety and vexation" (v. 16). Hannah's prayer of petition is different from Schleiermacher's ideal. Sometimes our desires do not subside, but intensify as we seek to follow God. The pious heart is not simply a placid one; often it is restless. At the beginning of St. Augustine's spiritual autobiography are these memorable words: "Our hearts find no peace until they rest in you."[10] This rest may not occur until the end of our days; in the meantime we desire, have desires modified, and experience the growth of desire. Our desires may even cause us to cry out to God for a change, just like Hannah.

Hannah makes a promise. Many of the promises in the Old Testament depict God as the originator of a promise: God pledges faithfulness to Israel and asks of Israel something in return: to keep the commandments God has given. But in this opening chapter, a person makes a promise to God. Hannah's prayer reminds us that one of the marks of personhood is our capacity for making and breaking promises. We are who we are, in part, because of the pledges that we make to one another and to God. Hannah's prayer is not so much a "bargain" struck with God, a tit-for-tat kind of exchange. Rather, it marks her profound sense of belonging: that she belongs—just as any hoped-for offspring—to the God who makes promises to Israel. Hannah's prayer is a reminder—uttered to God and to the reader—that the God of Israel remains true to promises. Hannah nudges God to be true to God's promise by looking with favor on

> **Prayer is an offering up of our desires unto God, in the name of Christ, by the help of his Spirit, with confession of our sins, and thankful acknowledgment of his mercies.**
>
> The Larger Catechism of the Westminster Confession, 7.288, in *The Constitution of the Presbyterian Church (U.S.A.)*, Part I, *Book of Confessions* (Louisville, KY: Office of the General Assembly, Presbyterian Church (U.S.A.), 1996), 7.288.

10. Augustine, *Confessions*, trans. R. S. Pine-Coffin. (New York: Penguin Books, 1961), 21.

her. She begins a dialogue and refuses to accept the conventional wisdom (given by her husband and perhaps Eli) that she should be content with her lot. God's promises, for her, mean something more than the status quo.

Eli, at least in part, recognizes the import of Hannah's prayer, as he tells her, "Go in peace; the God of Israel grant the petition you have made to him" (v. 17), whereupon Hannah's sadness evaporates and she regains her desire to eat and drink (v. 18). Her desires have all been spoken.[11]

1:19–28

An Answer to Prayer

Hannah, Elkanah, and the others rise in the morning, worship, and return home. In due course, Hannah's prayer is answered with the birth of a son, Samuel (vv. 19–20). His name is significant, meaning "name of God." In a subtle word play, Hannah's explanation of the name (and it is she who names her son, not Elkanah) is "He who is from God." Hence, both the name of God and Samuel's presence as one sent by God are bound together. Hannah has asked, and she has received. But the birth of her son also foreshadows the conflicted dynamics between parents and sons throughout the pages that follow (Eli and his sons; Saul and Jonathan; David and Absalom). Barbara Green writes, "Sons are a solution, but they are also the problem."[12] As Hannah gives away her own son, other sons that follow will take from their parents.

Hannah returns to Shiloh after Samuel is weaned. We do not know the exact duration of time, but the child is obviously still young (vv. 22–23). At Shiloh, Samuel is "given to the Lord" (v. 28), a further wordplay on Samuel's name. The one whose name evokes

---

11. Robert Polzin has claimed that the actions of Elkanah, Hannah, and Eli "set up a profound contrast between the God-centered perspective of Elkanah, on the one hand, and the human-centered perspective of Hannah and Eli on the other." *Samuel and the Deuteronomist* (San Francisco: Harper & Row, 1989), 30. Even if this reading exaggerates the perspective of each character, this contrast occurs over and again in subsequent sections (particularly in relation to Saul and David).

12. Barbara Green, O.P., *King Saul's Asking* (Collegeville, MN: Liturgical Press, 2003), 15.

God's name and is given by God is eventually given to God by his mother. Hannah, who at the beginning of the story has no child, receives a child only to give him away. The dynamic here is suggestive: receiving answers to prayer does not mean that one clutches what one receives as an answer, holding on to the precious gift at all costs. Rather, as one who has received a gift, Hannah is equipped to give in return. Hannah enacts and becomes a participant in the dynamics of divine giving. God does not give out of an assumption of scarcity: so that some have more while others have less. God gives so that all may participate in the abundance of life, an abundance that is approached and approximated when the receivers of gifts themselves become givers. Stephen Webb describes the divine economy of giving in this way: "We do not give in order to receive for ourselves but in order to give something back to God who gives. Our giving is not governed by the logic of compensation and return but by the desire to follow the essential dynamic of all gifts, which is to return them to their origin, in God, by giving them to others."[13] Hannah receives an answer to her prayer, the joy of the gift and the presence of the child's life, and then after a time she gives the child away to others. We should not underestimate the pain that Hannah's return gift entailed. What parent or caregiver of a child would not wince at "giving away" their child? But the Scriptures are filled with such instances. Indeed, the primary image for family in the Scriptures is not biological parentage but adoption (cf. Esth. 2:7; Rom. 8:14–17; Gal. 4:4–6; Eph. 1:5). Adoption is premised on one person giving a child to another. Hannah enacts the primary image for family in the Bible, giving her son to the Lord so that he might be adopted by God and raised by Eli. In the conclusion to this section there is interplay between giving and lending. "Therefore I have lent him to the LORD; as long as he lives, he is given to

> What is notable about Christianity . . . , what is unusual about it, is its attempt to institute a circulation of goods to be possessed by all in the same fullness of degree without diminution or loss.
>
> Kathryn Tanner, *Economy of Grace* (Minneapolis: Fortress, 205), 25.

13. Stephen H. Webb, *The Gifting God: A Trinitarian Ethics of Excess* (New York: Oxford University Press, 1996), 93.

the LORD" (v. 28). Gifts and lending are not diametrically opposed; rather, they are expressions of the divine economy that allows us, too, to become givers.

Hannah's prayer is answered as it equips her to become an agent of giving. The results of her prayer raise the obvious question of how prayer is answered and whether prayer is answered. Millions of prayers like Hannah's have been uttered across the ages. Many have been more fervent and countless prayers like it have gone unanswered, at least in the kind of resolution that Hannah experiences. Reflecting on these and other passages in Scripture where prospective parents pray for children, Jeanne Stevenson-Moessner writes, "There is not one woman recorded in either the Old or New Testament who, desirous of progeny, remained barren. There is not one model, mentor, or mother in Scripture with whom modern-day infertile woman can connect."[14] The Bible does not record the experience of women who pray but do not eventually give birth to a child. One of the unfortunate inferences often drawn in the history of the church is that God's answer to prayer is dependent on the degree of our faith or faithfulness. Such understandings can quickly become destructive and even demonic, where blessings and prosperity are the result of our purity of heart and where devastation, disease, and misfortune are the result of our sinfulness.

Schleiermacher's view of petitionary prayer provides a helpful counterpoint. For Hannah's prayer, in the end, does not lead to her clinging to the gift. The resolution of Hannah's prayer is not when she receives the gift of a child. Rather, it comes when she becomes a fuller participant in the dynamics of giving. Schleiermacher claims that petitionary prayer draws us closer to the posture of Christ, modifying our wishes so that we become more aligned with God's life, intent, and gift for the world. Prayer is not answered when we receive the thing that we ask for; prayer is answered when our prayers, by grace, lead us nearer to God. This is not something we can do on our own. It is possible, like in Hannah's case, only through the witness of others and the grace of God. Hannah's prayer finds its resolution in the hymn of praise she offers as she gives her son away.

14. Jeanne Stevenson-Moessner, *The Spirit of Adoption: At Home in God's Family* (Louisville, KY: Westminster John Knox Press, 2003), 23.

2:1–10

Hannah's Song

Hannah's song distills prominent themes that occur throughout 1–2 Samuel. Most scholars claim that it existed independently of the Hannah story, as a hymn or poem of thanksgiving perhaps used in worship or in settings where Israel remembered its history and covenant with the Lord. It stands out, like the Magnificat of Luke 1, as one woman's praise for God's mighty actions that are extended to those on the fringes of society, heralding the stunning reversals that occur whenever God's purposes are accomplished. God intervenes on behalf of the suffering and marginalized, breaking bonds that enslave, offering freedom to the oppressed. The prominence of texts such as these have led many African American theologians such as James Evans to conclude that the Bible is a text for outsiders: the Bible bears witness to God's liberation and is read most clearly by those who struggle for freedom.[15] As one who has experienced the gift of God and the new freedom that this gift has brought her, Hannah expresses these themes most vividly.

The hymn begins in exultation: Hannah is made strong "in my God" and she is able to look down on her enemies because of her victory (v. 1). This is not the gloating of a favored daughter. Rather, it is the legitimate experience of relief and newfound strength for one who has suffered extensively. The hymn points to a reckoning where those who have undergone oppression and those who have oppressed others come face to face, where oppressors are confronted by the humanity of the persons they oppressed. The nobodies become somebodies in Hannah's song.

The hymn contains memorable God-language. In the second stanza, we read, "There is no Holy One like the LORD, no one besides you; there is no Rock like our God" (v. 2). The images of Holy One and Rock stand out: they are not the most familiar terms for God in Scripture, but they do occur in other places (cf. Gen. 49:24; Deut. 32:4; Ps. 18:2; 89:18; Isa. 5:24). Hannah's lips convey expansive imagery for God, even in a patriarchal world. As Hannah names

---

15. See James H. Evans Jr., *We Have Been Believers: An African-American Systematic Theology* (Minneapolis: Fortress Press, 1992), 33–52.

God as Rock and Holy One, she expresses themes of God's activity that resound throughout the rest of 1 and 2 Samuel. First, the
God of Israel reverses the typical orders encountered in the world.
If the economy of wealth and prestige favors those with power and
means, God's hand is with those who suffer. Hannah claims that
the Lord "makes poor and makes rich" but that ultimately God will
uplift the downtrodden: "he lifts the needy from the ash heap, to
make them sit with princes and inherit a seat of honor" (v. 8). The
divine economy measures worth according to different criteria, by
sharing wealth rather than hoarding it. Hannah sings this topsy-
turvy theology at the beginnings of the story of monarchy in Israel,
but subsequent pages often reveal the reverse. In these stories, kings
figure much more prominently than the poor. As Steussy notes,
"When Lord does help underdogs, Lord is typically, as in the case
of Hannah's barrenness, responsible for the problems they face. . . .
The poor, in the books of Samuel, are most often casualties of Lord's
interactions with the elite."[16] Given these realities, we can rightly ask
whether Hannah's song is a faithful portrayal of God's actions or a
protest against them; a narration of God's involvement in history or
an ironic caricature of it; or perhaps a combination of all of these
themes.

Second, Hannah praises a God who attends to the details of
human life: "The LORD is a God of knowledge, and by him actions
are weighed" (v. 3). What happens on earth matters to the life of
God. God's guidance and providence, God's ability to make rich and
poor, lift up and bring low, does not mean that human actions are
irrelevant or inconsequential. God accounts for the actions of God's
people. This conviction is central to Deuteronomistic theology. If
Israel keeps the commandments, it will prosper and live well; if it
refuses its responsibilities and breaks covenant, it can expect loss.
Kings, prophets, priests, soldiers, and farmers are all bound by these
same promises. In many respects what happens in 1 and 2 Samuel is
the working out of this theology on a national scale.

Third, the God who weighs human behavior is a God in whom
there is life and death: "The LORD kills and brings to life; he brings

16. Marti J. Steussy, *Samuel and His God* (Columbia, SC: The University of South Carolina Press,
2010), 56.

down to Sheol and raises up" (v. 6). Sheol is a Hebrew expression for the realm of the dead; not a "hell," but a shadowy place that marks the end of earthly life. To choose God is to choose life; to turn from God is to choose death (cf. Deut. 30:19–20).

Finally, Hannah's song expresses confidence that God's purposes will be accomplished. Things often appear as if God has forgotten God's people. Hannah knows this well, as her longings for a child attest. But the Lord remains faithful to those who keep the commandments: "He will guard the feet of his faithful ones, but the wicked shall be cut off in darkness" (v. 9). Hannah concludes this song with an expression of hope in a king who is guided by God's wisdom and strength. Who is this one to come? Will the king be obedient to God's will? Is the people's longing for a king for Israel's benefit or not? What unfolds in the chapters that follow helps readers answer those questions. If Hannah's expression of praise is a model for Israel's praise, and if her expression of the way God overturns customary orders is in the name of justice, her expression of confidence in a king turns out to be somewhat ambiguous. Indeed, her son Samuel considers the dangers of kingship more carefully than any other human character in the pages that follow. As Hannah's song concludes, therefore, it is also cause for mourning. Wijk-Bos notes that the stories begin with a woman at the center who "is a sturdy sign of hope and human integrity" who all but disappears "with the mention of three male names,"[17] Elkanah, Samuel, and Eli. Biblical narratives are no stranger to the dynamics of patriarchy: here, as in so many other cases in history, men displace women and attempt to erase their contributions from the annals of time. In the stories that follow, Hannah will not be named ever again.

FURTHER REFLECTIONS
God-language

Hannah's song contains multiple images for God: Holy One, Rock, Most High, and Judge. The hymn, like many used in worship,

---

17. Wijk-Bos, *Reading Samuel*, 36.

expands rather than restricts the language we use for God. And, like much liturgical language, it makes us consider the truthfulness and limitations of words. Nearly every theologian in the history of the church has acknowledged the difficulty of using human language to refer to God. One of the most important series of reflections on the problem of God-language is found in the great medieval theologian Thomas Aquinas's magnum opus, the *Summa Theologica*.[18] In it, Thomas claims there are three ways of thinking about human language in relation to God. One is to claim that human language is always *equivocal* when it refers to God. Because God is infinite and we are finite, our language cannot express anything significant or ultimately true about God. The gulf between us and God is so great that our language constantly falls short of expressing God's nature. The only thing we can say about our language in relation to God is that it is perennially inadequate. Many of the great mystics of the Christian church have adopted a form of this view, often stressing that the most appropriate posture in relation to God is silence, the stilling of our speech, and "unknowing" our language as God reveals its inadequacies.[19] As important as this recognition of language's ultimate inadequacies is, however, this position can sometimes leave little room for truthful human speech about God. We are, after all, speaking creatures who need language to express basic convictions of truth, meaning, love, and even God's life.

Another position regarding human language is to claim that our words have a *univocal* quality when they refer to God. Certain words, particularly words found in Scripture, have precise meaning that describes the reality and being of God adequately (or at least adequately for us). A one-to-one correspondence exists between

---

18. See "The Names of God," in Thomas Aquinas, *Summa Theologica*, vol. I, trans. Fathers of the English Dominican Province (New York: Benziger Bros., 1948), 59–72.
19. The great fourteenth century mystical text, *The Cloud of Unknowing*, describes the journey into God in this way: "For when you first begin to undertake it, all that you find is a darkness, a sort of cloud of unknowing; you cannot tell what it is, except that you experience in your will a simple reaching out to God. This darkness and cloud is always between you and your God, no matter what you do, and it prevents you from seeing him clearly by the light of understanding in your reason, and from experiencing him in sweetness of love in your affection. So set yourself to rest in this darkness as long as you can, always crying out after him whom you love. For if you are to experience him or to see him at all, insofar as it is possible here, it must always be in this cloud and in this darkness." Edited by James Walsh, S. J. (Mahwah, NJ: Paulist Press, 1981), 120–21.

God's nature and human words. Some who adopt a version of this position claim that the "right" words for God are "God-given" and that they are rather few, such as Father and Lord. The advantage of this position is its seeming clarity and precision. Yet most versions of it have too much confidence in the ability of human language to express God's fullness.

Thomas rejects both of these positions and adopts what he calls an *analogical* approach to God-talk. Our words, because they are human words, will always be inadequate to expressing the fullness of God, but we have to use words to speak *of* God. Furthermore, God is able to express something truthful and meaningful about God's self in *our* speech. The analogical approach shares the concern with the limitations of language shown in the equivocal approach but also shares the concern with the ability of language to express truth in the univocal approach. The way it does this is to speak of God via analogy. Human language, in reference to God, operates with analogies: God is *like* something else encountered in human experience. In Thomas's approach, the primary meaning of any word we use for God (goodness, love, truth) is grounded in the nature of God. God is the fountain of goodness, truth, and mercy; our experience of other things as good, true, and merciful derives from God's primary goodness, truth, and mercy. When Hannah proclaims, "there is no Rock like our God" (v. 2), she speaks analogically. She is neither claiming that God is a literal rock nor claiming that the term "rock" has no meaning in relation to God. Rather, Hannah prays that God is *like* a rock in terms of stability, steadfastness, and permanence. For Thomas, moreover, the primary meaning of these rock-like qualities rests in God. Most theologians, in the wake of Thomas Aquinas, have adopted some form of this analogical approach.

The most prevalent analogies and names for God, in the tradition, are male names, such as Father and Son. Feminist theologians have documented the extensive problems that arise when God is referred to exclusively in male terms: it limits the broader portrayal of God found in Scripture and ignores experiences of God that do not conform to a male deity. These theologians have asked anew whether the church's reliance on male-language ultimately obscures the analogical quality of *all* God language. If God can only be referred to as male, has the church slipped toward univocal language? Has this preponderance of male language served to further limit women's leadership roles in the church while needlessly elevating men's? As Mary Daly has trenchantly observed, "If God in 'his' heaven is a father ruling 'his' people, then it is in the 'nature' of things and according to divine plan and the order of the universe that society be male-dominated."[20]

When Scripture refers to God, it is often with male language (cf. Matt. 28:19; Mark 13:32; John 8:54; Rom. 15:6; Rev. 1:6). Jesus called God "Abba" (Mark 14:36), a word for Father in his native Aramaic. But these words express only part of the biblical witness. The Old Testament, in particular, has a wide range of language for God that is seldom employed liturgically. Hannah's song includes expansive imagery, such as Rock, Holy One, and Most High. In other books of Scripture we hear God referred to as eagle (Deut. 32:11–12), nursing mother (Num. 11:12) and I am (Exod. 3:14). Jesus invites the comparison of God with a mother hen (Matt. 23:37). A close reading of the Scriptures yields surprising additions to the standard words and names that the church has used.

For the people Israel, God has a proper name, transliterated from the Hebrew as YHWH (cf. Exod. 3:13–15). But this name, because it is holy, cannot be uttered. Humans are inadequate to speak it. What are the implications of God's unnamable name? First, the God of Israel is personal, a God who establishes and maintains relationships with God's people. Israel encounters God not as an amorphous or impersonal force but as One with a name who is involved in Israel's history. Second, no matter how closely God reveals God's self to God's people, YHWH is also beyond Israel's experience. Whatever language we use for God, both of these aspects—God's incarnational, intimate presence and God's holiness and otherness—ought to be emphasized. A God devoid of mystery and holiness becomes an idol; a God without intimacy becomes a detached and impersonal force. When we employ the full range of scriptural imagery for God—and not one or two favored images—both of these aspects

20. Mary Daly, *Beyond God the Father: Toward a Philosophy of Women's Liberation* (Boston: Beacon, 1985), 13.

are expressed in worship and theology. Hannah's song contains both dimensions of God's holiness and nearness.

2:11–21
Corruption of Religion and a New Hope

The beginnings of these stories connect kingship and cultic worship: the one who becomes a kingmaker, Samuel, is the boy brought to the Lord as a gift. If Israel is to have a king, then that king will differ from the kings of the world by submitting himself to God's commandments. He will rule below—and not above—God's law. Right worship and right rule, for the Deuteronomist, go hand in hand.

As this story progresses, we encounter the corruption of worship. The first description of Eli's sons is not flattering: they are "scoundrels" (v. 12). This same term, literally "sons of Belial," is found in Deuteronomy 13:13–18, where the Deuteronomist stipulates that if persons lead inhabitants of a town astray and encourage them to worship other gods, an investigation shall be conducted, and if the charge is found true, then everything in the town—even the livestock—shall be destroyed by the sword. "Scoundrels" names the perpetuators of the worst kind of idolatry: religious deception of a people to worship something other than YHWH.

Eli's sons engage in exactly this kind of deception and abuse of power. They seem chiefly motivated by self-interest. As pilgrims come to make sacrifice, the sons take most of the offerings for themselves (vv. 13–15). The scene has an eerily contemporary ring to it. We have heard this story so much that we have become accustomed to it: the evangelist who crusades for the Lord only to take the bulk of the offering for himself and amass an unsightly fortune; the youth leader who is eventually revealed as a sexual predator; the preacher who is more concerned with her reputation as a gifted preacher than

> The entire world was created as an "altar of God," as a temple, as a symbol of the kingdom. According to its conception, it is all *sacred*, and not "profane."
>
> Alexander Schmemann, *The Eucharist* (Crestwood, NY: St. Vladimir's Seminary Press, 2003), 61.

in proclaiming the Word of God. The abuse of religious power has many faces, but at its root is the impulse to take from others and to seek chiefly one's own supposed good. For much of its history, the Christian church has stressed the unique responsibilities and demands of its clergy. John Chrysostom wrote that the priest "must be as pure as if he were standing in heaven itself."[21] The temptations of ministry, moreover, are great, chief of which is "vainglory, more dangerous than the Sirens' rock of which the poets have marvelous tales to tell."[22] Cognizant of clerical abuses of his time, Calvin emphasized not the personal authority of ministers but the authority of God's word: "Whatever authority and dignity the Spirit in Scripture accords to either priests or prophets, or apostles, or successors of apostles, it is wholly given not to the men personally, but to the ministry to which they have been appointed; or (to speak more briefly) to the Word, whose ministry is entrusted to them."[23] But each branch of the Christian church also knows the scandals of scoundrels who have fallen from grace. The leaders keep falling as the people keep attempting to live faithfully.

Eli's sons are bent on devouring the choicest meats. The author's deliberate use of the word "fat" (v. 16) is important. Regulations considering the treatment of fat were strict in cultic practice. Fat is the portion of the offering that belongs to God; it is not to be eaten but to be burned in a "pleasing odor" to God (Lev. 3:16–17). But the sons of Eli seem little concerned with this regulation. By taking meat from others they fatten themselves, with little regard for the regulations that maintain cultic order and protect the welfare of the people. Here, the people try to keep the commandments while the priests have little regard for them.

As Eli's sons make a mockery of sacrifice, the boy Samuel appears as a proto-priest, wearing a linen robe that Hannah has made for him. His garments represent an anticipation of his future status. The contrast between grown men's disregard for cultic practice and a young boy's sincerity is striking. Samuel is described as "ministering

---

21. John Chrysostom, "The Glory of the Priesthood," in William H. Willimon, ed., *Pastor: A Reader for Ordained Ministry* (Nashville: Abingdon, 2002), 280.
22. Ibid., 285.
23. Calvin, *Institutes*, 2:1150.

before the LORD" (v. 18), while Eli's sons flaunt regulation and treat offerings "with contempt" (v. 17). As Hannah and Elkanah return each year, Eli blesses them, taking note of the gift that Hannah has given. And as Eli blesses, Hannah receives yet greater gifts: three sons and two daughters. Abundance pervades the divine economy. Gift-giving has become contagious, as Hannah and Elkanah return to make sacrifice and the boy Samuel grows up "in the presence of the LORD" (vv. 20–21).

2:22–36

A Bold Prophecy

The contrast between Samuel and Eli's sons continues in this next section with even greater intensity. To this point, Eli has no reactions to his sons' behavior: was he ignorant of it? Did he choose to ignore the behavior like many parents are wont to do, believing his sons had the best intentions and that deep down they're really good boys? Eli is now "very old," perhaps suggesting that he is not fully aware of his son's sins. But he cannot claim ignorance, since he has now "heard all that his sons were doing to all Israel, and how they lay with the women who served at the entrance to the tent of meeting" (v. 22). Several details here are significant: He *hears* of this behavior. Others bring reports of his son's behavior that he cannot or will not see for himself. Here the priest is not aware of affairs in his temple; others must open his eyes. Second, his sons are not committing isolated offenses against individual worshipers, taking advantage of a few people and the choice sacrifices they bring; rather, they are offending *all Israel*, scarring the nation as a whole. Finally, we know that these sons are now taking advantage—by rape, most likely—of the women who serve as attendants at the entrance to the holy place. Their crime involves sexual abuse and the abuse of power, as men who manipulate women of lower cultic status. Again, the pattern is all too familiar, resembling male pastors who abuse pastoral confidence and their status in order to sleep with parishioners or other church employees. Such actions cause ruptures in the body of Christ and often cause those who experience or learn of such abuse to give up on the church altogether. Eli's sons, however, continue to take whatever they can get.

Eli rebukes his sons by claiming that what they have done is the gravest kind of offense. A sin against another person can be dealt with through intercession, "but if someone sins against the Lord, who can make intercession?" (v. 25). Here Eli connects sin against neighbor to sin against God. His sons take advantage of people: devouring sacrifices and taking others for sexual pleasure. But he also claims that the particular actions of his sons are grave because they are the ones who intercede for others before God. Their offense is not merely their disregard of religious ritual; by stealing and taking from others, they sin against God.[24] Yet this rebuke falls on deaf ears. Meanwhile, Samuel grows in stature and in favor with God and the people Israel (v. 26).

Then, without any narrative warning, an unnamed man of God appears to speak to Eli (v. 27). He resembles a prophet, one who offers a word from God to those who cannot hear it. The prophetic and priestly elements in Israel's history sometimes stand in tension with each other: the priest maintains ritual purity and proper worship practice while the prophet focuses on justice among the people of God and God's judgment on injustice. Both are indispensable to Israel's covenantal life, but here a prophet comes to admonish the priest. What he says is astonishing. First, he reminds Eli how God has chosen a portion of Israel, the Levites, to serve as priests (v. 28). Furthermore, this election of a particular tribe/family is perpetual: "I promised that your family and the family of your ancestor should go in and out before me forever" (v. 30). But then the prophet speaks a new word: a time is coming when Eli's family will no longer serve as priests, where their strength will be "cut off" (v. 31) and only one will not be "cut off" from the altar of the Lord (v. 33), a foreshadowing of Saul's massacre of the priests at Nob (22:16–19). This man of God prophesies nothing short of a revocation of God's promises to a particular family. The God who elects is also a God who will cut

---

24. Steussy notes YHWH's intervention as reason for Eli's sons' persistence in sin. "But they would not listen to the voice of their father; for it was the will of the LORD to kill them" (v. 25). She notes a double standard here, where God causes the hardening of the sons' hearts and later blames Eli for their failure. "This is a God who is not merely harsh, but one who shifts blame for divine actions onto humans," Steussy, *Samuel and His God*, 3.

off those who despise God's ordinances. This statement fits squarely within the Deuteronomist's theology, where faithfulness meets with blessing and faithlessness meets with disaster. As Walter Brueggemann has observed, "In this theological tradition, responsive obedience is required even for God's most sweeping promises."[25] God's promises, for the Deuteronomist, are for the sake of Israel's flourishing. When the priests have become corrupt, Israel has nowhere to turn unless God raises up "a faithful priest, who will do according to what is in [God's] heart and in [God's] mind" (v. 35). When the priests have forgotten the people, a prophet can remind Israel of the wider context of God's promises. This anonymous man of God points to the possibility that a priest can exist who also embodies the prophetic element. He points, in other words, to Samuel.

But he also points to a pattern that pervades Scripture: how God brings something new out of the ashes of the destruction. This is the story of Israel's exile into Babylon and their return; it is the story of the prophets' words that point to the new Zion; it is the story of Jesus' death and resurrection; ultimately it is the story of creation and new creation, where hope remains for all.

3:1–4:1a
Samuel's Call

Hope emerges anew as narrative attention shifts to the boy Samuel. This pivotal section is filled with contrasts: between young and old, between hearing and sight, between understanding and misunderstanding. Samuel "was ministering to the LORD under Eli" (v. 1). The prepositions are important: Samuel serves the Lord, but he is able to perform this service with Eli's tutelage. The narrator does not give Samuel's age but refers to him as a boy, as an apprentice, learning the priestly craft from a seasoned veteran.

God's word, according to the narrator, was a rarity "in those days,"

---

25. Walter Brueggemann, *First and Second Samuel* (Louisville, KY: John Knox Press, 1990), 23. Wijk-Bos writes similarly, "God's promises were not without the possibility of change insofar as they were connected to the way in which God's people lived up to their covenant commitments. . . . At times, the God of the Bible rues the choices God made." *Reading Samuel*, 42.

and visions "were not widespread" (v. 1). Note how both eye and ear are invoked: to hear God's word or to glimpse God in a vision are exceptional occurrences. This comment gives the reader a sense of the extraordinary events that follow. But it also forces us to ask when, if ever, such visions and hearings were *not* rare. Words from God and visions of God are often dismissed as hallucinations, perhaps especially today. The Scriptures are also aware of how often people mistake something else for a vision or

> Raising children also raises adults. Children dramatically transform the lives of adults who care for them.
>
> Bonnie Miller-McLemore, *In the Midst of Chaos: Caring for Children as Spiritual Practice* (San Francisco: Wiley, 2007), xv.

voice from God. Warnings against false prophets fill the Scriptures (cf. Lam. 2:14; Ezek. 13:9–10; 1 John 4:1; Rev. 19:20); sometimes "holy" visions lead folks down the wrong path. In the narrative that follows, Samuel is not immediately aware that the words he hears are the Lord's. Sometimes God's word takes a while to sink in.

Eli is a man who can no longer see; his capacity for glimpsing a vision has already disappeared. This loss of sight may foreshadow "Israel's diminishing insight about kingship,"[26] its stubborn demand for a king instead of reliance on YHWH. Sight is pivotal both to daily living and also to religious sense: seeing is believing. One way of understanding the fulfillment of life—personal eschatology—is that human beings will behold God "face-to-face," through sight (cf. 1 Cor. 13:12). But in the call of Samuel, *hearing* ultimately takes precedence over sight. Eli cannot see, but this lack does not obstruct him from hearing the word of God rightly.

Eli is lying in his room while Samuel is in the temple near the ark (vv. 2–3). Samuel's proximity to the holiest object in Israel offers a transition to the next section of the book (which is focused on the ark) and a reminder of where Samuel belongs: in the sanctuary but also *to* God. His nearness to this holy thing, in part, is what enables him to hear God's voice calling his name. God knows Samuel's name, an indication of intimacy and the particularity of Samuel's call. God issues a call to all Israel to keep the commandments, but God also

26. Polzin, *Samuel*, 54.

calls people individually. Samuel, however, does not yet know who is calling him. He responds "Here I am!" but runs to Eli (vv. 4–5). The scene repeats itself, as Eli tells his protégé to lie down again (v. 6). Here the narrator inserts a comment "Samuel did not yet know the LORD, and the word of the LORD had not yet been revealed to him" (v. 7). Samuel hears in part but does not yet see or understand. How is one to come to discern the call of God? For Samuel, it requires another person. Rarely in Scripture is a word of God meant for one person alone, in isolation. God's call is not eccentric, privy only to an isolated person. Rather, it is discerned with the help of others. Elizabeth Liebert notes the centrality of community in discerning God's call on our lives:

> Community carries our faith when we are weak, preserves the long tradition of listening for God, provides a collective interpretation of the Scriptures, and calls us to actions that are good for us and the larger community of living things. Cut off from its communitarian roots, the power and veracity of Christian discernment can easily stray into viewing our own idiosyncratic interpretations—and even downright evil—as God's call.[27]

Samuel learns to hear in full when Eli—who is functionally blind—helps him to hear. The third time that Samuel hears his name, Eli knows it is the voice of the Lord. He tells Samuel to speak so that he can hear: "Speak, LORD, for your servant is listening" (v. 9).

The fourth time that Samuel hears his name, he uses the words that Eli gives him to speak. What Samuel hears is enough to make him stop speaking and his ears "tingle" (v. 11). Here the words that the unnamed man of God spoke to Eli in chapter two get spoken as if they are already fulfilled: Because of the sins of the house of Eli, there will be no expiation of that house "forever" (vv. 12–14). It is hard to believe these words, even though readers are hearing them for the second time. The God who elects some for service is also a God who cuts off those who violate the commandments. The Deuteronomist displays a consistent theology: those who sow discord and

27. Elizabeth Liebert, *The Way of Discernment: Spiritual Practices for Decision Making* (Louisville, KY: Westminster John Knox Press, 2008), 10.

abuse and who disregard statutes and ritual can expect to fall. Eli's sons blaspheme God, and Eli has done nothing to intervene. He cannot claim ignorance, just as his sons cannot claim that they had good intentions. The God who makes promises to a people holds those who tend holy places to a high standard. Eli's house, once entrusted with the expiation of sins through sacrifices and offering, is never to be entrusted with these responsibilities again. This is surely a fall from grace. No future expiations can bring Eli's sons or their descendants back into the service of the Lord.

These are hard words for an apprentice to bring to his teacher: "Samuel was afraid to tell the vision to Eli" (v. 15). Perhaps discerning his apprentice's fear, Eli calls Samuel my son (v. 16; cf. v. 6), a term of affection, recognizing that his apprentice is the only one in the temple conducting himself as a priest. If Samuel is tempted to keep silent, the familial words of his supervisor encourage him to speak, not to hide anything from Eli. Hearing God's word requires Samuel to speak uncomfortable truths to others. And so Samuel tells Eli "everything." To which Eli can only respond: "It is the Lord; let him do what seems good to him" (v. 18). Eli's words are understandable: foreseeing the demise of one's household can hardly be welcomed as good news. But these words also convey something of Eli's culpability, not so much for his action but for his inaction. He acquiesces to what Samuel has told him as what *seems* good to the Lord; he does not accept these words *as* good. But Eli also utters no protest against God, just as he refused to protest his son's behavior. Eli's negligence is his inaction.

In most churches, the people of God name both sins of commission and sins of omission. Sins are not simply the active, willful behaviors that violate God's commands; they are just as often the things that we do not do: how we turn our head from poverty, how we choose to ignore how cheap clothes worn in North America are sewn by persons who are not making a living wage on the other side of the globe, locked in factories even when fire breaks out.[28]

---

28. The November 24, 2012, fire at a garment factory in Bangladesh is a haunting reminder of the connections between cheap consumer goods in North America and perilous working conditions for those who manufacture them. See http://www.nytimes.com/2012/12/07/world/asia/bangladesh-fire-exposes-safety-gap-in-supply-chain.html.

One prayer of confession in the Presbyterian Church claims, "We have left undone those things which we ought to have done; and we have done those things which we ought not to have done."[29] Eli's house falls as a result of both active and passive sin, with the sons representing the former and the father committing the latter.

As Eli fades from the narrative, the Deuteronomist focuses increasingly on Samuel, who grows and is surrounded by God's presence. God's presence, moreover, lets none of Samuel's words "fall to the ground," or be spoken without others hearing (v. 19). Just as Samuel cannot discern the initiating word from God without another, the words that he comes to speak more confidently are given to others. This vignette begins with words a boy hears and concludes with words a young man speaks to a nation: "And the word of Samuel came to all Israel" (4:1).

FURTHER REFLECTIONS
Sin

The sins of Eli's sons bring about loss in the household. If the sons commit iniquity, their father omits speaking out against them. The sons' actions *and* the father's inaction both display dimensions of the nature of sin. Eli's sons manifest the sin of *pride*, the willful assertion of oneself against God or over other people. Augustine claimed that pride inaugurated sin, "because it was this which overthrew the devil, from whom arose the origin of sin."[30] Though Augustine admits that not *every* sin that is committed is prideful, he holds special place for pride's toxicity. It is the form of sin most prevalent among human beings, rooted in the vain attempt to live apart from God. This view of sin has been enormously influential throughout the history of the church and is reflected in much of the church's theology and liturgy. But it is not the only way of considering the radical nature of sin, its causes, and its effects.

29. The Theology and Worship Ministry Unit for the Presbyterian Church (U.S.A.) and the Cumberland Presbyterian Church, *Book of Common Worship* (Louisville, KY: Westminster John Knox Press, 1993), 87.
30. Augustine, "On Nature and Grace," in *The Nicene and Post-Nicene Fathers: First Series*, vol. 5., ed. Philip Schaff. (Peabody, MA: Hendrickson, 2004), 132.

Many feminist theologians have called attention to how pride only considers part of the human experience of sin, primarily the experiences of those with a substantial degree of social power. The prideful assertion of oneself may have more in common with men's experiences than women's. These voices have rightly claimed that sin exhibits another face: not self-assertion, but self-abnegation. Sin is also the passive refusal to live into one's identity as a child of God, not arrogantly overasserting oneself, but dejectedly believing the worst about oneself. Valerie Saiving Goldstein, in an influential essay, writes,

> For the temptations of woman *as woman* are not the same as the temptations of man *as man*, and the specifically feminine forms of sin—"feminine" not because they are confined to women or because women are incapable of sinning in other ways but because they are outgrowths of the basic feminine character structure—have a quality which can never be encompassed by such terms as "pride" and "will-to-power." They are better suggested by such items as triviality, distractibility, and diffuseness; lack of an organizing center or focus; dependence on others for one's own self-definition; tolerance at the expense of standards of excellence; inability to respect the boundaries of privacy; sentimentality, gossipy sociability, and mistrust of reason—in short, underdevelopment or negation of the self.[31]

Such sin is as destructive as its prideful counterpart. If pride arrogates the self to the diminishment of others, passivity obliterates the self in relation to others. Both forms of sin wind up dehumanizing all people.

Other interpretations of sin pervade the tradition. One interpretation draws on disobedience, the violation of laws ordained by God, or our tendency to live without limits. This interpretation does not focus so much on rule-breaking but on the ways we withhold ourselves from God by ignoring the commands God has given us. If the sum of the commandments is "to love God with our whole heart and our neighbors as ourselves," then violation of the commandments

---

31. Valerie Saiving Goldstein, "The Human Situation," in *The Modern Theologians Reader*, ed. David F. Ford, Mike Higton, and Simeon Zahl (Malden, MA: Wiley-Blackwell, 2012), 266.

is any way that we do not love God and neighbor.[32] Others have suggested that sin is best expressed as *disbelief* or *despair*. This is a more nihilistic read of sin, a kind of purposelessness or living without hope. In the nineteenth century, when much of the world was exhibiting increasing confidence in itself, Søren Kierkegaard wrote, "Sin is: before God in despair not to will to be oneself, or before God in despair to will to be oneself."[33] If sin is living in despair, or living inauthentically, for Kierkegaard, the opposite of sin is faith: "Faith is: that the self in being itself and in willing to be itself rests transparently in God."[34] These are not the sole ways of interpreting sin, but they are some of the most significant ones that have proved influential in Christian theology across the ages. Perhaps the most significant thing we can conclude from these varied interpretations is that no single definition can describe all manifestations of sin. Sin, as it were, has many tortured faces. But what these understandings share in common is that sin in some way obstructs our relationship with God and others. We may experience sin as agents or victims, as willful perpetrators or in despairing passivity, but however it is experienced, sin cuts us off from God and others. Eli's sons are both "cut off" from the priesthood, but they also cut themselves off from God and others as they sin. Eli's sin might be considered a sin of weakness, of refusing to stand up to his sons' actions, of being a doormat to their abuses.

4:1b–11

Philistines Capture the Ark

The narrative shifts somewhat abruptly here; most likely this is the result of a combination of two story traditions. If the previous section was focused on people and God's action through people, this

---

32. Shirley Guthrie writes, "What God's law requires is *ourselves* . . . not just certain external actions. And what it forbids is the withholding of ourselves from God and other people, not just the doing of certain bad things." *Christian Doctrine*, rev. ed. (Louisville, KY: Westminster John Knox Press, 1994), 215.

33. Søren Kierkegaard, *The Sickness unto Death: A Christian Psychological Exposition for Upbuilding and Awakening*, ed. and trans. Howard V. Hong and Edna H. Hong (Princeton, NJ: Princeton University Press, 1980), 81.

34. Ibid., 82.

section is concerned with things and God's presence in those things. In this section readers also first encounter the Philistines, who abide as threats to Israel throughout the remaining story. At critical turning points in history, the Philistines crop up, foiling Israel's plans at least for a time. Indeed, this Philistine threat eventually leads Israel to clamor for a king.

Location may not be everything, but it does communicate much. The section begins with preparations for battle, occurring on the borderlands. Philistia is the threat posed to Israel from the West, along the Mediterranean coast. No reason is given for war: perhaps there are competing claims for land; perhaps each party sees the other as a threat to its existence. Aphek (v. 1), the place where the Philistines are mustering for war, is a strategic locale, on a highway connecting the sea to the inland hills. Battles over territory and national security have an ancient history—in this region and elsewhere. The first battle is disastrous for Israel: resounding defeat and substantial loss of life (v. 2). But when the beleaguered soldiers return to camp, the elders do not ask the soldiers what went wrong with their tactics but immediately point to God's will. They name not the Philistines as those who defeat them, but God: "Why has the LORD put us to rout today before the Philistines?" (v. 3). Their question is a theological one. Israel's defeat cannot just be a matter of military maneuvering but reveals something of God's presence and absence. Such is the case over and again in 1 and 2 Samuel: events that transpire between peoples are not simply politics or matters of human relationships; they are expressions of the relationship between Israel and God.

The elders, perhaps discerning God's absence from the battle, order the ark brought into the heat of the fight. They suggest the holiest thing in Israel's corporate life be brought into this most dangerous place. The ark represents the presence of God *with* the people Israel. Word is sent to Shiloh and Eli's sons Hophni and Phinehas: return with this holy thing of the living God (v. 4). In an ironic twist, Eli's iniquitous sons are entrusted with God's throne as Israel faces an ominous threat.

Shouts emerge from the Israelite camp that the Philistines overhear but do not understand (vv. 5–6). Their first reaction is fear, pointing to the "gods" that have come into the Israelite camp, the ones who defeated the Egyptians. They know of the plagues inflicted on Egypt and suspect that something similar may be their fate (vv. 7–8). But they are also told to maintain courage not to be slaves "to the Hebrews as they have been to you" (v. 9). Both Philistines and Israelites fear being made subservient to the other.

How are we to interpret this presence of holy things in the midst of battle? Clearly there are elements of religious practice here that are somewhat remote from the lives of today's synagogues and churches. But what is most significant is how God's presence is made known *through* concrete things. The God of Israel is a God who chooses, who enters into relationship and is revealed through people and things. This is both the result of God's "accommodation" to our humanity[35] and a revelation of the kind of God YHWH is. God speaks, works, and makes God's self known through things that are not God. Reverence of holy things is not a remnant of primitive religion; it is one of the chief expressions of an incarnational faith, recognizing that God comes near to God's people: indeed nearer than that people's breath. A people that neglects reverence of holy things renders God distant from the everyday affairs of peoples and nations.

After a significant build-up, the narration of battle is a surprisingly terse two verses: the Philistines fight (Israel is not described as fighting) while Israel is defeated and flees. Thirty-thousand Israelite foot soldiers die: a stunning number, probably a narrative exaggeration to demonstrate the extent of catastrophe (vv. 10–11). This humiliation is magnified by the Philistines' capture of the ark. But whereas the earlier battle was interpreted theologically (as God routing the Israelites), this second battle is interpreted militarily, without reference to God. The rationale that impelled the Israelites to carry the ark into battle suddenly vanishes. Fulfilling the previous prophecy, the sons of Eli die in battle. As the ark moves from Shiloh and the

35. One of Calvin's insights is that God cannot be fully comprehended by human beings. God is God; we are us. But God overcomes the gulf between us and God by accommodating God's self—in revelation, in Scripture—to our weak and partial ability to understand. For Calvin, God's "essence is incomprehensible; hence, his divineness far escapes all human perception." *Institutes*, 52. But God also "accommodated diverse forms to different ages, as he knew would be expedient for each. . . . In the fact that he has changed the outward form and manner, he does not show himself subject to change. Rather, he has accommodated himself to men's capacity, which is varied and changeable." Ibid., 462–63.

house of Eli, it falls into enemy hands. The capture is surely catastrophic, but perhaps the only way to remove the ark from the hands
that have abused Israel's worship is to lose it to an enemy.

4:12–22

Eli's Death

If the battle is narrated tersely, the subsequent effects on Eli's family are treated with greater detail. Eli watches and waits at his seat
by the side of the road. His heart—the center or core of the person in much of Scripture—is trembling for the ark (v. 13). This
aged priest has premonitions of what has already occurred. A messenger's disheveled appearance is visual confirmation of what has
occurred, but Eli cannot see (v. 15). He hears, however, the uproar
that the messenger's words have brought to the town. When the
messenger comes to Eli, the news hits as death. Eli dies almost as
violently as the contestants in battle (perhaps in the way that his
sons did)—in a fall that breaks his neck (v. 18). The battle has carried forth even to Shiloh, it seems, killing the man entrusted with
the center of Israel's worship. Only upon Eli's death does the narrator first number him as one of the judges. He is not referred to
as such earlier in the story, but he has judged Israel for forty years,
nearly half of his long life. Eli's backward fall off his "throne," in
Polzin's view, represents the Deuteronomist's "view of kingship in
a nutshell" in all its "burden and doom."[36] Who will emerge in Eli's
place? If the characters in the story do not know yet, the readers
already do. All signs point to Samuel.

The catastrophic loss of the ark, an army, a judge, and two sons
ripples further into Eli's family. Phinehas's wife, on hearing that her
husband and father-in-law are dead, goes into labor (v. 19). Catastrophe begets birth, as she is on the brink of death herself. Even the
child's name reflects the swirling chaos of events: Ichabod ("Alas for
the glory")—a name that is an expression of lament. The birth of a

---

36. Polzin, *Samuel*, 64.

child in Eli's family is mixed with tragedy, or in the words of Phinehas's wife, "The glory has departed from Israel" (v. 21).

Eli's death is narrated without explicit theological referent. God does not cause Eli to die as God routed the Israelites by the Philistines. But it would be a mistake to interpret Eli's death simply as an accident, for the overarching narrative relays much about God's activity. What begins with the prophet's words in chapter two gains momentum in Samuel's call, crescendos in the capture of the ark, and climaxes in Eli's death. These are not random events but reveal something of God's intent to "cut off" the house of Eli from the priesthood. The lengths to which God goes to accomplish this may be direct or roundabout, but they are accomplished nonetheless. Discerning the hand of God in these events, however, does not lessen the sense of tragedy. The narrator does not celebrate the death of Eli's sons, even though they are scoundrels. Breaking a neck in a fall seems an ignoble end to this judge in Israel. If God's purposes are accomplished in the Deuteronomistic History, it is not without attention to the tragic and human dimensions of the story. This makes the Deuteronomist more than a rosy-eyed Pollyanna, where all works out in the end and no one gets hurt. Rather, the history of the world is shot through with suffering and tragedy that cannot always be explained away. Each historical event, however, consistently shows forth two dimensions—the human interactions that brought about the event and God's providential hand, in, with, and under all things and interactions. Both are essential for the history.

Eli, in the four chapters in which readers encounter him, is a complex character. Most of what we read about him is laudable— his consoling of Hannah, his supervision of Samuel, his aid in discerning Samuel's call, and his stint as judge of Israel. But he also exhibits a tragic flaw: his obliviousness to his sons' abuses of their duties. Yet in the end he is a sympathetic character, one who readers are apt to understand. Most parents believe the best in their children, even when signs point otherwise. Sometimes parents are the slowest to respond to signs of warning. But it is this flaw that leads to the downfall of his house and sets the stage for tragedies yet to come.

5:1–12

The Ark in a Foreign Land

The scene shifts now to Philistine country, where the portrayal of God's activity in human affairs becomes more direct and dramatic. Here the ark experiences exile, recalling the experiences of Israel in Egypt and foreshadowing them in Babylon. Polzin writes, "The story of the ark not only looks backward in time to Israel's enslavement in Egypt, it also looks forward to Israel's exile from its proper place, the land."[37] But what is exile for Israel is cause for triumph in Philistia: on their triumphal return, the Philistines take the ark and place it in the most sacred space on their soil—the temple of Dagon in Ashdod. This placement is possibly a mixture of triumph and reverence: either showing the inferiority of Israel's YHWH by placing the ark before Dagon or showing some reverence by setting it in the holiest place in the land. We read that the ark was placed "beside Dagon" (v. 2), however, indicating some degree of honor. But this side-by-side arrangement is blasphemous to the readers of the text, and the action that proceeds is swift. When the Philistines return to the temple the next morning, Dagon is face-first on the ground, a posture that connotes humiliation or subservience (v. 3). Throughout this narrative, moreover, the statue of Dagon is never referred to *as* a statue. The statue does not represent Dagon; it *is* Dagon according to the narrator. The contrast is stark: whereas the ark represents YHWH and serves as a throne, a holy thing in service of the Lord, the Philistine god is nothing more than an inanimate object. This characterization verges on lampoon and serves the narrator's purpose well. The God of Israel is a God of history; the god of the Philistines is an empty vessel.

The action repeats itself in more dramatic fashion: after Dagon is restored to his place, overnight he falls again, this time with his hands and head "cut off" (v. 4). What is sacrilege to Philistine religion is yet further demonstration of YHWH's power over lesser gods. Though the narrator does not describe either of these incidents as God's action, there is no doubt in the reader's mind: even in a foreign land,

---

37. Ibid., 66.

the hand of YHWH rules supreme. When the Israelites are nowhere to be seen, God accomplishes a victory over the Philistines, beginning with the humiliation of an empty god. These dramatic actions, according to the narrator, continue to have effects in this foreign land. The priests of Dagon do not step on the threshold of Dagon "to this day" (v. 5). The action of YHWH even changes the practice of foreign priests who do not worship the living God.

God's activity among the Philistines intensifies as the story progresses: "the hand of the LORD was heavy upon the people of Ashdod" (v. 6) as the people become terrified and afflicted with tumors. Hans Wilhelm Hertzberg notes how the Masoretic Text describes the tumors as boils and sores on the anus, "an epidemic which brings added shame to the Philistines because of the part of the body which is affected,"[38] as if the hand of YHWH is ravaging Philistines from the inside out. The parallels with the plagues of Egypt are also apparent. If the Philistines feared such plagues as they prepare to battle Israel (4:8), they eventually experience them in the aftermath of their victory over the Israelite army. The plague this time, however, is localized, confined to Ashdod and the surrounding territory. Popular demand forces the ark to move to Gath. Here the scene repeats itself: more tumors, widespread panic, and popular uproar (5:8–9). Young and old are afflicted and the ark has to move on. By the time the ark arrives in Ekron, the people of that city clamor for it to be sent away immediately, as panic reaches an apex (v. 10). The ark begins as a threat to the statue of a foreign god, emerges as an instigator of plague, and now is the hand of God who will "kill us and our people" (v. 11). The longer the ark stays in Philistine lands, the more destruction it unleashes. No wonder the Philistines utter a cry to heaven (v. 12). The victory tour has become a tour of horrors.

If Israel's loss to the Philistines and loss of the ark is initially experienced as tragedy, this chapter narrates the beginning of a victory and the assured triumph of God's purposes. Even in the most humiliating circumstances, where the central relic of Israel's worship is confiscated by pagans, God's trustworthy hand is at work. The hands of Dagon are cut off while God's hand is sure and steady. The hope

---

38. Herzberg, *I & II Samuel*, 54.

uttered in this vignette is the hope of the millions upon millions of oppressed people throughout history: a confidence that victory does not belong to those with the most advanced armies, the deepest pockets, or the easiest access to the corridors of political power. Victory, instead, belongs to God who establishes justice among God's people even when injustice is all that seems visible. JoAnne Marie Terrell describes the God of biblical faith in this way: "Because the God of the Bible made and makes impossible things possible, God continuously demonstrates love for God's people, asserts the justice of God beyond the will of their oppressors, and maintains for God's sovereignty over their enemies."[39] God is the power for the impos-

sible, who brings people out of slavery into freedom, who makes a way out of no way, who brings sight to the blind. Those who wait on this God do not do so passively, but are equipped to be agents against impossible odds.

> **The God who is and suffers with the oppressed is the God of life, the liberator God.**
>
> Ronaldo Muñoz, *The God of Christians,* Paul Burns, trans. (Maryknoll, NY: Orbis, 1990), 87.

6:1–7:2

The Ark's Return

The Philistines' "victory tour" has turned into a rout but not in the anticipated way. In a stay of seven months, the ark has brought panic, disease, sacrilege, and even death. The people demand that the ark be sent back to its place; they do not ask the priests and diviners for permission. But they do ask these tenders of the sacred what should be sent *with* the ark. The priests then urge the people to also send a guilt offering (vv. 1–3). The booty of war gets transformed into an offering—not of peace, but of the guilt of a people, all in the hopes that the hand of the God of Israel will no longer torment them. Since the coming of the ark to their land, the Philistines have only experienced the hand of the Lord as heavy; they now seek a lighter burden as they send away the ark. The five gold tumors and five gold mice

---

39. JoAnne Marie Terrell, "God," in *Handbook of U.S. Theologies of Liberation,* ed. Miguel A. De La Torre (St. Louis: Chalice Press, 2004), 12.

they offer (vv. 4–5) are odd but symbolic, signifying the five major cities and the five lords of Philistia. The offerings are reminders of the very things that have inflicted suffering and death on the people. Casting these images is a gesture of humiliation and guilt by the Philistines, as it memorializes in gold the plague and the victory of YHWH. In crafting these images, the Philistines seek to be different from the Egyptians, those who hardened their hearts in the face of multiple plagues. Here only one plague is sufficient to turn a people and free what had been lost.

The imagery of burdening and lightening continues: the Philistines lighten their load by yoking two milch cows, two beasts who have never felt the burden of human labor (v. 7). They are to be separated from their calves, yoked to a cart with the ark and the guilt offerings in tow. The milch cows represent purity: if the Philistines have defiled the ark by confiscating it and placing it in a pagan temple, they return it with these spotless animals. If they carried the ark into Ashdod by their own hands, they return the ark without touching it. The reversals are indeed dramatic and the irony pointed: Philistine priests are now behaving piously, in marked contrast to an Israelite priesthood that has already been revealed as corrupt.[40]

Yet there is dispute in Philistia over the origin of the recent catastrophes. The people blame the ark, but the diviners appear less certain. In a rhetorical flourish, the diviners instruct the people to set the yoked cows on a direct road leading to Israel. They are not to lead the calves, but see where they journey of their own accord. If the cows journey on the road toward the land of the Israelites, then YHWH has brought this about. But if the cows turn aside (as a milch cow would be expected to do and return to her calf), then catastrophe was by chance (vv. 8–10). Of course, the narrator claims that nothing occurs by chance. The cows are unwavering in their journey and do not as much as turn to the right or the left (v. 12).

When the Israelites behold the ark's return, their first act is to make sacrifice, using the milch cows and cart. The offering occurs somewhat hastily, perhaps without the proper priestly supervision: those who see the ark are reaping wheat and cease their labors to

---

40. Wijk-Bos, *Reading Samuel*, 52.

make sacrifice and rejoice. The ark stops in a field of Joshua of Beth-shemesh, a person not mentioned elsewhere in Scripture, on the edge of Israelite territory. Wood is already being split and cows are being offered before the Levites are mentioned (vv. 14–15). These members of the priestly tribe, however, handle the ark and the symbolic gold offerings. The five lords of the Philistines who have accompanied the ark on its journey observe the ritual. No words are exchanged among themselves or between them and the Israelites; they simply return to their home as the ark has returned home (v. 16). The scene in the wheat fields and at the impromptu altar is joyous. Even in this somewhat marginal place—on the edge of Israel, at some distance from the centers of political and religious power—the ark is back where it belongs, a home that is memorialized "to this day" in the field of Joshua (v. 18).

But apparently there are some in Israel who do not celebrate the ark's return. In a textually difficult section, beginning with verse 19, we encounter "descendants of Jeconiah" who refrain from rejoicing; God's response to their restraint is to kill seventy men. In one version of this story, contained in the Masoretic Text, the people are killed because they looked into the ark. But other versions say nothing of this sort, rendering the cause of their death difficult to establish. Their deaths, moreover, elicit mourning from those who had been rejoicing. Life and death accompany each other as the ark returns home. In this difficult section, the return of the ark is also a return of the Lord's holy and terrifying presence, a presence that had never wholly departed Israel but is now manifest again as power over life and death. The return of the ark is not merely the long-anticipated homecoming of a religious relic; it is Israel's coming face-to-face with the life-giving power of God, a power that can also take away life.

The makeshift altar and the somewhat hasty sacrifice, if necessary as an immediate response, soon become inadequate. The people who have been rejoicing in Beth-shemesh ask who is worthy to stand before the Lord, implying that no one present is worthy. They even ask how they might "be rid" (v. 20) of this God: a perplexing query that is perhaps understandable in light of the seventy who are now dead. They send word to other Israelites in Kiriath-jearim—further to the north and east—to take the ark, where a priestly consecration is performed. With Eli now dead and his house in disarray, a new priest, Eleazar, emerges from the house of Abinadab "to have charge of the ark of the LORD" (7:1). We hear little more about this family in the story, but their presence signals something new and something old: a departure from the family of Eli but a return to the Levitical moorings of Israel's worship. As the ark returns, a split in Israel's leadership emerges, "royal (in the person of Samuel) and priestly."[41]

The episode concludes with a puzzling statement: "and all the house of Israel lamented after the LORD" (v. 2). Biblical scholars debate this verse and most agree that the meaning of "lament" is uncertain. But the term "lament" is strangely appropriate to the story, since the return of the ark does not amount to spoil for the victors. God has triumphed over the people who seized the ark in battle. But the ark's return is also a return of a terrifying holiness that brings with it a loss of life. The people lament those who have died as they rejoice the return of God's throne. This people that laments is a people that remembers and stays connected to its past. Faithfulness to the God of Israel is not simply "forgiving and forgetting" but remembering, staying connected, and standing in awe of the God of heaven and earth. The God who acts in history elicits our response, in rejoice and lament. As Israel looks to its future (and its desire to have a king like other nations) it will also be tested in how it remembers to rejoice and lament.

7:3–17

Judge Samuel

We last encountered Samuel at the beginning of chapter 4 (where the word of Samuel came to all Israel), and the opening sentences of this section flow rather smoothly from them. It is highly likely that the interlude of chapters 4–6 were originally an independent set of stories, distinct from the Samuel material of chapters 1–3. This

---

41. Green, *Saul's Asking*, 32.

section resumes the narrative trajectory that was cut off in chapter 4. But the interlude is significant to the story as a whole, for it names a Philistine threat that surfaces over and over again throughout subsequent stories, often at transitional points in the narrative.

After the ark/Philistine interlude, however, Samuel occupies a new role as judge with some kind of influence over military affairs. The narrator gives no account for how he assumed this role, but the shift is significant. Now Samuel assumes all of the central civic roles: warning Israel against unfaithfulness (prophet), presiding over religious rites (priest), and leading people as the head of the nation (judge, and a foreshadowing of king). For the Deuteronomist, Samuel personifies the coalescence of these roles. He is consistently regarded as a model in subsequent narratives and in many ways stands as a contrast to the kings who follow: more modest in political trappings, more measured in his military responses, less lenient in matters pertaining to law and the commandments. Even when Samuel dies, the narrative recalls him. If David becomes the chief human protagonist in subsequent chapters, these early depictions of Samuel pave the way for David by showing the reader the importance of the traditions that root Israel in its covenant with God.

Samuel's first words to the people are to put away foreign gods. It is a call *back*. The mention of these foreign gods is somewhat surprising at this juncture: nothing in the narrative thus far (apart from the abuses of Eli's sons) has suggested that Israel has engaged in idolatry. But its placement here indicates that part of the reason why Israel fell in battle with the Philistines and why the ark was captured was that Israel was honoring other gods. Samuel's words condense the Deuteronomist's promise: *if* you put away the foreign gods, *if* you seek only the Lord, *then* you will be delivered from the hands of the Philistines (v. 3).

Samuel's words and actions mark him as a traditionalist. He is not so much a conservative resistant to change as he is one who honors traditions because they have served Israel's benefit. Traditions, in this view, are not for the sake of tradition but for the sake of *life*. Israel does not need anything more to live in faithfulness—no novel deities, no political innovations gained from other nations—the law, the prophets, and the sacrifices are enough. Samuel's first act as judge is to call Israel back to the traditions that give it life.

As he gathers Israel at Mizpah, a town noted for its position on a hilltop, he performs a ritual that adds force to his already spoken words. The action of pouring water before the Lord is somewhat anomalous (vv. 5–6), since we do not find many similar actions elsewhere in Scripture. But the actions are consistent with the notion of sacrifice at times of confession. Samuel's words and actions here, at the beginning of his judgeship, are calls to confession: he performs a libation that summons Israel to fast before God.

Just as suddenly as the Philistine threat disappears (with the return of the ark), they appear on the horizon again. Philistines get word of Israel gathering on the hilltop to worship, spurring these foes to gather against Israel. Word gets back to Israel about the gathering military force and Israel is afraid, clamoring for Samuel to cry out to God without ceasing (vv. 7–8). But the ensuing engagement with the Philistines differs from the skirmishes of chapter 4. In the previous narrative, Israel faces the Philistine threat by mustering an army. Here, it responds by clamoring for Samuel to intercede on its behalf. If Israel is often summoned to war in the chapters that follow, the first act of this new judge and the nation he leads is to entrust the battle to God. Samuel offers a lamb instead of mustering troops, and the result is swift and devastating. As Samuel is in the midst of the offering, God thunders "with a mighty voice" against the Philistines and throws the raiding party into a state of confusion, routing the attackers (vv. 9–10).

The narrative of Samuel as judge thus begins with markers of Israel's lack of trust in God (idols and foreign gods) and turns to a consummate gesture of trust: prayer and intercession in the face of a raiding army. Only after God's first act do the Israelites engage in battle: after the confusion sets in, the men of Israel pursue the Philistines and strike them down (v. 11). But it is clear to whom the battle belongs and who has won it. The army can take little credit here, for there is really only one Warrior who defeats adversaries by the power of a voice. Much has been made about God the warrior in the Scriptures; many debates have been staged over whether such passages justify or condone military violence. But the battle here is not glorified in the ways that modern readers often look back on the "good wars" of history, such as World War II. Battles may be profuse, but the victor in battle is consistently God. This section does not depict the apotheosis of military tactics, but faith in the ultimate triumph of God's purposes, in One who can accomplish those purposes simply by uttering a word.

God's victory over the Philistines evokes yet another ritual: Samuel raises a memorial stone, "Ebenezer," or stone of help (v. 12). A new marker calls Israel back to its moorings in the God who helps. The victory also brings an increase in territory, as Israel claims cities that only a chapter earlier were in the hands of Philistines: Ekron and Gath. But again these territorial gains are interpreted not as the result of military campaigns but the hand of YHWH, that is with Israel and "against the Philistines all the days of Samuel" (vv. 13–14).

Land figures prominently here and in many other sections of 1 and 2 Samuel: the loss of land and its reclamation, rival claims over land, battles that settle questions of land ownership. The faith of Israel is deeply rooted in the land. Some Christians have difficulty grasping the centrality of land and place. They may read sections of the New Testament, such as Jesus' claim that the "Son of Man has nowhere to lay his head" (Luke 9:58), as the ultimate statement of Christian placelessness. It can be tempting to overstate a contrast between a supposed Jewish fixation on place—temple, holy land, diaspora—and a Protestant observation that any place can be holy and that therefore no place is really all that privileged or special in the end. How is the church to read narratives that remember place so intensely? What do these stories that long over the loss of place and rejoice over the regaining of place mean?

For more than forty years, Wendell Berry has rooted his life and work in a particular place, a small plot of land in rural Kentucky. He writes how this attachment to place opens his eyes to the unique features of this landscape and the miracle of life that emerges anew in this place:

> Today as always I have been aware of what has been happening beyond this window. The ground is whitened by patches of melting snow. The river, swollen with the runoff, is swift and muddy. I saw four wood ducks riding the current, apparently

for fun. A great blue heron was fishing, standing in water up to his belly feathers. . . . I see that the life of this place is always emerging beyond expectation or prediction or typicality, that it is unique, given to the world minute by minute, only once, never to be repeated. And then is when I see that this life is a miracle, absolutely worth having, absolutely worth saving.[42]

When we remember, revere, and pay attention to sacred places, we are bound more tightly not only to our ancestors and traditions, but to the living God who meets us in our place. God's call on human life is not only to a task or a mission but to a place: to care for, to tend, to till. Christians lose sight of the incarnation when they claim that place, in the end, does not really matter. God comes to the world in a place, in a person. If all places become holy because of that embrace, it is because the Creator has touched a distinct place and a distinct person. Honoring certain places as holy does not denigrate the rest of the world as "unholy." Rather, it opens our eyes to the holy in the midst of all things and all places.

We glimpse that holiness of all places when we return to familiar places and familiar rituals that we regard as especially holy. In sharing the Lord's Supper week after week, Christians recognize that holiness does not end with the bread and wine at Table, but is encountered whenever food and drink is shared with the hungry and celebrated as a gift from God. As the Deuteronomist names places—Ekron, Gath, Bethel, Gilgal, Mizpah—we are reminded how God is concerned with the particular. Samuel's gestures and words connect Israel to its past and its place; but ultimately they direct Israel to YHWH, who is the Lord of all places and holds out a special concern for the places Israel calls home. Christians ignore place at their peril, because the God of Israel and the God of Christian faith is a God who is revealed in particular places.

> [We] should often be exhorted to seek God our Lord in all things.
>
> Ignatius of Loyola, "Constitutions of the Society of Jesus," in *Ignatius of Loyola: The Spiritual Exercises and Selected Works*, ed. George E. Ganss, S. J. (New York: Paulist, 1991), 292.

42. Wendell Berry, *Life Is a Miracle: An Essay against Modern Superstition* (New York: Counterpoint, 2001), 43–45.

But there is another side to place in the Scriptures: how often place becomes a site of struggle, argument, and even displacement. Israel is promised a place, a land flowing with milk and honey, but there are people already living in that place. Israel finds its place as it displaces others. Israel, too, knows the pain of displacement, as it serves in slavery in Egypt and experiences exile in Babylon. The narrative of place in the Scriptures is not finding a romantic place of one's own that is never contested; it is more like finding a place in order to lose it and losing it in order to find it again. Struggles between peoples over place have continued unabated since these narratives were written. They are woven into the fabric of the Middle East and so many other places around the globe, including the North American continent that has its own ugly story of forcible displacement of Native peoples. We do a disservice to biblical narratives if we do not also recognize the tragedy and contestability of the places named in its pages. Perhaps we best read them by keeping the themes of place and displacement close together. Home and homelessness are not simply opposites, but held together in tension, as they are in the experience of Israel. When we read these stories only in terms of finding a place of one's own, we risk absolutizing and valorizing our place, forgetting that God also works through displacement and the loss of home. But the stories are also not only about displacement: when we neglect the importance of place, we forget how God enters into and cares for distinct places. Places, as they surface in biblical text, are bitterly contested as much as they are promised by God. We read stories about place best when we remember all of the people involved in those stories: the peoples who find home and the people who are displaced, knowing often that most peoples experience place and displacement during the long course of their lives. The history of Israel, if nothing else, shows how God is present with a people in the joy of finding a place and the despair of losing one's place.

At the conclusion of this cycle of stories, Samuel returns to his place in Ramah and builds there an altar to the Lord (v. 17). From this place he judges Israel. And from this place he observes Israel's longing to be like peoples from other places in their hunger for a king. That, as we shall see in the next section, is an ambiguous longing.

1 Samuel 8–15:33
King Saul

In this next section of the narrative, the longings begin not with the prayer of a woman but with the cries of a nation. Thus far Samuel has served as a wise judge. But for a people anxious about their own status in relation to surrounding peoples, his leadership is not enough. Israel longs for a king who will lead them in military victory against enemies, one who will make them "like the nations." This desire to become like the nations is a decidedly mixed blessing: if it brings initial victory on the plain of war, it also leads Israel away from fidelity to its covenant with God. Hearing Israel's longings, however, God relents by choosing a man who replaces Samuel as Israel's first king.

These next several chapters focus, accordingly, on Saul, who is one of the more intriguing characters in the Hebrew Bible. Externally, he embodies much of the kingly ideal: physical attractiveness, strong military leadership, public piety, even a regal air. His story begins with humility and modesty, and he shows great concern for Israel's covenant. But as his reign progresses, he becomes an increasingly tragic—and at times, detestable—figure. As the initial promise of his reign grows into fruition, he also embodies envy, deceit, and treachery. The office has changed him or at least brought out aspects of his character that were hitherto invisible. We do not see the full extent of these personal failings until later chapters, but here they have their beginnings.

As the narrative focuses on Saul, however, not all of the blame for his downfall lays at his feet. Saul only comes to be king because the people clamored so loudly for one. Israel is hardly an innocent bystander to royal shenanigans. Indeed, the people have created a king in their own likeness. By thinking that a leader will provide the solution to the nation's problems, the people also stand judged. Though these subsequent stories provide a framework for considering the successes and failures of kingly leadership, they also suggest that kingship, at best, is a second best arrangement that already signals a compromise between Israel and its God.

8:1–22

Longing for a King

Samuel's stint as judge, narratively speaking, does not last long. What we know of his judgeship is auspicious: he addresses the Philistine threat, performs sacrifices rightly, and—most pivotally—administers justice and builds an altar to the Lord in Ramah. The house of Israel appears in order. The turn is sudden in chapter 8, where Samuel is advanced in age and steps down so that his sons may judge in his stead. Their behavior recalls that of Eli's sons (2:11–17). Where Samuel administers with justice, Joel and Abijah pervert justice and take bribes (8:1–3). Money, rather than wisdom and faithfulness, becomes the arbiter of what is fair, good, and right. Joel and Abijah "turn aside" (v. 3) from justice to seek personal gain. What is most eerie about this opening is that the corruption of these two sons sets the stage for the inauguration of kingship. Will Israel's kings prove any different than Eli's sons?

Elders come to meet the old judge Samuel (not the present judges Joel and Abijah). The account is intriguing, as if these elders and Samuel constitute the power structure behind the figures in power. Nearly every leader has a cabinet; some cabinets work at cross-purposes to the leader. This cabinet, however, works behind the scene by consulting with the former leader, constituting an "old guard." Their remarks are direct: Samuel is old, his sons do not follow him, the time is ripe for a change. And then, most decisively, they urge Samuel to "appoint a king to govern us, *like other nations*" (v. 5, emphasis mine). This desire to be like the nations is almost never interpreted positively. In its desire to become like the nations, Israel ignores the particularity of its call, the way it is called to be a signal to another way of being and doing rather than replicating what others do. The desire to be like the nations is the desire to escape from God's claims on Israel. This is what disturbs Samuel. Demands for a king are more than a personal insult to his judgeship; they forget the way that God has ruled over Israel in ways that no king ever could. In the face of these demands, Samuel prays (v. 6). Even the old guard of elders seems to be rejecting him.

God's answer to Samuel's prayer, however, is even more striking: It is first a call for Samuel to listen to the people. In the face of a demand that seems inconsistent with the

> It is most natural for me to think of prayer in terms of the open hand.
>
> Howard Thurman, *Meditations of the Heart* (Boston: Beacon, 1981), 174.

life of a covenant people, God tells Samuel to pay attention. But in listening, Samuel will also discern that Israel's demand is a rejection of YHWH as king, a rejection that falls in line with the seemingly countless ways Israel has turned aside from God ever since the Exodus (vv. 7–8). This is an exceptionally strong statement: In asking for something, Israel is *rejecting* God. The judgment has already been made, even before a king comes to their midst. The monarchy could hardly have begun with less divine enthusiasm. If God is to choose or anoint a king, that anointing occurs only in the context of Israel's rejection of YHWH's kingship. In listening to Israel's demands, Samuel may pave the way for the first king, but he is also prepared to warn Israel about the consequences of their demands (v. 9).

Samuel's words to the people are not the stuff of royal pageantry. By reporting God's words to the people, he indicates the character of the king who will come. The description is vivid and one verb dominates: *take.* The king who will come will take Israel's sons: for the military, for agriculture, for industry. Kings take from their people and bolster the kings' power through the waging of war and harnessing the means of production. But the king's taking will not cease there: Israel can expect its daughters to be taken as well, in household duties for the good of the kingdom (v. 13). The king will also "take the best of your fields and vineyards and olive orchards" (v. 14) to give to his underlings. Here the king's taking is less for the good of the nation and more for the self-aggrandizement of the royal court. And yet this king will keep on taking: property, livestock, possessions, levies, taxes. The ultimate effect: Israel will experience itself as slaves to the king (v. 17). In demanding to be like the nations, Israel wills itself back into slavery, revoking the liberation that God has brought. If Israel complained during the Exodus that they had it better back in Egypt (cf. Num. 20:5), in their desire for a king they will finally get their wish: slavery at the hands of their own people rather than at the hands of foreigners. Their present cries *for* a king will soon become cries *because* of a king, cries that God will not answer (v. 18).

Samuel has warned the people of the assured consequences of their longings, but the people refuse to listen. Instead, they add another justification for their demand for a king: to "fight our battles" (v. 20). War nearly always provides justification for a powerful leader. Peoples often surrender liberties (or have their freedoms taken from them) in the face of war or the threat of war (witness the Patriot Act during the war on terror and the imprisonment of Japanese Americans during World War II). This justification, however, rings hollow in Samuel's context. It is hardly an argument for a king; it is more aptly a further mark of Israel's rejection of YHWH. The battles that Israel has won thus far in the story have been won by God. But apparently, that was not enough. War, or the threat of war, quickly causes Israel to forget where it came from, and to whom it owes its life: someone other than a king.

Yet the demands keep coming. Samuel hears the protests of the people and repeats them to God. God's response to these demands, given the strong words against kings thus far, is as surprising as it is brief: "Listen to their voice and set a king over them" (v. 22). What is going on here? On the one hand, God relents. In the face of stubborn demands, however unwise, God simply accedes to the demands and lets the people act against divine will. Or perhaps God is acting as teacher here: "You want a king? I've already told you what a king will do. You still want a king? Okay, then I'll send you one and you'll see for yourself what a king will do." Either of these interpretations is certainly possible; both seem true to the story thus far. But another interpretation is also plausible, one that also accounts for the story yet to come. For in the pages that follow, readers learn how much kings fall short *and* how kings can be the recipient of divine blessing.

In this interpretation, God's statement "listen to their voice and set a king over them" reveals a God who revisits and reassesses for the sake of the covenant God has made with God's people. The God of Israel is a God who *responds* to people in relationship. The divine will of this covenantal God is not a will of iron, fixed for all eternity, immovable in its tracks, forever ordaining things one way and in one way only. That view of divine will is more like fate than providence. Or, as Catherine Keller has put it, "Once the doctrine of divine all-control is locked in place, both the biblical concepts of divine love and of sin are undermined. Love and responsibility go down the tubes. . . ."[1] God's power in Scripture, she suggests, reveals itself differently, by responding, yielding, and empowering: "The power of God, if it is a response-able power, *empowers* the others—to respond. In their freedom. God's will is indeed God's will! But the term *will* derives from *voluntas*, from which also comes 'voluntary,' which means not control but *desire*. What God *wants*."[2] God wants the people to flourish; God knows that a king will often cause them not to flourish. But God does not impose God's kingship on Israel. God is also willing, for the sake of relationship, to live with Israel's demand. This says something remarkable about the power and providence of God: that it is unlike the power of earthly kings. Whereas earthly kings are prone to wield power over their subjects, the power of God is power *with*. In comparison to the supposed power of kings, it often seems weak. But the ways of God typically confound those bent on a will to power. Few places in Scripture emphasize this as much as Paul, "For God's foolishness is wiser than human wisdom, and God's weakness is stronger than human strength. . . . God chose what is low and despised in the world, things that are not, to reduce to nothing things that are, so that no one might boast in the presence of God" (1 Cor. 1:25, 28–29). If God's weakness is stronger than human power, God's power is also perfected by weakness: "My

---

1. Catherine Keller, *On the Mystery: Discerning God in Process* (Minneapolis: Fortress Press, 2008), 79.
2. Ibid., 89.

grace is sufficient for you, for power is made perfect in weakness" (2 Cor. 12:9).

In this pivotal conversation between God and Samuel, God is willing to relent for the sake of covenant, or as Walter Brueggemann writes, "Yahweh is willing to let Israel choose, and then Israel must live with its choice. . . . Yahweh is rejected (v. 7). How remarkable that Yahweh concedes everything, does not resist, does not argue, does not rage, does not retaliate."[3]

> **The power made perfect in weakness may belong to a congregation that loses members because of a courageous stance.**
>
> Catherine Keller, *On the Mystery* (Minneapolis: Fortress, 2008), 85.

This decision, even if it is for the sake of relationship, also conveys much sadness and loss. Israel is losing something in its desire for a king: some of its innocence, some of its blessing, much of its security. Perhaps that sadness is best captured in Samuel's response to the people. He does not repeat YHWH's words but instead simply tells the people to return home (v. 22), as if he cannot bear hearing those words again.

9:1–10:8

Finding and Anointing a King

The warnings have now been uttered. Nonetheless, the beginning of Saul's story is auspicious. His genealogy is strong: he is a Benjaminite and his father, Kish, is very wealthy. Saul comes from a family with name and money, and he is also tall and good-looking (vv. 1–2). This is someone who *looks* like he could lead. The narrator makes similar comments on David's appearance (cf. 16:12). But looks can also be deceiving, hiding flaws in character and leadership. At least Saul looks the part.

Kish has lost his donkeys. The text is ambiguous: Have *all* of Kish's donkeys strayed? If so, then this loss would be catastrophic, at least in economic terms. Have *some* of the donkeys strayed? If so,

---

3. Walter Brueggemann, *First and Second Samuel* (Louisville, KY: John Knox Press, 1990), 68.

the economic damage would certainly be less yet still significant.[4] Kish sends his son and a boy to go in search of the donkeys. This beginning rings like a fable: a son goes in search of some donkeys and finds something else instead. The search takes the two companions through many different lands (vv. 3–4), ostensibly to recover the livestock but in actuality to familiarize Saul with the land that he soon will reign over.

The search proves increasingly fruitless, so much that Saul suggests to his companion that they return home, lest Kish's worry over the donkeys be replaced by worry over Saul and the boy. The boy, however, has a different suggestion: to inquire of the man of God nearby (vv. 5–6). Much like the boy Samuel leads adults in proper worship, this boy leads Saul to the one who will anoint Saul. Indeed, the story has come full circle, with a child showing the future king the way and a new hope. As a child leads a future king, we are reminded of the king who comes as a child: "The wolf shall live with the lamb, the leopard shall lie down with the kid, the calf and the lion and the fatling together, and a little child shall lead them" (Isa. 11:6).

Because he is empty-handed, Saul is initially hesitant to meet the man of God who will tell him about his journey. But the boy who has accompanied Saul has a quarter shekel of silver: enough, it seems, to honor the seer. At this point, the narrator inserts a historical aside that equates seer with prophet. Perhaps this is done to reinforce the point that the one whom they seek, a seer/prophet, is also what Saul becomes (vv. 7–10).

Two girls appear to aid in the search. They tell the companions where to find the seer and inform the travelers that a sacrifice will take place on that day. The girls point the companions in the right direction, and as they enter town, they encounter the seer, who is now identified as Samuel (vv. 11–14). The delay in mentioning the seer's name is intriguing. Perhaps the story circulated in earlier times without naming Samuel. Perhaps there is literary artistry and suspense building as Samuel is named at this later stage. But the name certainly raises the stakes, for here the two companions encounter one who has judged Israel just as he is moving toward the shrine, the

4. P. Kyle McCarter, "1 Samuel," textual notes in *The HarperCollins Study Bible,* ed. Wayne A. Meeks (New York: HarperCollins, 1993), 428.

locus of religious obligation and ritual. It makes for a riveting scene: a boy, a man who will soon be king, and a king maker.

Samuel has already been prepared for this moment; God told him the previous day that Samuel would meet the future king. But the God who speaks now strikes a different tone from the warnings of the previous chapter. God instructs Samuel to anoint the Benjaminite he is to meet to be "ruler" over God's people Israel, one who will save the people from the Philistines (vv. 15–16). The cries of the people for a military protector are not simply the ravings of insecurity. God perceives the threat as well, and presents a future king not merely as a concession to people's demands but also as a response to legitimate cries for help. This is the shape of God's covenantal love: to respond to the voice of God's people with compassion and aid.

As Saul searches for the seer, Samuel finds the would-be king. Saul does not know who Samuel is, but Samuel knows him. He tells Saul to give no further thought to the donkeys, "for they have been found" (v. 20). But of course the one who has really been found is Saul. Samuel's words to Saul are lofty, that Israel's desire is fixed on Saul. Desire has a complicated history in the church. It has sometimes been viewed with suspicion, either because it is too strong a passion or because it has been linked inextricably to sex. But the God of Israel's history is a God who desires the people's flourishing, a God who seeks God's people with passion. Much of the narrative tension of the Deuteronomistic History can be linked to whether or not Israel's desires are in line with God's desires for Israel. In the case of Samuel's affirmation of Saul, there are traces of desire for good *and* ill. The people seek a leader, and these desires find their answer in God's choice of Samuel. But it is also the case that these desires are not innocent: they stem, after all, from the intent to be like the other nations. Yet as Samuel speaks these words to Saul, they single out Saul as someone special, someone chosen, someone who may assuage some of the people's desires and even express the desire of God.

Saul's response to these lofty words is humble. He claims to be from the least of Israel's tribes and a lowly family (v. 21, although the reader already knows that his father is wealthy). Saul may be engaging in unwarranted self-deprecation here, but there is also something positive to these words. Saul is presented, at least initially, as a leader who does not arrogate power to himself but as someone who receives the mantle of leadership from another. He responds to Samuel's words of acclamation with diffidence, humility, and even wonder. These are traits that can serve leaders well. Polzin notes how Saul "appears to be exactly the kind of man whom Samuel would have every hope of molding into a compliant king."[5]

After speaking these words of acclaim, Samuel leads Saul and his servant to dine, giving them a place (symbolically) at the head of the table. Here we see Saul occupying another role as he performs actions typical of priests. He is given the portion of thigh meat set aside, a reserved portion that a priest would eat. His actions indicate that the future king will also occupy a priestly role (just as Samuel did before him). Saul's embodiment of the priestly ideal, of course, is rather deficient, as subsequent episodes in his life indicate (cf. 13:1–15). But at the beginning of his story, he is presented as both honored guest and as host, leader and priest, offering and receiving hospitality. The meal ends; Samuel escorts Saul from the shrine to his house, and Saul is given the place of honor for the night: on the roof, where the temperature is best for sleeping (vv. 22–25).

The confirmation of Saul's election as king comes the next day with an anointing that happens not in the presence of all Israel, but in private. Even the boy who accompanies Saul does not witness it. The word that Samuel speaks to Saul comes both in speech and in action. It is first a word encountered in oil and a kiss, a word that becomes flesh (10:1). These acts of bodily affection and care prepare Saul for hearing the word. The liturgies of synagogue and church consistently remember that word does not only encounter us audibly: word is also tasted in a meal (Passover and Eucharist) and felt in a bath (baptism). The word that Samuel speaks comes after the word touches him,

> How holy, just, and worthy must be the person who touches [Christ] with his hands, receives [Christ] in his heart and mouth, and offers [Christ] to others to be received.
>
> Francis of Assisi, "A Letter to the Entire Order," in *Francis and Clare: The Complete Works*, trans. Regis J. Armstrong and Ignatius C. Brady (New York: Paulist, 1982), 57.

5. Polzin, *Samuel and the Deuteronomist* (San Francisco: Harper & Row, 1989), 104.

a word that claims Saul will reign over his people and save them from their enemies.

This anointing, which has been performed in private, will eventually result in public acclamation. The word that is used to describe the land of Saul's reign is an interesting one: heritage, connoting something acquired as a gift or inheritance. This further indicates the graciousness of Saul's reign: it is something that he receives on behalf of others, not something that he seizes.

Donkeys have been lost, but now they have been found, just as Kish has lost a son who has now been found as a king. Saul will also receive offerings from three men of Tabor (vv. 2–3) in a manner akin to a priest. Samuel further tells Saul that he will also act as prophet, as Saul encounters a disruptive spirit of the Lord, which will make him a "different person." But in the midst of that disruption, Samuel promises Saul that God will be with him. As Saul is sent to Gilgal and told to wait seven days for Samuel so that proper sacrifices can be made (vv. 5-8), the reader senses how auspicious the beginning is. It has all the marks of true kingship and the seal of God's blessing. All that it needs now is public affirmation. But there is also a shadow side to Samuel's instructions to Saul: Samuel may be seeking "personal control" over Saul and a "warrant for royal dependence."[6] Samuel expects Saul to obey his every word.

FURTHER REFLECTIONS
Christ as Prophet, Priest, and King

Here, at the "birth" of kingship in Israel, the Deuteronomist portrays Saul in multiple lights: anointed king and ruler, quasi-priest who consumes the reserved meat, and—in the next section—as ecstatic prophet. Kings in Israel sometimes play more than one role. In its interpretation of Christ, the new king, the Christian church has looked to the Hebrew Scriptures to interpret the one they also proclaim as prophet and priest. The Reformed tradition, in particular, is

---

6. Ibid., 106.

known for emphasizing these threefold offices, placing the ministry of Jesus in continuity with Israel's worship and adherence to Torah.

In this tradition Jesus acts as prophet to the world, "revealing to us, by his Word and Spirit, the will of God for our salvation."[7] Christ is the one who both *denounces* the powers that enslave human beings to sin and *announces* the Good News of salvation in and through him. As prophet, Jesus shows us the way into the fullness of God's promises. His prophetic word encompasses his life and ministry, judging a world of corruption and oppression, offering a vision of God's reign where peace, justice, and abundance are shared with all creation.

As priest, Jesus intercedes for us, offering a sacrifice "to satisfy divine justice, and reconcile us to God."[8] Christ provides the ultimate priestly offering of himself: "By the sacrifice of his death he blotted out our own guilt and made satisfaction for our sins."[9] This sacrifice reflects not so much God's demand of a payment as much as it does the enormity of sin, its cost to all forms of life on earth. Christ's sacrificial death illustrates the extent to which Christ goes to be with us in solidarity, even unto death.

Christ's kingly office emphasizes his lordship of the world, his governance of the cosmos, and his transformation of death into life. As king, Christ calls "out of the world a people to himself" and gives them laws, preserves and supports them "under all their temptations and sufferings . . . powerfully ordering all things for his own glory and their good."[10] The kingship of Christ is illustrated in his resurrection from the dead, the effective triumph of the gospel over all that would enslave, destroy, and bring death. From the shadow of the grave, God raises Jesus to new life that will abide until the end of days. Christ's kingdom is not a magnification of earthly kingdoms but represents an entirely different order. As Calvin writes, "Christ's

---

7. The Shorter Catechism of the Westminster Confession of Faith, *The Constitution of the Presbyterian Church (U.S.A.)*, Part I, *Book of Confessions* (Louisville, KY: Office of the General Assembly, Presbyterian Church (U.S.A.), 1996), 7.024.

8. Ibid.

9. John Calvin, *Institutes of the Christian Religion*, ed. John T. McNeill, trans. Ford Lewis Battles, LCC (Philadelphia: Westminster Press, 1960), 502.

10. "The Larger Catechism," in the *Book of Confessions*, 7.155.

Kingdom lies in the Spirit, not in earthly pleasures or pomp. Hence we must forsake the world if we are to share in the Kingdom."[11]

Each of these offices is prone to distortion in our day. Jesus the prophet can be twisted into an unyielding moralist fixated on right behavior (What would Jesus do?) whose denunciations of sin blind us to the grace in our midst. Christ the priest can be manipulated into a masochist who valorizes all sacrifices as signs of redemption, when in fact many sacrifices inhibit life rather than enhance it. Christ the king can mirror the structures of power in a capitalist society, emulating a C.E.O. As Joerg Rieger writes, such a Christ "stands for those who believe that they have pulled themselves up by their own bootstraps, and who advocates the survival of the fittest when economic times are tough."[12] What is to prevent the church from distorting Christ's offices? One way is by reading the accounts of prophecy, priesthood, and kingship in the Hebrew Scriptures. There we see prophecy in the service of a life of a people, priestly sacrifice that calls Israel back to its God, kingship that stands under God's Word—even when kings such as Saul fail—and thereby reorients the structures of power in the world. Jesus is prophet, priest, and king not because he departs from Israel's conceptions of these offices, but because he embodies them in their fullness and offers them to the world for the sake of life. The One whom Christians call prophet, priest, and king is also the One who comes from Israel, whose disciples called him "rabbi."

10:9–27a

Prophetic Frenzy, Public Acclamation

Saul turns from Samuel, and in his turning something astonishing happens: God gives Saul a new heart (v. 9). In Israel's understanding of anatomy, and indeed in the broad arc of Scripture, the heart occupies center stage. It is not, as in much Western thought, the seat

11. Calvin, *Institutes*, 500.
12. Joerg Rieger, "Christ's Offices Reconsidered," in *Constructive Theology: A Contemporary Approach to Classical Themes*, ed. Serene Jones and Paul Lakeland (Minneapolis: Fortress, 2005), 192.

of the affections and emotions but "characterizes humans first and foremost as 'rational beings' that are susceptible to teaching and learning." The heart represents human conduct and our capacities for acting consciously and strategically.[13] Where the heart leads, there the person will go. In Ezekiel, the prophet foresees a restoration of Israel that is symbolized in God's creation of a new heart: "I will give them one heart, and put a new spirit within them; I will remove the heart of stone from their flesh and give them a heart of flesh, so that they may follow my statutes and keep my ordinances and obey them. Then they shall be my people, and I will be their God" (Ezek. 11:19–20). God can change the heart, even the heart of the most hardened. "Create in me a clean heart, O God, and put a new and right spirit within me," rings the psalmist (Ps. 51:10), echoed in many Christian congregations as a prayer of confession, a chorus that expresses the hope that God transforms the hearts of sinners. Wherever we find ourselves, God's renewal is never far away. At this turn in the story, Saul has been acknowledged in private as Israel's future king, a calling that requires nothing less than a new heart, a change that provides the internal confirmation that Saul is God's chosen.

Internal transformation leads to an encounter with prophets. As soon as Saul meets them, the spirit of God possesses him as he falls into frenzy (v. 10). Again, YHWH proves the pivotal actor in the story: whatever prophetic gifts Saul can claim are the result of God's activity. The movement of the spirit is multifaceted in Saul's life; often it is disturbing. Later in the narrative Saul is tormented by an evil spirit sent by God (16:14). Here the spirit's aim is more benign, but it is nonetheless disruptive. Saul does not seem himself, and those who have known him are also perplexed. Their questions, "What has come over the Son of Kish? Is Saul also among the prophets?" (v. 11) reflect surprise rather than confirmation of his newfound role. This frenzy seems ambiguous, even embarrassing. Polzin claims the incident expresses "a central problem with the reign of Saul . . . the disastrous confusion of monarchic and prophetic offices" in his person.[14]

---

13. Andreas Schuele, "Heart," in *The New Interpreter's Dictionary of the Bible*, vol. 2., ed. Katharine Doob Sakenfeld (Nashville: Abingdon, 2007), 764.
14. Polzin, *Samuel*, 101.

Saul does not give a message amid his seeming madness. The image is chaotic and ecstatic, of a man on the brink, a foreshadowing of his own reign that is often precarious, as his grip on the monarchy will soon start slipping from his hands. Saul seems at the edge of sanity in this vignette; subsequent chapters will reveal a man who seems to have succumbed to insanity. But his head and his heart are sustained by the spirit of God, which upholds kings just as surely as it can bring down kingdoms.

The frenzy subsides and Saul returns home. Upon entering his hometown he first meets not his father but his uncle. Is Kish embarrassed over his son's behavior? Perplexed over the word of the prophetic incident?

The uncle's question, "Where did you go?" is also a bit odd. Surely, he knew that Saul had been dispatched to find the donkeys.

> And [Jesus] said, "Truly I tell you, no prophet is accepted in the prophet's hometown."
>
> Luke 4:24

Saul reveals to his uncle that he went to Samuel, but the only thing Saul tells his uncle about Samuel's words is that the donkeys have been found. About the weightiest matters, Saul is silent (vv. 13–16). Whether Saul's silence represents appropriate modesty or the beginnings of an evasion of responsibility is not clear. But at this point silence speaks more loudly then words.

Silence over kingship, however, cannot be kept for long. Samuel summons the people to the Lord. The gathering has a touch of the mythic: "all the tribes of Israel" (v. 20) are there—a gathering that is as much symbolic as it is factual history. At this gathering to proclaim a king, however, the first words are of remembrance. Samuel recalls God's mighty acts of deliverance that brought a people out of slavery into freedom. This liberation that ought to have engendered faithfulness in God's people instead has bred departure from the covenant. The choosing of a king is marked with these inauspicious words: "Today you have rejected your God" (v. 19). Again, the nod toward monarchy is reluctant, at least on the part of the religious authority. Coronations are meant to revel in pomp and national pride; how different Israel's first coronation is, by looking backward rather than

forward, in confession rather than celebration. Samuel's words provoke many questions about the nature of political authority. Is political leadership, whatever form, a concession to human sinfulness? Or
are there systems of political power that are closer to God's intent
for human society? The answer to both of those questions, at least at
the outset of Saul's kingship, appears to be "yes." For, if the demand
for a king is the result of sin, God is able to work even within a monarchy to accomplish good. Political theorists of the past, however,
who saw in these pages an endorsement of the "divine right of kings"
took many liberties with the text. Words about kingship in the Bible
begin with warnings about kingly power and hesitancy over the idea
of monarchy itself rather than celebrations of royal prerogatives.

Though the reader knows who is to be king already, the gathered
tribes do not. Lots are taken, a common ancient practice of discerning God's will (cf. Acts 1:21–26, where Matthias is chosen by lot
to replace Judas among the disciples). For many of us, the practice
seems arbitrary and governed more by fortune than the Spirit. But
for a community that senses the movement of God's spirit in all
things, the practice reflects careful discernment. As the lots narrow
to the tribe of Benjamin, the family of the Matrites, and ultimately
to Saul, at the pivotal moment Saul has disappeared. The crowd
does not even know whether he accompanied them to the assembly.
His location is not made known until YHWH reveals his location:
among the baggage, an appropriate spot for hiding. Amid these piles
of stuff for the journey, they find the future king, already weighed
down with the baggage of his newfound responsibility. As he rises
from the baggage of the crowd into the burden of a new role, the
reader notices one thing: his appearance, a man who is taller than
anyone else (vv. 21–23). Samuel claims there is no one like him, an
ambiguous endorsement at best. As the good-looking man towers
over the crowd, the acclamation rises up, "Long live the king!" (v.
24). The rabble's enthusiasm has already drowned out the pious old
man's words. But at last what has been made known in private is
affirmed in public.

Saul does not speak, but Samuel continues: telling the crowd of
the duties and responsibilities of kings, recording these words for
posterity. And then the people go home; Samuel sends them home

(not Saul). We read of no fanfare, no dancing, no celebration. The people have received what they wanted, and now it is time to move on. Of note is Saul's choice of warriors. Every leader needs a few strong men to serve the political cause (vv. 25–26). Yesterday's men with swords are not much different from today's political strategists and spin doctors. But these men are also those who have had their hearts touched by God. Even amid this concession toward monarchy, God works within the system, touching hearts and bringing treasure out of trash. Even when Saul is accosted by detractors, those who despise him, "How can this man save us?" (v. 27), Saul holds his tongue. The first threat to his office is met with royal restraint. Perhaps it will turn out well after all. He stands head and shoulders above the crowd and does not say rash things.

10:27b–11:15

Military Success

Samuel has claimed that the new king will save the people from "the hand of their enemies all around" (10:1). Saul's first act as king is to deal with a foreign power, the Ammonites, and he does so successfully. Whatever his faults, Saul is a keen military man, a strong commander who knows the craft of war. If he is to serve as king, he must dispatch the dangers at hand on the edges of Israelite territory, both east and west.

The setup is gruesome. Nahash, the king of the Ammonites, is oppressing the tribes of Gad and Reuben, who live east of the Jordan. To make matters worse, he is gouging out their right eyes (v. 27). The act is both sadistic in its wanton infliction of suffering and symbolic in that loss of an eye leads to the loss of depth perception. To see with only one eye is to lose the fullness of sight. The Gadites and Reubenites are thus marked as belonging to Nahash and demeaned as less than full persons. This forcible dismemberment of the body also mocks Israel's covenant. If part of the aim of covenant is to present the whole of oneself and the nation before God, the sadistic dismemberment of the body renders the Gadites and Reubenites somewhat less than whole before God and before each other. The inhabitants of Jabesh-gilead seem to have internalized this oppression and degradation, as they seek a treaty with Nahash so that they might serve him (11:1). Better to make a pact with the enemy than to suffer continued humiliation and degradation at his hands. But the offer to make a pact will only result in continued dismemberment. Nahash agrees to the treaty, but only on the condition that he will gouge out everyone's right eye and "put disgrace upon all Israel" (v. 2). Now the logic of the invading king is clear: to inflict bodily harm on the entire covenant people.

The timing of this military challenge is intriguing. Chapter 11 begins with the phrase "about a month later," connecting the Ammonite threat to the public acclamation of Saul as king (10:17–27). But earlier, Samuel has instructed Saul to wait for him at Gilgal for seven days (10:8), a meeting that does not occur until the end of chapter 11. This literary inconsistency, again, is likely due to the original independence of each narrative. If chapter 10 indicates Saul's prophetic bent and his acclaim in the sight of the people, chapter 11 offers an interlude of his military prowess.

News of the oppression and cruelty reaches Saul as he is coming in from the field. He hears the news with an immediate surge of emotion induced by the Spirit. Again, Saul seems on the edge of self-control as the Spirit disrupts the customary order. His response is a vivid display of anger that demonstrates both how Israel is bound together as a people and the wrath of the man who is now king. Though Saul is not foaming at the mouth, he is not far from it in his fury (vv. 5–6). What is the role of anger in the Christian life? Some strands of the Bible warn against anger: "Those with good sense are slow to anger, and it is their glory to overlook an offense" (Prov. 19:11). Often the church has perceived anger as remote from the work of love, that the saints eventually transcend anger for the sake of love. Others, such as Beverly Harrison, connect the power of anger directly to love: "Anger is not the opposite of love. It is better understood as a feeling-signal that all is not well in our relation to other persons or groups or to the world around us. Anger is a mode of connectedness to others and it is always a vivid form of caring."[15]

15. Beverly Wildung Harrison, *Making the Connections: Essays in Feminist Social Ethics* (Boston: Beacon, 1985), 14.

In Saul's case, the origin and direction of his anger are not all that clear. Certainly, his anger is connected to his concern for justice in the land.

He is rightly incensed that his fellow Israelites are being brutalized by a cruel king. But his display of anger, cutting oxen in pieces and sending them throughout the kingdom, is also accompanied with a threat: whoever is not with me in this battle, so shall it be done to his oxen! (v. 7). Saul's action is both a symbolic display of the interconnection of Israel's tribes (yoked together as oxen are, so that whatever affects one tribe also affects the others) and a rash display of anger, as a man unhinged. Is this a clear-eyed military commander, the ravings of a strong man, or a little of both? However we answer that question, Saul emerges in this vignette with formidable physical strength and decisiveness that hovers on the edge of sanity.

> We Christians have come very close to killing love precisely because we have understood anger to be a deadly sin.
>
> Beverly Wildung Harrison, *Making the Connections* (Boston: Beacon, 1985), 14.

Saul summons hundreds of thousands and the battle is swift. Word is sent to those suffering in Jabesh that they will soon experience deliverance. Details of the battle are not even reported (vv. 8–10). Saul's army attacks the camp and cuts down the Ammonites, scattering them so that "no two of them were left together" (v. 11). The victory could not be clearer. It is a decisive show of force by an imposing man capable of summoning the allegiance of multitudes. Whether there is literary hyperbole in the numbers of soldiers assembled does not really matter. The Saul who emerges from this skirmish is a man to be reckoned with.

After the battle, the people are both intimidated by and enthralled with Saul. They ask Samuel (who appears again) about those who questioned Saul's reign, demanding that they be put to death (v. 12). The people have seen the success of the leader and now reckon that questioning the leader is an act of treason. The echoes of their words are haunting in this day, where questioning of national security policies or lampooning those in power is likely to raise charges of disloyalty to country. The political intrigue of ancient Israel is not that remote from the present day. Saul's response, however, immediately defers that demand: "No one shall be put to death today" (v. 13), though the reader wonders whether some will be put to death in the future. On a day when his troops seem invincible, Saul claims that the Lord has brought deliverance for Israel.

Now, after a vivid display of military prowess, after public acclamation in the sight of all Israel, is the full investiture of the king ready to commence. And it proceeds like the old guard would have it: Samuel summons the people to Gilgal to make sacrifice (vv. 14–15). There is something poignant in this scene, of the last judge offering sacrifices with the people as the new king is installed. The king cannot simply revel in military success (even if national security is his chief raison d'être); he must also orient the people to worship of God. Only then can Israel rejoice in its king.

12:1–25
Samuel's Farewell Address

Sacrifices have been performed and now it is time for Samuel to address the crowd at this pivotal moment of transition. Though Samuel is not disappearing from the scene, his role from here forward will differ. His words sound like a last testament, but they are also a call to remembrance and confession. At this time of looking toward Israel's future, Samuel calls the people to look back on what they have done, and most importantly on what God has done. Samuel begins by reminding the Israelites of his own role. He has listened to the people and set a king over them. The king leads now, but intriguingly, the king is not named (vv. 1–2). The circumspect nature of Samuel's speech is enhanced by this device. In refraining from naming Saul, Samuel adds a touch of wariness and suspicion. Indeed, this will only intensify as the address progresses. At this time of coronation, the king is not celebrated. This day is no cause for jubilation; instead it is cause for regret.

Samuel begins his address by noting how he has listened to Israel. By listening to Israel's cries, Samuel has set a king over Israel. The subject of this sentence—I (Samuel)—is intriguing. Prior narration has claimed YHWH has made Saul king, as a divine concession to Israel's relentless demands. If the people were not content with YHWH as king, then perhaps God can work through a human king. But at the beginning of his address, Samuel presents himself as the one who sets a king over Israel. Perhaps he cannot bear the thought of public proclamation of the new king as YHWH's anointed. Perhaps this is a way of pointing to the interconnection between God's work and Samuel's own. At the very least, the portrait is of a leader who attends to his people, even when that attention results in choices that the leader himself would not have made.

Much of the beginning of Samuel's address is occupied with self-defense. He poses questions to the crowd, asking whether he had ever stolen, defrauded, or oppressed the people. The people respond negatively. The point is contrast with the kings who are to come, who will take from Israel. Samuel's defense concludes with the claim that the people have "not found anything in my hand" (v. 5). Samuel leaves the scene empty handed, holding on to nothing save his integrity. Good leaders are not noted for accumulation but for how much they leave behind for their people and how little they leave for themselves.

Samuel transitions from an assessment of his leadership to an account of YHWH's dealings with Israel. Instead of looking forward, Samuel begins retrospectively by calling the people to remember God's faithfulness and their own tendency to turn away. He recites the heroes of the faith—Moses, Aaron, Jacob, judges like Jerubbaal, Barak, and Samson—and recalls God's saving deeds. The human characters in each account are different but the pattern the same: God is faithful, bringing God's people out of bondage and oppression, but the people forget God's faithfulness and long after other things, falling away from God and into the hand of enemies. But God will not give up on God's people. This pattern will continue in the future. Even if their demand for a king represents a lack of faith, God will redeem God's people and work through a king for Israel's benefit (vv. 6–13).

The God who will not give up on Israel also places requirements on the people. These requirements are central to the next section of Samuel's address and point to the crux of Deuteronomistic theology:

"If you will fear the LORD and serve him and heed his voice and not rebel against the commandment of the LORD, and if both you and the king who reigns over you will follow the LORD your God, it will be well; but if you will not heed the voice of the LORD, but rebel against the commandment of the LORD, then the hand of the LORD will be against you and your king" (vv. 14–15). The pattern of "if . . . then" holds the key. And it all depends on whether or not Israel—and its king—will listen to God.[16] Not whether the king proves charismatic, a good military man, or a bringer of prosperity to the land; not whether Israel listens to its king, but whether Israel listens to God and obeys the commandments. Israel's king is not set over the law, but under it. The beginning of kingship in Israel is marked by an address that adds the king almost as an afterthought. Things will go well, and God will be with the people if the people heed God's voice and follow the commandments. Kings only matter and are only beneficial if they instruct a people to listen to a voice other than their own.

Added to this effective afterthought of a king is the blunt claim that the demand for a king is wickedness in the sight of the Lord. These are hardly words of coronation! Accompanying this dismal claim is ominous weather: on a day of wheat harvest, the most important day of the year for clear weather, Samuel implores God to send thunder and rain (v. 17). Here is a final glimpse at Samuel's priestly power in relation to the divine. His proximity to God makes him capable of bringing God's blessing and judgment in ways that others cannot. The king who will come will not have these same capabilities. But it seems that only this dramatic gesture will bring the people to recognize the error of their demands. Nowhere in the narrative until now—despite Samuel's warnings, despite the narrative judgment against kingship—do the people ever recognize the destructive nature of their demands for a king. Only when faced with the destruction of their harvest are they able to listen and confess, asking Samuel to intercede for them, claiming that they have added to their sin by demanding a king. They confess out of fear that the harvest will be destroyed, fear of God's wrath, fear of their own

16. "Everything depends on Israel listening or not listening." Brueggemann, *First and Second Samuel*, 93.

sin, and perhaps fear of Samuel's power. But Samuel's closing words for them are not to fear. He calls for them not to turn away from fulfilling the Lord's commandments, and if they do so, God will not cast them away (vv. 19-22).

The farewell address closes with prayer. If Samuel is no longer the judge over the people Israel, if many of his roles are to be supplanted by Saul, he will remain as long as he lives as one who prays for his people and instructs them in what is good and faithful. Israel's obligations to listen to God and follow the commandments will be aided by one who is a teacher, who will teach and pray for the king as well. In the end, the king who remains unnamed throughout this address, too, stands under the obligations of listening to God, sage teaching, and following the commandments.

> The prophets themselves were certainly the first people to realise that their own lives were totally dependent on Jahweh.
>
> Gerhard von Rad, *Old Testament Theology*, vol. 2, trans. D. M. G. Stalker (San Francisco: Harper & Row, 1965), 92.

Samuel's address that accompanies a coronation turns out to have little to do with kingship and everything to do with the law and the commandments. Samuel will pray for the nation, but he will also instruct them "in the good and right way" (v. 23). This does not seem to be a "farewell" speech, since Samuel will be sticking around. As Steussy observes, "Samuel has no intention of relinquishing his position as speaker for God."[17]

13:1–15a

A Religious Mistake?

The Deuteronomist often introduces or concludes narratives of kings with their ages at the beginning of the reign and the length of it (cf. 1 Kgs. 14:20; 14:21; 15:1-2), but these have been lost in Saul's case. This absence of a chronology (13:1) is oddly appropriate to Saul, since his reign is marked by gaps and missteps. The ambiguities

17. Marti J. Steussy, *Samuel and His God* (Columbia, SC: The University of South Carolina Press, 2010), 84.

of Saul are often on the surface, and hence the introduction to his reign is unable to mark a beginning or an end.

But Saul excels in war. He assembles an army to combat the Philistines alongside his son, Jonathan, whom we encounter for the first time. Saul has the larger army, but Jonathan emerges with the initial victory, defeating a garrison of Philistines at Geba. Word of this victory travels quickly—both to the other camps of Philistines and to Saul. Saul's trumpet blast is a call not only to those who recognize him as king but to the Hebrews: "Let the Hebrews hear!" (vv. 2–3), an indication that the tribes are not fully unified. Though ethnically related, the peoples do not yet constitute a nation, as rivals jockey for power and kindred people throw their weight behind different leaders. The emergence of monarchy in Israel is hardly a seamless process throughout 1 and 2 Samuel. Jonathan's initial victory calls others to recognize the new king and signals to the Philistines that their days are numbered. Indeed, the people Israel have become "odious" in Philistia's sight. As Israel basks in this initial victory, Saul gathers the people at Gilgal, the place where Samuel has told him to wait, the place of ritual sacrifice and a reminder of the One to whom Israel really belongs (v. 4).

As the call to join Saul in Gilgal goes out, the Philistines reassemble. Their numbers are greater—at least twice as large—than those summoned by Saul. Faced with this disparity, the Israelites quaver before the enemy, with some retreating to caves and holes and others crossing the Jordan. Saul remains at Gilgal, while the people who follow him tremble (vv. 5–7). Saul seems to be on the verge of losing his people and his army. Jonathan's initial victory has led not to confidence in the final vanquishing of the Philistine threat but to terror in the face of a more powerful adversary.

Saul tries to keep the promises he made to Samuel, to wait seven days in Gilgal, in order that Samuel might perform the sacrifices that establish Saul's reign. But in the intervening time, things have become more urgent. Saul is faced with his first difficult decision as king, confronted by many salient realities: an assembled enemy, a fleeing people, and an army on the verge of collapse. Seven days have passed, the time appointed by Samuel, but the old judge has not yet appeared. The people, moreover, are slipping away from Saul. What is a leader in peril to do? We read of no deliberation on Saul's part; instead we read of his instructions to bring the burnt offerings to him (vv. 8–9). If the appointed priest is not available, then resort to the next best option: the king who can perform sacrifice in his stead. The decision is fraught with *Realpolitik*: it is a political and military decision. In order to stanch a hemorrhaging people, in order to begin the battle that will slip from Israel's grasp if it waits any longer, the sacrifices must be made. And if Saul's sacrifice does not follow the letter of the law, then at least it seems in tenor with its spirit. Better for the wrong person to make sacrifice than not to make any sacrifice at all. The decision is also an emergency measure, a way of seeking God's blessing before battle, even if the proper celebrant is not present.

Saul's decision is understandable, and there is much to sympathize with in it. What, after all, were the alternatives? To sit around and wait for the right man who has not arrived on time? To allow the Philistines to rout the Israelites while the bulk of the populace flees or hides? Saul makes a calculation that seems astute politically and militarily. This is one way to rally the people—around religion and ritual—and to keep the Philistines at bay. God has carried Israel to victory before. Saul's calculation, however, proves to be the wrong one. As soon as Saul finishes performing the sacrifice, Samuel appears. Saul, after violating the terms of his agreement with Samuel, now plays the appropriate role, going out to meet Samuel and saluting him, paying homage to the kingmaker. Saul's explanation of his actions is clear enough: he performed the sacrifice because Samuel had not appeared at the appointed time (vv. 10–12). Polzin indicates that the blame rests equally with Samuel: he has encouraged Saul's prophetic indulgence; he has failed in his role as prophet by not arriving when he said he would and thus placed Saul in a "double bind."[18] Furthermore, it is not clear that Saul has actually done any wrong, as Cheryl Exum notes: "the narrative records no instructions from YHWH but only from Samuel (10:8). In fact, Samuel had earlier given Saul confusing instructions."[19] There may be more than a hint of Samuel's

---

18. Polzin, *Samuel*, 107.
19. J. Cheryl Exum, *Tragedy and Biblical Narrative: Arrows of the Almighty* (Cambridge: Cambridge University Press, 1992), 27–28.

jealousy of Saul revealed in their interactions. The charges Samuel lodges against Saul appear "trumped-up" to "keep Saul on the defensive" and under Samuel's control.[20]

The words of Samuel, the prophet with complicated motives, are unequivocal. Saul has not kept the commandments (though that charge is still unclear to the reader), and for this transgression, his kingdom will not continue. Nearly as soon as Saul's reign has begun, its demise is foretold. Had Saul listened and upheld the commandments, his kingdom would have been established "forever." But this is precisely what Saul did not do, even if his intentions were within the spirit of the law and politically astute. The king who has just ascended will not pass his reign to his own house; indeed, he will see it slip from his hands as God finds another (vv. 13–14).

This seems unfair. The character of God's actions, indeed, is difficult to discern. Saul's actions seem politically wise and appropriately reverent, if not ritually correct. Further waiting for Samuel would have likely resulted in further attrition in the ranks. On one reading, Saul is the victim not only of Samuel's failure but also of a divine setup: for violating a technicality in the law, Saul paves the way for one who is God's favored. Is God playing favorites? In much of what follows, this seems to be the case. In later chapters, David commits far more disturbing transgressions but does not lose his kingdom. Saul was not stealing, oppressing, or murdering; he was only trying to fulfill a religious obligation. Dwelling on the technicalities fails to render an adequate interpretation of the story. At best, God appears in this light an inflexible rule-giver or one who plays arbitrary favorites.

Perhaps the key to interpreting this story lies with Samuel's claim that the Lord seeks a "man after his own heart" (v. 14). When all is said and done, the leadership of God's people is not a matter of political or military calculation, or even religious sensibility, but a matter of the heart. God seeks one whose heart is directed toward God. Saul, in making political and military calculations, reveals himself as one whose heart is often not clearly directed toward God. "For where your treasure is, there your heart will be also" (Luke 12:34). The disposition

---

20. Polzin, *Samuel*, 129.

of the heart is what is paramount: whether a leader relies on God (not as a mere preparation for battle, not as a way of bolstering political support), but whether in the face of threats, internal and external, the leader knows that trust in God is already enough.

Shrewd political tactics and regular religious observations cannot, in the end, cover up the inclination of the heart. Samuel leaves by uttering these judgments, but the people follow Saul (v. 15). If Saul is to lose the kingdom, it will not be without a fight.

> **To take heart is to gain courage. Our lives bloom in fullness from the heart, the core of our being, which is created and sustained by interconnection.**
>
> Rita Nakashima Brock, *Journeys by Heart* (New York: Crossroad, 1988), xiv.

13:15b–22

Military Preparations

The outlook for battle with the Philistines does not look auspicious: six hundred men are with Saul in the face of the thousands of Philistines. The armies are encamped a few miles apart, in Michmash and Geba. Philistines come out in three companies, as the Israelite army seems surrounded (vv. 15–18). To make matters worse, the Philistines have superior weaponry. Metalworking is controlled by the Philistines, as there is "no smith to be found throughout all the land of Israel" (v. 19). Swords and spears are in Philistine hands, while the Israelites are relegated to sharpening their farming implements at the hands of their enemies. The scene recalls the various peasants' rebellions and popular uprisings throughout history that have been squashed by superior military technology—German peasants in the sixteenth century, protesters against the Vietnam War at Kent State in 1970, peaceful demonstrators in Tiananmen Square in 1989. Empires and occupiers control people by controlling access to products: food, technology, natural resources. The story is as old as history itself. Yesterday's metalworking is today's access to technology and state secrets. It looks like a hopeless case. Only Jonathan and Saul possess a sword (vv. 20–22).

13:23–14:23
Jonathan's Stratagem, Israel's Victory

The odds are stacked against Israel. The Philistine army has assembled and gone out to the pass (v. 23). The opposing camps are within sight of each another, separated by a ravine with a treacherous path between them (v. 16). When armies can see one another, the first volleys are often psychological. The technological prowess of the Philistines was probably demonstrable even at a distance.

Jonathan is the first to take action but does it in secret, without revealing his plans to his father. On the surface, the plan is foolhardy: two men, Jonathan and his armor-bearer, sneaking up on the Philistine camp. Whether to spy or to attack, such plans seem unwise without consulting the military commander. Saul, meanwhile, has brought the religious apparatus that he consults to bolster his kingship. But that apparatus is ambiguous, as he brings Ahijah the priest, a member of the house of Eli, one who has been included in the oracle against Eli uttered in chapter 2 (14:1–3). The reader knows that this priestly house is destined for demise; Saul is unaware of this and brings with him the vestiges of a religious old guard. The contrast is marked: Saul, surrounded by six hundred soldiers, with the trappings of official religion meant to protect; Jonathan going out alone with one armor-bearer traversing a craggy and rocky path. The contrast is made more explicit by Jonathan's confidence in YHWH's guidance. Whereas Saul relies on the trappings of religion, Jonathan places his trust in God alone: "nothing can hinder the LORD from saving by many or by few" (v. 6). Jonathan knows that he and his armor-bearer are not traveling alone.

This confidence translates into Jonathan's discernment of a sign. He sees two options: waiting for the Philistines to come to them or coming into their camp. The word of the Philistines will provide the sign of what they are to do: to wait or to approach (vv. 7–10). Confidence in sensing a divine sign in others' seemingly chance words may strike contemporary readers as odd. Indeed, the biblical record often discerns signs where we are prone to see none. But the world of the Deuteronomist is not a world governed by chance or even primarily by human calculation. History is molded and shaped by a God who acts in history, who works through improbable people, even Philistines. The eyes of faith often see things that others do not. Friedrich Schleiermacher criticized those who see only isolated events as miraculous or as evidence of the hand of God, claiming that for the faithful *everything* that happens in history and human life is miraculous. "To me everything is a miracle. . . . The more religious you would be, the more you would see miracles everywhere."[21] Jonathan is both one who expects the miraculous (victory over the Philistines) and sees the miraculous in everything (God as the governor, author, and sustainer of history). The true mark of religion and of faith is not how many religious artifacts we surround ourselves with, how many rituals we properly perform, but to what extent our eyes are open to the miraculous beauty of the everyday, the world as it is—and as it will be—under the care of God. If this is the mark, then Jonathan has religion, even if the ark and the ephod are far from him.

The sign is for Jonathan and his armor-bearer to approach. The Philistines see the two men and their words convey mockery: the Hebrews are coming out of their holes. They call out further that they want to show the Israelites "something" (vv. 11–12). Hardly a convincing statement, but it is signal enough for Jonathan. The two Israelites attack the camp and chaos ensues. The two underdogs kill twenty men; indeed, the attack bears the traces of legend, as earth quakes and raiders tremble (vv. 13–15). Saul and his men witness the skirmish from their camp, and when the king determines that Jonathan is not in the camp, he consults the trappings of establishment religion. Some versions of the text state that Saul instructs his priest to bring the ark, others that he tells them to bring the ephod. Like Jonathan, Saul is trying to discern a sign from God. But in Saul's case, there is no clear sign. Indeed, while Saul is consulting with the priest, the tumult in the opposing camp increases, and Saul's words are abrupt: "Withdraw your hand" (vv. 16–19). Saul's company launches into battle and greater confusion results. But the net effect is rather auspicious politically: Hebrews who were with the Philistines are now convinced to join Saul and Jonathan. If Saul

---

21. Friedrich Schleiermacher, *On Religion: Speeches to Its Cultured Despisers*, ed. Richard Crouter. (New York: Cambridge University Press, 1996), 49.

stumbles in his religious leadership, his military and political tactics frequently prove effective. The rallying of ethnic relatives who were not yet allied with Saul's kingdom is the result of somewhat bumbling religious devotion. As victory is assured and relatives are rallied, a full ten thousand have joined in the cause as the battle spreads over the hill country (vv. 20–22).

14:24–46

Saul's Oath and Its Consequences

Military success and devotional incompetence are further juxtaposed in this next section. Saul makes an oath, though it is not clear *why* he does. Religious devotion—or at least the appearance of devotion—tends to make for good politics. People want to see integrity, faith, and even piety in their leaders. Candidates for president in the United States, though they often claim that religion is a private affair, know that church usually provides a good photo op. Saul knows this and makes an oath that presents himself in a pious light and demands piety from his troops. Such an oath, moreover, adds an aura of sanctity to the battle: the troops are not to eat a morsel until Saul has been avenged on his enemies. As if tempting the oath-takers, honeycomb appears on the ground as the battle continues. The appearance of honey is significant, for it is a food that delights the tongue, a delicacy rather than a staple. Savoring honey would constitute a seemingly greater violation of the oath than scrounging a scrap of bread. None of the troops succumb to the temptation, but the one who has not heard of the oath—Jonathan—does, and the effects of this choice food are narrated vividly. Jonathan's eyes grow bright as he dips his staff and tastes the honey (vv. 24–27). Rules about how soldiers should engage in war were specific in Israel's history: they included regulations for keeping the camp holy and the requirement of sexual abstinence (Deut. 23:9–14). Good soldiering, in this view, requires a degree of withdrawal and asceticism, both as a military tactic and as a way of marking the soldier as belonging to God.

On seeing Jonathan eat, one of the soldiers tells him that Saul has strictly charged no one to eat: "And so the troops are faint" (v. 28).

This last sentence conveys a question. Is the one who catches Jonathan in the forbidden act also begrudging the king's seemingly arbitrary oath? Jonathan's words, however, convey even a greater sense of dissatisfaction. In his eyes, the oath—which he did not hear—was stupid. He claims that his father "has troubled the land" (v. 29). The Bible often focuses on land: who belongs to the land and how to tend it. To claim that one has troubled the land is to recognize that something serious is amiss. Jonathan claims that the Israelites' victory has been jeopardized by Saul's oath: troops would have been better served had they been allowed to eat. This interchange between the soldier and Jonathan conveys two things: the people's slipping confidence in Saul (who has heretofore been the object of public affection) and the beginnings of a rift between son and father. Both will prove decisive in the coming events and both are rooted in Saul's own religious and political miscalculations.

The narrative shifts momentarily from Jonathan to the troops, who advance westward toward Philistine territory. They experience success (the Philistines are "struck down" from Michmash to Aijalon), but these victories are narrated incidentally, devoid of battle scenes or testimony. Yet readers can feel the exhaustion of the troops, as the narrator is more concerned with describing their condition than the waging of battle. Having experienced victory, however, the troops are no longer bound by Saul's oath. Ravenous, the soldiers descend on the spoil of battle: livestock that is devoured almost as soon as it is slaughtered on the ground. An oath, which has caused exhaustion among the troops, now leads to a serious violation of Israel's law: the troops eat meat with blood, consuming the part of the animal reserved for God. One result of Saul's showy display of piety is greater offense. He appears pious in the eyes of would-be beholders, but such religious acts lead to a breakdown in Israel's cultic relation to God. It is hard to blame the soldiers for their actions: in the field there are few of the implements for the proper rituals surrounding dietary regulations. Moreover, they have gone without food an entire day, exerting themselves enormously. Nonetheless, what they have done constitutes a breach. Saul sees it as sin but does not connect the troops' lawbreaking to his own supposedly righteous behavior. He describes their action as "treacherous" and attempts to salvage the situation by instructing his underlings to roll a large stone before him, which will allow the troops to slaughter animals and allow the blood to drain to the earth. No further ritual violations occur, as the animals are brought toward the stone, and the troops sate themselves. This episode is resolved with Saul's further display of piety: construction of an altar to the Lord, the first that he has built (vv. 31–35). Saul knows well the power of religion in political hands. The reader, however, is left wondering: Is the construction of the altar the mark of genuine piety, the manipulation of religion for political and military gain, or perhaps a little of both? Part of what makes Saul such a tragic figure in this story is that he usually tries to do the right thing, and much of the time his motivation is pious. But these very same acts can also be seen as the marks of a man desperately grasping and clinging to power, even as it starts slipping from his hands.

The move from ritual to further military tactics is sudden. Saul suggests that the Israelites pursue the Philistines further, under cover of night and "despoil them until the morning light," leaving no survivors. Readers get the impression of a giddy military man, inspired by initial success, desiring more. The soldiers, moreover, seem willing and give the king a blanket endorsement to do whatever seems good in his sight. But again, cultic factors intervene. The priest urges Saul to "draw near to God" (v. 36), and Saul, pious leader that he appears, agrees. The king pauses to ask God whether to pursue the Philistines and whether God will deliver them into Israel's hand. The theology here is straightforwardly Deuteronomistic: victory is assured not by military tactics, strategic leadership, or raw concerns of power but by God's steady hand. Fresh from initial victory, Saul pauses in prayer. But his prayer is not answered (v. 37). His attempt at divination is futile. Here Saul experiences divine silence and interprets it, consistent with the Deuteronomistic History, as the result of sin among the people or in his own family.

Saul makes a bold acclamation in the face of the soldiers gathered: he will find out the source of the sin, and whoever is responsible—even if it is his own son Jonathan—will die. Nothing will get in the way of his piety, even the ties of blood and kin. In response to Saul's acclamation, however, not a single soldier answers him.

Having experienced the silence of God, Saul now experiences the silence of his troops. No one, it seems, is listening, let alone answering. This silence both indicates the innocence of the troops (in relation to Saul's oath) and to the beginnings of a people that listens to its king less and less. At this moment, even in a crowd, Saul is a man alone. But the sin must be in the group somewhere, perhaps even in the king. When the lot points to Saul's family, and eventually to Jonathan (vv. 38–42), the son presents himself to his father-king and tells him what he has done. There is no embellishment in his words: he tasted the honey, "Here I am, I will die" (v. 43). Jonathan does not excuse himself from the oath because he had not heard it. Indeed, Jonathan upstages his father in both his trust in God and military skill.[22] In the name of piety, and in the name of his people, Jonathan is willing to submit to death. His father is ready as well, but the people are not. What happens next renders the story more complex. The story of Saul's oath and Jonathan's violation of it is not merely a story of responsibility in the face of promises made to God. Rather, it is also a story of how God acts in history and how God sometimes favors those who are not the established leaders.

Indeed, it is difficult to answer the question of who holds the power in this pivotal narrative: On the one hand, Saul has the power of kingship and military commander, even if cracks are beginning to appear in his leadership. On the other hand, Jonathan has power as the one who has secured a strong victory for the Israelites. In another regard, the soldiers (the people) have the power as they contradict their king: "Shall Jonathan die, who has accomplished this great victory in Israel? Far from it! As the LORD lives, not one hair of his head shall fall to the ground; for he has

> The question is not whether we will choose to take part in God's plan but whether we will embrace who we are as carriers, bearers, irreplaceable participants in the life of the unnamable God, who calls us by name by becoming a particular human being, called by a particular name.
>
> Cynthia L. Rigby, "Mary and the Artistry of God," in *Blessed One*, ed. Beverly Roberts Gaventa and Cynthia L. Rigby (Louisville, KY: Westminster John Knox Press, 2002), 146.

22. Johanna W. H. van Wijk-Bos, *Reading Samuel: A Literary and Theological Commentary* (Macon, GA: Smyth & Helwys Publishing, Inc., 2011), 83.

worked with God today" (v. 45). Surrounding all of these various actors, however, is the power of God who can take power away from those in power. This is a God who works through people to accomplish God's purposes, a God who anoints the powerful but who also empowers the weak and oppressed.

The people, in the end, ransom Jonathan from Saul's oath. The conclusion to this episode is Saul's withdrawal from further pursuit of the Philistines. A final victory over them eludes him. Indeed, when the Philistines go "to their own place" (v. 46), we see that much is escaping Saul's clutches. He has not only lost further victory over the Philistines, he is now losing his son and beginning to lose his own people. A supposedly noble act of piety winds up costing him dearly, as God's favor seems ever more remote.

14:47–15:9
Details of a Military Man and an Ambiguous Victory

Saul's oath has resulted in a promise that he cannot fulfill. His subjects have spared him from killing his own son, one of his most effective warriors. This next section considers Saul as a military king who fights enemies "on every side" (v. 47). Recent defeats, however, have now turned to successes. If the Deuteronomist's portrayal of Saul is often disparaging, it can also be adulatory, as it is here. Saul does "valiantly" and rescues "Israel out of the hands of those who plundered them" (v. 48), expanding the nation's territorial footprint. He achieves success but experiences rejection in spite of it, sometimes by his own people, but most significantly by the God of Israel. He is the king whom YHWH has reluctantly agreed to, but he is not a king after the Lord's heart. This is part of what makes Saul a tragic figure: he brings tragedy on himself but also experiences the tragic results of others' actions against him: within his own family and from the hand of the living God. In Saul, we witness the complex interaction of personal responsibility and tragic circumstance. He is the one who is both responsible for his demise and a victim of it. And in this regard he reveals much of the human condition: how we both experience the tragic (and at times glorious) results of our own behavior and bear the traces of actions beyond our control.

The brief enumeration of Saul's military success is followed by a list of family members and his military commander. Saul has a wife, three sons, and two daughters (vv. 49–50). Yet we hear mainly from one son, Jonathan, and one daughter, Michal, in subsequent narratives. Saul is a man with a name and a family, but that family is not always allied with him. His most prominent son often acts against him, while Michal marries his rival to the throne. The houses of Saul and of David, as we shall see, are interwoven, revealing conflicted loyalties. The commander Abner, however, remains true to Saul until the bitter end, seeking to keep the throne within the house of Saul, even when all hope is lost (2 Sam. 2:8). This list of family members and subjects concludes with further reminders of enemies that surround Israel. Israel experiences "hard fighting" with the Philistines all of Saul's days (v. 52).

Fast upon this enumeration of Saul's household Samuel appears somewhat suddenly. The relationship between the one who anointed and the one who received anointing has been complicated from their first meeting. The prophet of the old guard and the king of the new are cut from different molds. Samuel reminds Saul that God—and no one else—is the kingmaker, the one to whom Saul should hearken. The word from the Lord that Samuel brings is uncompromising. Saul is to go out in battle against the Amalekites, the nomadic tribe that waged war against Israel as it journeyed in Exodus (Exod. 17:8–13). Saul is to avenge Israel against the Amalekites for their attack against Israel long ago. If Moses foresaw war with Amalek "from generation to generation" (Exod. 17:16), this episode offers the ultimate resolution to that conflict. This is more than a generations-old grudge; this is the hand of God dispensing with those who would destroy the covenant people. The word Samuel brings is staggering and difficult to fit into any theology of divine goodness. Saul and his troops are to wage war against Amalek, utterly destroy them, sparing no person or animal: man, woman, child, infant, and every single livestock (15:1–3). They are to wipe Amalek from the face of the earth.

The words ought to give any reader enough consternation to pause. What kind of a God would command this? What kind of military campaign is this? How is God, in the end, present in the most horrific acts of violence that human beings can commit? Are the deaths of infant enemies really the signs of divine favor? Even asking these questions risks the demonic distortions of God's will that have arisen over the centuries. Time and again, military leaders, convinced that God was on their side, have committed atrocities against the innocent. American notions of "Manifest Destiny," cloaked in supposedly Christian fervor, resulted in annihilation of native peoples. Islamic fundamentalists on September 11, 2001, murdered nearly three thousand people in an act of jihad. Is what is being offered here simply another, much earlier version of religious slaughter? This is a question that has haunted many interpreters. Barbara Green claims that the "whole issue of obedience to God" here is constructed on "genocide."[23] However one reads the story, one cannot escape the fact that God here commands an atrocity.

The Deuteronomist does not spend much time justifying war with the Amalekites; the chief reason for war is rooted in God's command. But Saul does not fulfill this command. As the battle rages, Saul spares many. The Kenites are spared because they are not members of the Amalekite tribe, even though they live among them. Because the Kenites showed kindness to Israel (in contrast to Amalekite hostility), they will be spared. He takes Amalekite King Agag alive and saves the choicest livestock (vv. 4–9). Though the narrator does not give reasons for these actions, we may sense in them a political and economic calculus: choice livestock are worth money and represent wealth and prosperity, and a vanquished king is a potent political symbol and perhaps a potential ally or advisor. Saul's subsequent defense of himself is clear. His sparing of these lives was for cultic reasons: to sacrifice the choicest to the Lord in a display of public piety. The narrator, however, deems any of these reasons less than faithful. His actions against the Amalekites seal his subsequent rejection. Even in the midst of overwhelming military triumph, Saul shows that he cannot obey the word of God consistently.

23. Barbara Green, O.P., *King Saul's Asking* (Collegeville, MN: Liturgical Press, 2003), 110.

FURTHER REFLECTIONS
Pacifism, Just War, and Crusade

The military campaigns that saturate the pages of 1 and 2 Samuel are varied: some are defensive wars to repel foreign invaders, others satisfy expansionist aims, and yet others seem entirely gratuitous. The campaign against the Amalekites is brutal in scope and difficult to interpret, especially because Saul is judged for not bringing about total annihilation. How are we to read such texts? Some in the church consider the text as a foil, that it outlines war as a departure from God's intent. Many early Christians espoused pacifism, such as Hippolytus of Rome, who wrote in the third century: "A soldier who is in authority must be told not to execute men; if he should be ordered to do it, he shall not do it. . . . If a catechumen or a baptized Christian wishes to become a soldier, let him be cast out. For he has despised God."[24] During the Reformation era, Menno Simons presented a renewed version of Christian pacifism in the face of religious wars sweeping across Europe: "The regenerated do not go to war nor fight. They are the children of peace who have beaten their swords into plowshares and their spears into pruning hooks and know of no war."[25] Mennonites, Brethren and Quakers continue this powerful witness in the present day, reminding us that the lordship of Christ stands against all powers and principalities that would claim equal allegiance. For them and others, the Amalekite campaign might represent an old order overturned by the Prince of Peace.

Other Christians, suspicious of both war and absolute pacifism, have developed accounts of "just war" that strictly limit the waging of war by outlining criteria for its appropriate use. The Catholic Reformation theologian Francisco Suárez represents this tradition:

> Is war intrinsically evil? . . . Our first conclusion is that war, absolutely speaking, is not intrinsically evil, nor is it forbidden to Christians. . . . First, the war must be waged by a legitimate

---

24. Gregory Dix, ed., *The Treatise on the Apostolic Tradition of St. Hippolytus of Rome, Bishop and Martyr* (London: SPCK, 1968), 26–27.
25. Menno Simons, *The Writings of Menno Simons*, in William C. Placher, ed., *Readings in the History of Christian Theology, Volume 2* (Philadelphia: Westminster Press, 1988), 33.

power; secondly, the cause itself and the reason must be just; thirdly, the method of its conduct must be proper, and due proportion must be observed at its beginning, during its prosecution and after victory.[26]

This tradition stipulates defensive—rather than preemptive—war and rejects any casualties among civilians. Judged by these criteria, however, the Amalekite campaign fails miserably: it is hardly a "just" war.

Many have claimed to espouse a just war view when in actuality they veer toward crusade, or holy war, the third historical view of war. This view understands combat to be a fight between good and evil. It tolerates preemptive war and acknowledges the necessity, at times of "collateral damage," the euphemism for civilian casualties, often on an enormous scale. Most, if not all, of the wars the United States has engaged in bear traces of a crusade: from World War II's Hiroshima and Nagasaki to the war on terror's preemptive strikes. The classic example is the Medieval Crusades, a series of wars that combined religious fervor and imperial expansion. Bernard of Clairvaux's sermon preached at the dawn of the Second Crusade is representative:

> "Clothe yourselves in sackcloth, but also cover yourselves with your impenetrable bucklers. The din of arms, the danger, the labors, the fatigues of war, are the penances that God now imposes upon you. Hasten then to expiate your sins by victories over the Infidels, and let the deliverance of the holy places be the reward of your repentance."[27]

That Jesus lived and taught nonviolence seems generally, if not universally, accepted. What has been almost universally doubted, it seems, is that Jesus' example and teaching apply to the contemporary church.

J. Denny Weaver, *The Nonviolent Atonement* (Grand Rapids: Eerdmans, 2001), 12.

---

26. Francisco Suárez, from *A Work on the Three Theological Virtues: Faith, Hope, and Charity*, in William C. Placher, ed., *Readings in Christian Theology, Volume 2*, 52–53.
27. Bernard of Clairvaux, cited in James M. Ludlow, *The Age of the Crusades* (New York: The Christian Literature Co., 1896), 166–67.

Crusades have constituted a minority theological position in the church but a majority of actual battles. If few theologians have advocated crusades, they have been more common than any other war in the history of the church. If we are revolted at the sound of the Lord's command to Saul to eliminate the Amalekites, then we ought also be repulsed by the history of warfare in our church, nation, and world.

15:10–33

Saul's Rejection

This episode offers closure to Saul's life, even if he occupies many subsequent stories. What follows after Saul's rejection by God, in other words, are details. God's word comes, reliably, to Samuel, who is more adept at hearing than anyone else in the story. The gist of this word is God's regret over making Saul king. Samuel's response to YHWH's regret is anger that impels him to cry out to the Lord all night (v. 11). Samuel, of course, was never keen on the idea of a king in the first place. Perhaps his cries to the Lord convey some of this disappointment, a bit of the "I told you so" that can be common among the devout. Perhaps the disappointment is in himself, for not mentoring Saul. Certainly the anger is directed to Saul, who has failed to obey God's word.

After a night of outcry, Samuel rises in the morning to find Saul and bring him God's word. This initial search yields critical information: Saul has gone to Carmel, "where he set up a monument for himself" (v. 12). Leaders know that monuments can foster their legacies. Saul, fresh from military victory, seems focused on enshrining it for posterity. Saul, who previously built an altar for God (14:35), now constructs an edifice for himself. This is the way of the nations, the way of other kings who are concerned with consolidating power and prestige. Though Saul eventually goes to Gilgal—the place of sacrifice to the Lord—this intermediate stop in Carmel reveals that he cares a bit too much about his own legacy.

Kingmaker and king meet, and it is the king who speaks first. Saul's words both bless Samuel and claim that he has carried out the Lord's command. These are suitable statements for a king concerned with maintaining the blessing of the religious establishment. Perhaps Saul thinks he *has* carried out God's command, or at least carried it out better than others who have heard it. The narrator does not pronounce judgment on Saul's words here, leaving readers open to a number of interpretations: Saul is speaking truthfully, in that he thinks he has carried out God's commands faithfully; or, alternatively, he has spoken deceptively and is trying to hide his failure from Samuel. Even more likely, however, is that there is *both* truth and deception in Saul's words. Leaders can speak truth and use the truth for deceptive ends. What appears as piety is often a mask for lesser motives. The sound of cattle and sheep, however, leads Samuel to believe Saul is deceiving him. Saul, however, maintains that these animals are destined for sacrifice (vv. 13–15). They are the choicest animals, confiscated from the Amalekites after their decisive defeat, reserved as a gesture of thanksgiving to the Lord.

Samuel dismisses Saul's explanation: what Saul has done directly violated God's command. And Saul, on hearing that Samuel heard the voice of the Lord the previous night, orders (or relents) Samuel to speak. Samuel's initial words remind Saul of his humble beginnings: "Though you are little in your own eyes" (v. 17). His recent actions, moreover, reveal that his kingship has also been held with little regard. However much Saul may excuse or regard his actions as a slight violation of God's command, this "little" thing has revealed a much larger issue. Indeed, Samuel claims that what Saul has done was not a mere trifle, but doing "what was evil in the sight of the LORD" (v. 19). A harsher verdict on allegedly pious behavior is hardly imaginable.

Saul, however, is still unable to hear this verdict and maintains that his actions were not only defensible but somehow laudable: the best things *ought* to be sacrificed to God in Gilgal (vv. 20–21). Samuel's retort is striking, especially for one serving in a priestly role. His language resembles the anti-cultic language prevalent in many of Israel's prophets. If it comes to a choice between ritual sacrifices and hearing the word of God, the latter is always preferable: "Surely, to obey is better than sacrifice, and to heed than the fat of rams" (v. 22). In this passage, readers witness a priest criticizing priestly activities, even when the sacrifices are choicest! Sacrifices are subservient to hearing and doing the will of God. Samuel's words here trigger questions about the role and purpose of worship. Some Protestants have seized on Samuel's words (as well as the words of Amos[28]) as justification for worship devoid of much ceremony, as if ritual distracted from the hearing of the word. But liturgy, at its root, means "work of the people" (*leitourgia*, from *laos* and *ergon*, people and work). To hear God's word is also to offer labor unto God. Read thusly, Samuel's words here are less a condemnation of ritual and more a placing of liturgy in its proper context, people's work given to God. By refusing to hear and obey God's word, Saul has refused to worship, even if he made choice sacrifices.

The consequences of Saul's action are drastic: he has *rejected* God's word. And because he has rejected God's word, God will reject Saul as king (v. 23). From here, there is no turning back: not a second (or third) chance for Saul, not a reconsideration of Saul's kingly role. The end is already here. God will find another to serve as king.

If Saul has appeared deceptive or disingenuous in some of his earlier actions, his response to Samuel is forthright and remorseful. Hearing these devastating words, Saul confesses honestly and directly: He has *sinned*, he has *transgressed*. He has feared people and obeyed their voice (v. 24). Saul seems to be seeing and hearing rightly for the first time. He admits his behavior, asks for Samuel's pardon, and asks the former judge to return with him. Though one might read his actions as yet another example of a desperate king seeking priestly imprimatur (It would look good for the king to return from military victory and priestly sacrifice with the one who anointed him as king!), they are striking in their lack of self-justification. The practice of confession depends, at least in part, on personal honesty: laying bare one's actions and responsibility before God and neighbor. And here, Saul seems to do that. But here, penance yields nothing but the face of Samuel's and God's stubborn rejection. As Polzin notes, "everything in the text leads toward a repentant Saul

---

28. "I hate, I despise your festivals, and I take no delight in your solemn assemblies. Even though you offer me your burnt offerings and grain offerings, I will not accept them; and the offerings of well-being of your fatted animals I will not look upon. Take away from me the noise of your songs; I will not listen to the melody of your harps" (Amos 5:21–23).

at odds with an unmerciful God."[29] Saul admits his "guilt"—a term I use ironically—in failing to wipe the Amalekites from the face of the earth while God remains unyielding against him. Samuel will not grant Saul's request for the prophet to return with the king, uttering decisive words: Because Saul has rejected the word of God (but has he really?) and God has rejected Saul, Samuel cannot return with the king. As Samuel turns away, Saul imploringly grabs Samuel's robe, ripping it. The king who clings to a garment has it torn away; the land, like this robe, will also be torn from Saul and given to another (vv. 25–28). A sincere confession cannot change the fact that the kingdom has already been lost.

For Samuel, the God who rejects Saul "will not recant or change his mind" (v. 29). The same God who was willing to compromise with God's people in granting Israel a king will not revoke Saul's rejection. This declaration points to a theological struggle within Deuteronomistic history. Does God change? Previously in the narrative, God appears to change God's mind by relenting to Israel's demand for a king (8:7–9). This change is not arbitrary or capricious but a mark of YHWH's responsiveness to the people Israel. Samuel's claim, however, is more unyielding: God will not recant or change God's mind.

This remark stands in tension with the God who accedes to Israel's demand for a king. First and Second Samuel describe a God who will not change and yet yields to human cries, however misguided those cries might be. How, and in what way, God both changes and is unchanging is the subject of ongoing internal debate within many of these stories.

> You are unchangeable and yet you change all things. You are never new, never old, and yet all things have new life from you. . . . You are ever active, yet always at rest.
>
> Augustine, *Confessions*, trans. R. S. Pine-Coffin (New York: Penguin, 1961), 23.

Having established the trustworthiness and unchanging nature of God's Word, however, the narrator ends this episode on a surprising note. Samuel, who has just told Saul that he cannot accompany him

---

29. Polzin, *Samuel*, 141.

home, now has changed *his* mind. Verses 30–33 may entail an independent tradition more favorable to Saul than the rest of this section. For here Saul again confesses, which leads to Samuel's change of heart. The two men return in order to worship God but also in order to "honor" Saul before the elders (v. 30). Public piety and popular approval are never far from Saul's eyes. Perhaps there is hope that the king might also change, even if God's decree is already set. But a final display of the difference between Samuel and Saul is striking. Samuel obeys the command that Saul could not, summoning Agag the king and slaughtering him brutally. The language invokes a ritual killing—hewing the king to pieces before the Lord. It is told without detail or commentary, other than a single note of retribution. As Agag has made many women childless, Agag's mother will now also be childless (vv. 32–33). We may attribute this killing to the reprisals of ancient peoples; we may also regard it as a distant form of piety difficult to understand. But it is also narrated without graphic detail and certainly without the exultation of a people or leaders (nothing akin to the public celebration that accompanied the capture and executions of Saddam Hussein or Osama bin Laden). Perhaps Samuel's actions are a vivid reminder of the self-destruction that death-dealing eventually breeds. The Amalekites sowed death rather than life in their dealings with Israel. Perhaps Agag stands for his people's own disregard of Israel. At the very least, the story is a stark reminder of the violence and brutality of human life, especially among kings and warring peoples. In this regard, the ritual killing is not at all foreign to our day, as violence continues unabated, now on a colossal scale. It is no coincidence that Saul's rejection is punctuated by horrific violence, for the rejected king will breed more violence in the episodes that follow.

1 Samuel 15:34–2 Samuel 4:12
The Rise of David

This section marks a transition in kingship—and in God's blessing to the new king—by focusing on the actions of three characters: Saul, Jonathan, and David. In actions both public and private, these three act in ways that have far-reaching implications. Their stories are woven with royal intrigue, military strategy, family rivalry, and psychological struggle. Motivated by high ideals and base instincts, these three men express some of the pain and promise of what it means to be human. Their biographies illustrate conflicts between family loyalty and bonds of friendship. They reveal much about the nature of political power and how those who have tasted power often cling to it at all costs. Finally, by example and counterexample, these characters show some of the marks of trust in others and trust in God. The story of Israel, in part, is figured in these three characters' actions, for what they do does not remain a private affair. The story of these three is also the story of a nation as it struggles with its distinctive obligations in light of God's covenant.

As the initiator of covenant, God, the most intriguing character of all, shows again that God's purposes are not enacted vertically, as if God simply decrees something that automatically happens. The God of Israel, as shown in these pages, does not act as a puppeteer or magician but summons flawed and conflicted people (and nations) to take part in the accomplishment of God's purposes for the world. The Deuteronomist assures us that God's purposes will be done, that we can trust and rely on God. But as we trust, we also become actors in the ends that God has in store for us. God will establish a king in Israel, a king who more fully embodies the promise and grace of God toward Israel; but in the story of blessing and the loss of blessing, human actors play a significant role. In the intriguing, conflicted, and riveting stories that this section comprises, we see how interwoven our actions and God's actions can become. The actions of Saul, Jonathan, and David are further reminders of that.

15:34–16:13

David Is Anointed

The conclusion of the previous section reached a brutal climax: Saul, who does not follow God's command by destroying the Amalekites, is rejected by God, while Samuel fulfills God's command by slaughtering Agag, the Amalekite king. In this next section, no further words are exchanged between the king and kingmaker. After the ritual slaughter of Agag, Saul and Samuel go their separate ways, Saul to his home, Samuel to Ramah. Their parting is fatal: the two will not to see each other again until the day of Samuel's death. At this parting, Samuel grieves over Saul and God regrets "that he had made Saul king over Israel" (v. 35). There is both striking similarity and a subtle difference in the narrator's depiction of Samuel's and God's regret. On the one hand, the God of Israel mourns with God's people, as God takes Samuel's grief as God's own. On the other hand, YHWH's response is different from Samuel's. God is sorry that God *made Saul king*, while Samuel grieves *over Saul*. Here is the difference between regret over a person's station and lament over a person. The first displays sorrow over the effects of a person's actions while the second expresses empathy with a person and his or her condition. Both of these sorrows, of course, are significant: one displays great concern for the broader social impact of a person and the other for the life of a unique child of God. YHWH's grief is more comprehensive; Samuel's is more intimate. Saul's kingship, of course, has resulted in much to grieve; here we see two sides of a grief that affects a person and a nation in relation to God.

God, however, does not linger long over grief, at least in this instance. YHWH's question to Samuel, "how long will you grieve over Saul?" conveys a message that the time to grieve is over. By instructing Samuel to fill his horn with oil, God is preparing Samuel for the new thing and the new king. In fact, God's words already employ the language of kingship for someone other than Saul: "I have provided for myself a king among [Jesse's] sons" (16:1). This leaves the reader with no doubt: even if Saul continues to function as king, he no longer is the king. We have not met David yet, but he is already the king in God's eyes. The promise of a new king does not, however, comfort Samuel. God's summons for Samuel to go to Bethlehem is dangerous: "How can I go? If Saul hears of it, he will kill me" (v. 2). God's answer to this question is a subtle deception: if questioned, Samuel is going to Bethlehem to perform sacrifice.

Jesse hails from the southern tribe of Judah. This is the region that eventually favors their native son, David. David's ascension to the throne will not be universally heralded in Israel and results in division in the kingdom. Samuel's journey to Bethlehem is a reminder of David's home and his closest allies. Both divine blessing and tribal struggle factor into the making of a king. Furthermore, the stories of David and Saul, as they have come down to us, have been written chiefly by David's partisans. Samuel's journey to Bethlehem also reminds us which people were responsible for writing these stories and how our understanding of the characters within them is undeniably affected by their own alliances, biases, and predilections.

Samuel follows God's command and makes his way to Jesse's city. The elders who meet him there appear alarmed and afraid. They worry whether Samuel comes in peace. Echoing the words that God has given him, Samuel professes his peaceful mission and the invitation to sacrifice—sanctifying Jesse and his sons (vv. 4–5). But the reader knows that even if Samuel's initial mission was peaceful, it will eventually result in much war and struggle. The transition from one king to another will not come easily. The elders should not worry over their lives now, but they will definitely need to worry about them in the days to come.

Of the actual sacrifice, we read nothing. The real point of Samuel's journey will now be revealed to all who have assembled for sacrifice (the elders, Jesse, and his sons). Samuel looks upon Jesse's eldest son, Eliab, and assumes that he is the chosen one. The Lord's words to Samuel, however, are otherwise, indicating that he is not to look upon appearance or stature as a mark of God's anointed: "The LORD does not see as mortals see; they look on the outward appearance, but the LORD looks on the heart" (v. 7). The heart has figured prominently in what has preceded this moment: God promises a priest, Samuel, who will do what is in God's heart and mind (2:35); upon being anointed, Saul is given a new heart (10:9) as a sign of renewal and faithfulness; in his farewell address, Samuel adjures the people Israel to serve God with all their heart (12:20, 24); as he experiences rejection, Saul is told that God has sought another king, one after God's own heart (13:14). Here is the resolution of God's search. The buildup is formulaic: seven sons of Jesse are brought before Samuel, but none of them is the chosen one. Stories about the youngest or the seventh son abound in world folklore. Often they reveal a special mission or ability of the youngest son that none of the rest has. Samuel asks Jesse whether all of his sons are present. The youngest, apparently, had not even been considered mature enough to take part in the sacrifice. He is with the sheep (vv. 8–11). But this is the one whom God has chosen. And if God looks chiefly upon the heart, in David's case, God also seems to regard appearances: "He was ruddy, and had beautiful eyes, and was handsome" (v. 12). When he appears before Samuel, the reader cannot but notice his face.

As he is anointed by Samuel, the spirit of God comes "mightily upon David from that day forward" (v. 13). Saul, likewise, is the recipient of God's spirit. But the difference between their experiences of the spirit is great. For Saul, his anointing leads to prophetic frenzy (10:9–13); for David, it leads to comfort of a king tormented by the spirit. While Saul often experiences the spirit in isolation and desperation, David experiences the spirit as guide, bond of community, and strength. There is not one way the spirit acts in Scripture; but, in these men's cases, the nature of the spirit makes all the difference.

[T]here is nothing more astonishing than a human face...You feel your obligation to a child when you have seen it and held it. Any human face is a claim on you, because you can't help but understand the singularity of it, the courage and loneliness of it.

Marilynne Robinson, *Gilead* (New York: Picador, 2004), 66.

FURTHER REFLECTIONS
The Authority and Inspiration of Scripture

Spirit courses through the lives of David and Saul: inspiring, disrupting, renewing, and depleting. God's Spirit does not move uniformly in their lives but blows where it chooses (John 3:8). Throughout its history the Christian church has closely linked interpretation of Scripture to the work of God's Spirit. Despite their frequent arguments over biblical interpretation, most Christians agree on at least two things about the Scriptures: they were written by human beings *and* in some way inspired by God. But even if Christians use the words "human authorship" and "divine inspiration" to describe the texts of the Bible, they often draw very different conclusions from them. The meaning of these terms has become especially contentious in the churches over the last 150 years as historical-critical, sociological, and literary studies of the Bible have become more prominent.

In the nineteenth century, at the dawn of modern biblical scholarship, Charles Hodge offered a defense of the classic Protestant understanding of scriptural authority and inspiration. For Hodge, the Bible is the supreme authority for Christians "due to the fact that [its words] are the word of God; and they are the word of God because they were given by the inspiration of the Holy Ghost."[1] The Scriptures are authoritative—and, in Hodge's understanding, infallible—because they are the direct testimony of the Spirit. This does not mean that the human writers were passive vessels. In Hodge's words, "The sacred writers were not machines. Their self-consciousness was not suspended; nor were their intellectual powers superseded. Holy men spake as they were moved by the Holy Ghost."[2] In this "high" view of scriptural authority, human agency has a direct role. Nonetheless, the words of Scripture are without error, regardless of subject: "All the books of Scripture are equally inspired. All alike are infallible in what they teach. . . . It is not confined to moral and religious truths, but extends to the statements of facts, whether

1. Charles Hodge, *Systematic Theology,* vol. 1 (New York: Charles Scribner's Sons, 1911), 153.
2. Ibid., 157.

scientific, historical, or geographical. . . . It extends to everything which any sacred writer asserts to be true."[3] This strong affirmation of biblical infallibility is often referred to as the plenary inspiration of Scripture.

Hodge's view continues in many fundamentalist churches but has been widely discredited in light of (1) historical-critical studies of the Bible that document the evolution of biblical texts rather than their fixed nature and the multiple traditions within Scripture that often clash with each other and (2) the centuries-old history of abusive readings of Scripture and how the Bible has been used to justify horrors, including slavery, xenophobia, sexism, and persecution of LGBT persons. Some strands of the Bible (to take one example, cf. Titus 2:9: "Tell slaves to be submissive to their masters and to give satisfaction in every respect; they are not to talk back") run so contrary to freedom in Christ that it is problematic to consider them inspired or authoritative. In light of the horrors perpetuated in the name of the Scriptures, some theologians such as Carter Heyward have argued for dismantling the notion of biblical authority. The texts of the Bible contain good and bad news and can easily "become a spiritual license to build the world in the image of one's own self."[4] Heyward is skeptical of any book—however holy—as being inherently authoritative. In her view, "Christians would do well to speak less of 'the bible' and more of justice."[5] What is authoritative, in her view, is less the content of specific writings and more the experience of liberation and being freed for mutual relation with others. Much can function as Scripture in Heyward's view, not merely the canonized texts of the Christian church: "Whether it be the biblical creation stories, the book of Ruth, *The Color Purple*, or our mothers' letters to their friends, Scripture reveals God's involvement in our efforts to cocreate right relation."[6]

Heyward's proposal for radically revising what constitutes Scripture, however, causes its own difficulties: one of which is that we simply favor selected texts so that the Scriptures become a reflection of

3. Ibid., 163.
4. Carter Heyward, *Touching Our Strength: The Erotic as Power and the Love of God* (San Francisco: Harper & Row, 1989), 77.
5. Ibid., 84.
6. Ibid., 85.

oneself, and we lapse into the idolatry that Heyward warns against. Amy Plantinga Pauw, in a recent essay, argues for a more nuanced view of scriptural authority and inspiration than either Hodge or Heyward. Cognizant of the idolatries and horrors perpetuated by biblical texts and readings, she centers her understanding of Scripture on the work of the Holy Spirit. The Spirit inspired the authors of Scriptures, just as it inspires our reading of Scripture today. But this recognition offers no guarantee that *we* will read Scripture rightly. Pauw notes that the book of life has often become a poison book in the history of the church. As we read Scripture, one role in our interpretive life is to test the Spirit, to see whether our readings of it are in accordance with the movement of God's spirit. Three images for the Spirit, she claims, may help us in this discernment. First, our readings of Scripture ought to accord with the Spirit as the bond of love. Does our reading of the Scriptures lead, in other words, to greater love for God and others? Or does it merely wind up justifying ourselves? Second, our reading of the Bible ought to correspond to the Spirit's presence as the giver of all life, which liberates all for fuller life. Finally, our reading of Scripture ought also to heed the movement of Holy Spirit as exorcist, freeing us from oppressive readings of the Bible that produce "deep and long-lasting harm . . . freeing us from the interpretive demons that possess us personally and communally."[7]

Because it was written by human beings, Scripture is not immune from the predilections and biases of its human writers. Certain texts within the canon have been dangerous historically and have constituted "bad news" for many groups of people. In Pauw's view, however, this exorcist Spirit does not excise problematic texts from the canon but better enables the church to struggle with these texts: "The Spirit's work of exorcism is aided by keeping troubling texts before the church, rather than excising them from lectionaries and Sunday school curricula, as a reminder that the roots of demonic readings lie finally not in particular texts but in the human

---

7. Amy Plantinga Pauw, "The Holy Spirit and Scripture," in David H. Jensen, ed., *The Lord and Giver of Life: Perspectives on Constructive Pneumatology* (Louisville, KY: Westminster John Knox Press, 2008), 36.

heart."[8] Our reading of Scripture, therefore, is always provisional and never final. We read faithfully when we read together, open to new insights that are the work of the Spirit. As we read the human words of Scripture, which are inspired by the Spirit in their ongoing reception, the Bible can become good news for us all over again. Perhaps this approach best addresses the conflicted narratives of 1 and 2 Samuel. They are neither unadulterated testimonies of God's Spirit nor outmoded stories that are no longer sources of liberation. Instead, they interweave raw political ambition and divine inspiration, the biases of partisan writers (such as the Deuteronomist) and a Spirit that is capable of speaking through them. In such an approach, both exorcism and the rule of love are needed and will doubtless lead to multiple—rather than singular—interpretations of stories.

16:14–23

David in Saul's Service

"Now the spirit of the LORD departed from Saul, and an evil spirit from the LORD tormented him" (v. 14). This verse has vexed interpreters for centuries. If God is good and the fruits of the Spirit are "love, joy, peace, patience, kindness, generosity, faithfulness, gentleness, and self-control" (Gal. 5:22–23), then is it not contradictory to claim God sends an *evil* spirit responsible for torment and lack of self-control? The Deuteronomist, however, seems less concerned with defending God's goodness than with documenting that what happens with Saul (and with David) is according to the divine will. When Saul experiences torment, this is because he has lost divine favor, the very thing that has established kingship in the first place. The question is less about theodicy than it is about history. God will act to achieve God's purposes in history by sending a spirit that can torment, disrupting and confounding the aims and ambitions of people. If Saul continues to cling to power, he can expect further disruptive—and painful—eruption of the spirit.

8. Ibid., 37.

The Heidelberg Catechism describes God's providence in this way: "Whatever evil [God] sends upon me in this troubled life he will turn to my good, for he is able to do it."[9] It is difficult to say whether Saul's experience of the evil God sends upon him is in accord with this Reformation-era document. Clearly, God's sending of an evil spirit upon Saul is ultimately for Israel's good, as it paves the way for King David. But is it for Saul's good as well? Cheryl Exum suggests that here Saul "encounters God's dark side." It might even be described as "demonic" because Saul experiences "divine absence" and "YHWH's persecuting presence in the form of an evil spirit."[10] This is a God who haunts and torments as well as providing comfort.

Saul's servants recognize the spirit's divine origin and they also name its remedy: music. The Christian tradition has long simultaneously celebrated and expressed wariness over the power of music. Augustine, though he defended the practice of singing during worship, claimed that raising one's voice in song could also invite spirits antithetical to Christian faith. He was suspicious of music that would "set aflame . . . revelries by the singing of songs that are merely human compositions."[11] Such song, moreover, is closely linked to "the pestilential rowdiness of dancers," which can infect worship with the rhythms of "impious songs," when worshippers should be dancing "not with the body but the mind."[12] Music, though a powerful form of religious expression, could just as easily lead Christians astray, making them move to passions not ruled by reason. The Augustinian monk (and composer) Martin Luther, by contrast, enjoyed robust singing and playing, not only religious harmonies but also secular titles: "Music is the greatest gift, indeed it is divine; and therefore Satan is extremely hostile to it, because by its influence many great temptations overcome. . . . Music is the highest art, the notes of which cause the words of the text to live. . . . How does it

---

9. *Constitution of the Presbyterian Church (U.S.A.)*, Part I, *Book of Confessions*, (Louisville, KY: Office of the General Assembly, Presbyterian Church (U.S.A.), 1996), 4.026.

10. J. Cheryl Exum, *Tragedy and Biblical Narrative: Arrows of the Almighty* (Cambridge: Cambridge University Press, 1992), 40.

11. Augustine, "Letter 55," in *Letters 1–99*, ed. John E. Rotelle, O.S.A., trans. Roland Teske, S.J., *The Works of Saint Augustine: A Translation for the 21st Century* II/1 (Hyde Park, NY: New City Press, 2001), 234.

12. Augustine, "Sermon 311: On the Birthday of the Martyr Cyprian," in *Sermons*, ed. John E. Rotelle, O.S.A, trans. Edmund Hill, O.P., *The Works of Saint Augustine* III/9 (Hyde Park, NY: New City Press,1994), 73–74.

happen that with reference to secular things we have so many a fine poem and so many a beautiful song, while for spiritual edification we have such wretched, cold things."[13] These differing attitudes toward music reverberate down to the present day, with some traditions disallowing instrumental music in worship and others employing organs, trumpets, and—more recently—electric guitars and drums. Christians often are deeply suspicious about the "wrong kind" of music but have also produced some of the most passionate stanzas known to humankind. Who cannot help but stand, for example, during a performance of Handel's Hallelujah Chorus? From Mozart to John Coltrane, from Gregorian chant to U2, the Christian story has erupted in music: sometimes frenzied, sometimes calm; in voice and in instrument; in whispers and in shouts.

Music, undoubtedly, often speaks more clearly than words: in praise and in lament. Karl Barth began each day by listening to Mozart, who "did not produce merely his own music but that of creation, its twofold and yet harmonious praise of God."[14] Given music's power to move and sustain the human spirit, it is no wonder that Saul's servants recommend not religious counsel, but chords played on strings. When words fail to alleviate his condition, music can.

> If God could employ flawed instruments like Moses, David, and Paul, why can't divine grace be channeled through rock and roll?
>
> Don Compier, *Listening to Popular Music* (Minneapolis: Fortress, 2013), 14.

Saul agrees to his servants' suggestion: "Provide for me someone who can play well and bring him to me" (v. 17). One servant answers that he knows a son of Jesse who is not only skilled at the lyre but is a man of valor, a warrior who is prudent in his words. But, even more significantly, this servant notes that the Lord is with David (v. 18). The very presence that has fled Saul is now with David. Saul will thus be comforted by one who cannot escape YHWH's presence.

Saul sends messengers to Jesse, who ask for David to come to court. Two things are noteworthy about this incident: (1) Saul

---

13. *Conversations with Luther*, ed. Preserved Smith and Herbert Percival Gallinger (New Canaan, CT: Keats Publishing, Inc., 1979), 98, 100.
14. Karl Barth, *Church Dogmatics*, III/3, *The Doctrine of Creation*, ed. G. W. Bromiley and T. F. Torrance (London: T. & T. Clark, 2004), 298.

names David, though his servants have not. This indicates that Saul already knows of David. Jesse's son, in other words, is not an anonymous innocent, but one whose resourcefulness in battle is already well-known. This contrasts with the depiction of David as inexperienced shepherd in the following chapter. (2) Despite David's renown, Saul seems to give David backhanded treatment when he instructs his messengers to bring him the one who is "with the sheep" (v. 19). David is full of contrasts: he is a valiant warrior and a simple shepherd; he is the military man who is also a musician; a violent and at times ruthless leader who grieves deeply over his own sin. His subsequent actions reveal both pastoral sensitivity and raw political strategy. In this case, however, Saul appears to be slighting David: after hearing of his valor, he describes David as one who cares for domesticated animals. The traces of Saul's jealousy have already emerged before the two ever meet.

David's arrival in court evokes immediate affection: Saul "loved David greatly" (v. 21). David's name, after all, means "beloved," and he seems almost irresistibly lovable, regardless of what he does. The tale of love in what follows, however, becomes conflicted, pitting family members against one another. From this moment forward, Saul and David are bound by love: even when they are pitted against one another, the tattered bonds of love remain. For the moment, Saul's love for David results in David becoming the king's armor-bearer, near to Saul's heart. David's position at court, if initially envisioned as temporary, soon becomes permanent, as Saul sends word to Jesse that David has found "favor" in Saul's sight. Only after this request for David's permanent stay in court, however, do we hear of his effectiveness in the role for which he was originally requested. David's musicianship relieves Saul and causes the evil spirit to depart (vv. 22–23). The spirit that haunts Saul responds to David's gentle touch on strings.

17:1–58
David and Goliath

Of all the episodes in 1 and 2 Samuel, the battle between David and Goliath is undoubtedly the most widely known. People who have never read a word of the Bible are familiar with David and Goliath, as their names have infused cultural vocabularies: any underdog struggle—political, economic, or athletic—gains inspiration from David's victory in the face of staggering odds. The story is masterfully told, with suspense and compelling character studies. The story, as it appears in Scripture, is a combination of multiple traditions, which the editor has not harmonized into a seamless whole. David, for example, is reintroduced to readers in verse 12 as if he had not been mentioned before. No wonder this legend has taken on a life of its own. There are multiple traditions surrounding it within the cadence of Scripture itself.

The Philistines, who never seem to be far away, gather for battle at Socoh, in the borderlands of Judah and Philistia. The narrator claims that the town belongs to Judah, though it was likely disputed territory. Saul and the Israelites assemble nearby, as each army faces the other on opposing mountainsides (vv. 1–3). Goliath, whose imposing stature is described in great detail, advances toward the Israelites. Differing traditions record different heights: the Masoretic Text reads six cubits and a span (almost ten feet, or a fabled giant), while the Septuagint indicates four cubits and a span (over six and a half feet, or a rather large man). His stature provokes fear and serves as a symbol of the Philistine's superior strength. We already know of the Philistine's technological advantage in metallurgy: their effective monopoly on the production of iron (cf. 13:19–22). In the description of Goliath's equipment, we see this technological capability brought to full force. Outfitted with bronze helmet, a coat of mail, greaves, and a javelin, he also wields a massive spear made of iron, which is stronger than bronze. Waging war typically depends on technological prowess. Arms races of today are hardly remote from ancient stockpiling of iron spears. Technology, then as well as now, can demonstrate superior power as well as undue confidence that a nation is invincible. In Goliath we have an example of both: an army that is superiorly equipped in comparison to its foes, breeding warranted assurance and unwarranted arrogance.

With his shield-bearer before him, Goliath utters the taunt of a champion assured of victory: "Why have you come out to draw up for battle?" (v. 8). Before we read of any battle between the armies,

Goliath issues a challenge for a single man to fight him. The proposal is for a proxy battle, with the losing nation agreeing to serve the victor. Goliath's taunt and proposal only serve to heighten Israel's fears, as "all Israel heard these words of the Philistine" (vv. 8–11). No one accepts Goliath's proposal. Thus far, the battle is all buildup and no action.

Verse 12 marks an abrupt transition and the beginning of a second rendition of the story, as David gets reintroduced to the reader. Three of Jesse's eldest sons have joined Saul's army, but David stays at home to tend the sheep. Here David is not described as a warrior (as in chap. 16) but as a boy attending to domestic duties (vv. 12–15). As David is occupied with these tasks, Goliath, who is referred to here and elsewhere as "the Philistine," comes forward each morning and evening for forty days (v. 16). Two things stand out in this description: (1) the impersonal reference of "the Philistine," which conveys that what is most significant about Goliath is that he stands for a people who threaten Israel. The depersonalization of foes is the norm in battles. Both Israel and Philistia practice it, since killing is easier when armies refer to one another only as "the enemy," nameless entities without stories, families, or histories. The forty days symbolizes a period of trial and waiting in anticipation of God's intervention. The most obvious parallel is the forty days of the flood, where all seems lost amid the storm (Gen. 7–8). But, just as the story of Noah shows, in this story a long period of waiting is followed by a new beginning.

David enters this scene as a youth bringing his brothers and their commander food (vv. 17–18). David appears as a servant, a role that will accompany him as he becomes king. When he serves Israel, all will be well. When he serves himself, he will fail as king. The description of the army camp suggests that Israel has done more than wait in response to Goliath's threats. David arrives as the Israelites shout a war cry and troops are poised for battle. Goliath repeats his ritual of words, which David hears for the first time. The Philistine's words strike fear in the Israelites' hearts but also kindle discussion of the reward that the Philistine's slayer will receive from Saul (vv. 19–25). David, who apparently is not privy to their discussion, asks what shall be done to the man who kills Goliath, but his question is less motivated by reward than it is by offense at the Philistine's words. David is not intimidated by Goliath but appalled by his ignorance of the God of Israel, how he defies the army of "the living God" (v. 26). David puts faith in God's direct involvement in Israel's affairs. David already stands out from the soldiers surrounding him: his first instinct is not to flee, but to confront what is sacrilegious and blasphemous in his sight.

But if David's questions distinguish him from the soldiers, they are dubious to his brothers. The exchange between David and his brother Eliab indicates some degree of family rivalry. Angry that David is talking with soldiers, Eliab is perplexed that David has arrived at all and wonders who is tending his father's sheep. He furthermore considers David's actions to be presumptuous rather than faithful, claiming to know the "evil" of David's heart (v. 28). This testimony from David's own kin stands in direct opposition to the Deuteronomist's portrayal of David. For the uprightness of David's heart is part of what distinguishes him as God's anointed. David's family, however, interpret him as having other motives: of merely being a spectator to the battle. Family loyalties and rivalries are complicated. Sharing the same space with others can bind family members together in trust and generate profound distrust. We are not told why Eliab responds in this way: jealousy, presumption, or perhaps Eliab's experience with David on prior occasions. But where the Deuteronomist painstakingly outlines David's faithfulness, a brother who knows him well can only see ulterior motives. David, in turn, plays the role of innocent: "What have I done now? It was only a question" (v. 29). Perhaps the question conveys both innocence and ambition, for David is one willing to take up the Philistine's challenge. His brother's rebuke will not shake David's determination to face this taunt of the living God. But the exchange between Eliab and David may also foreshadow something more tragic. Despite David's present reliance on God, this youth will commit evil when he becomes king. Perhaps the heart that Eliab discerns is the heart of the king who seizes the wife of his best soldier and plots murder. Eliab may recognize something about David that the reader does not yet know: that the pure heart is also capable of evil, even the heart of God's anointed.

Saul hears of David's words and summons the boy to him. David offers to fight Goliath, an offer that Saul initially spurns, since David is a boy and Goliath has been a warrior since youth. But David will not countenance the king's rejection, claiming his experience as a shepherd will serve him well in battle. The "uncircumcised Philistine" is like the lions and bears he has killed while tending sheep (vv. 31–37). What distinguishes David from all the other characters in this episode is his trust in God: Goliath is confident in his stature and weapons; the Israelite soldiers lack confidence in themselves and lack trust in YHWH; Saul seeks to protect David with his own armor. But David is different: his trust in YHWH is complete, and in this trust he offers both a model for kingship and a posture for the people Israel. For those who trust in the Lord, the Lord will provide protection and salvation. When Saul clothes David with his own helmet and armor, girding him with his own sword, the picture is comical: David cannot walk. In defiance of military protocol, David sheds these arms and advances toward Goliath with a simple shepherd's staff, a sling, and a few stones in a pouch, armed with the living God (vv. 38–40). As David casts off Saul's armor, however, we witness something else: Saul is giving David symbols of his royal identity, which David refuses to take "from the proffered hand" in order to earn them "on his own terms."[15] Indeed, David's battle against Goliath serves as a kind of proxy battle between David and Saul, as it demonstrates David's destiny to become king and supplant Saul.

Though Goliath is confident of victory, his shield-bearer walks before him. He disparages David's youth and appearance, which is "ruddy and handsome" (v. 42). Apparently David's looks are also striking to his enemies. The Philistine is offended, curses the youth, and claims that David's paltry defenses mean that Goliath is being treated as a dog. Goliath taunts that the boy will become food for wild animals. David's response is lengthy, summing up his trust in YHWH. The battle between them, in David's eyes, is not merely a

15. Barbara Green, O.P., *King Saul's Asking* (Collegeville, MN: Liturgical Press, 2003), 67. J. Cheryl Exum notes that the contrast between David and Saul might be described in this way: "Unlike his tragic predecessor Saul, David does not seek out his destiny but rather lets events unfold as they will" (*Tragedy*, 146). David's refusal of Saul's arms may thus demonstrate his receptivity to God's will rather than his resistance to it.

symbol for the war between Philistia and Israel, it is so that "all the earth may know that there is a God in Israel" (v. 46). David turns Goliath's taunt on him: it is not just Goliath who will die, but also the soldiers who stand behind him, and they will become the food of wild animals.

After the prolonged buildup, the battle itself is extremely short. In sparse prose, the narrator recounts David's actions in a series of active verbs: he runs, places his hand in the bag, takes a stone, slings it, and strikes the Philistine. When the stone sinks into Goliath's head, he falls. There is no circling of the combatants, no further words between them, no blood. David moves quickly and confidently, without a word or sword. But there is also a moment of exultation and the spoils of the victor. In a final gesture, David takes Goliath's sword and beheads the Philistine warrior. There are no more skirmishes or words exchanged between armies; once their champion is felled, the Philistines flee. The Israelites pursue their enemies, inflicting more casualties and plundering the Philistine camp as the shepherd becomes a warrior and takes the victory trophy—Goliath's head—to Jerusalem (vv. 48–54). The city of David appears here anachronistically: David hails from Bethlehem, and Jerusalem is not established as an Israelite city until after David assumes the throne. After all, this episode is as much allegory as it is history. David's victory over Goliath offers further evidence of David's anointing, the new thing—and the new city—that God is establishing through him.

Saul, who has already been introduced to David twice, asks his right-hand military man, Abner: "Whose son is this young man?" (v. 55). The question only makes sense if we consider the multiple versions of the story contained in the present narrative. When Abner brings David (with Saul's sword in hand) before the king, David answers directly: "I am the son of your servant Jesse the Bethlehemite" (v. 58). David is not a youth panting after the throne but a valiant soldier who is primarily a servant to the king. But the combination of several versions of the story leaves nothing in doubt: something new is being done in this servant who appears as a warrior, a soldier who is also a shepherd, a loyal son who is also a family rival, a youth who trusts in the Lord but is also swift to act.

18:1-16

David, Jonathan, and Saul: Friendship and Jealousy

The servant who is a warrior attracted others' notice, even in the king's own family. As soon as David finishes speaking with Saul, "the soul of Jonathan was bound to the soul of David" (v. 1). There have been no prior meetings between David and Jonathan, but the ties between them are already strong and will only get stronger. Jonathan "loved him as his own soul" (v. 1). Interpreters have posed innumerable questions about this love over the centuries (What kind of love is it?), but the intensity of their love is rooted first in friendship. Friendship is basic to life: we are creatures who need others in order for life to flourish, persons who will stick with us through thick and thin, who challenge us to reach further and accept us for whoever we are. Given the significance of friendship in so much of the biblical canon (not only here, but also in the ministry of Jesus, cf. John 15:13–15), it is surprising that theologians have often avoided friendship as a theological topic. One recent exception is Sallie McFague, who writes that in distinction to many other kinds of relationships (such as parent-child), friendship entails mutual responsibility and reciprocity. "Friends are mutually interdependent in a way characteristic of adults."[16] Friendship may be the kind of relationship that most nearly resembles the reign of God, the new thing that God is doing in the world to tear down the barriers that make some oppressed and others oppressors. The relationship between David and Jonathan offers one pattern of friendship, to pledge one's life to be with another, despite physical distance or family loyalty. Friendship of this sort also entails risks: to love another as oneself risks loss as well as conflict with one's family of origin. In the end, Jonathan experiences both of these risks.

> [H]uman nature is something social, and hath for a great and natural good, the power also of friendship.
>
> Augustine, "On the Good of Marriage," in Philip Schaff, ed., *Nicene and Post-Nicene Fathers*, First Series, vol. 3 (Peabody, MA: Hendrickson Publishers, 2004), 399.

16. Sallie McFague, *Models of God: Theology for an Ecological, Nuclear Age* (Philadelphia: Fortress, 1987), 165.

This friendship also reveals a shadow side in a patriarchal milieu. Exum describes the relationship between David and Jonathan as male bonding, which "characteristically excludes and undervalues women." Jonathan ultimately replaces his sister, Michal, as David's love object.[17] Ultimately, Michal becomes a victim to the power struggles between Saul and David and the love between Jonathan and David, as she is left bereft of children. If we are stirred by the language that describes the attraction between David and Jonathan, we should also note who it leaves behind.

Saul is also attracted to David. By refusing to allow David to return to his father's house (v. 2), Saul makes a claim on David as well. Henceforth, David belongs in the house of the king, whether as a servant or eventually as king. Jonathan then establishes a covenant with David that represents not only friendship but also a gesture of fealty to the one who will be king. As Jonathan takes off his robe, armor, weapons, and belt and gives them to David (vv. 3–4), the son of the king transfers signs of his inheritance of the throne to the one whom he loves as his own soul.[18] Indeed, the conflict of Jonathan's loyalties becomes all the more intense in the ensuing drama. By making a covenant with David, Jonathan not only bears witness to friendship but to political realities. The question of Jonathan's true loyalty will drive much of the narrative ahead.

The political intrigue soon becomes more intense. Saul sets David "over the army," an appointment that appears to supplant Abner. Here, the one who remains loyal to Saul unto the end is replaced by a youthful upstart. David's military success, however, is immediate, and "all the people, even the servants of Saul" approve (v. 5). Interpreting Saul's appointment of David is difficult: it may be the calculation of a shrewd king (immediately placing the new hero in a position of prominence to bolster the king's image), or it may be due to affection for the new warrior. Whatever the case, the people's acclaim cannot hurt the king. Or can it? As David returns

17. Exum, *Tragedy*, 73.
18. P. Kyle McCarter, "1 Samuel," textual notes in *The HarperCollins Study Bible*, ed. Wayne A. Meeks (New York: HarperCollins, 1993), 446. And Exum notes that "though he earlier refused Saul's armor (17:38–39), David accepts from Jonathan these royal symbols—a sign that what he could not *take* from Saul, who wants to retain the kingship, he can *receive* from Jonathan, who is willing to give it up" (*Tragedy*, 78, italics in original).

from "killing the Philistine," women come out "of all the towns of Israel," singing and dancing, exulting that Saul has killed thousands and David ten thousands (vv. 6–7). The comparison evokes Saul's jealousy and rage. His question of what more David can have but the kingdom is eerily prescient. For as desperately as Saul will cling to the throne, David, who shows little ambition for it, will receive it. Saul's jealousy, from this point on, begins to tear him apart: he eyes David from that day on (vv. 8–9).

The day after their return, jealousy intensifies. This, too, is from the hand of God: "an evil spirit from God rushed upon Saul, and he raved within his house" (v. 10). But this time David's music can do little to soothe the madman. This spirit is forceful, beyond human control, beyond even the ministrations of the one anointed by God to be the new king. Saul's rage is uncontrollable, as he tries to kill David with his spear. Welcomed into the house of the king, David now experiences the king's hospitality as a death threat, as he eludes Saul's spear twice. Conflicting passions are swift in this narrative: Saul's welcome of David turns to jealousy and finally to a fear that consumes Saul for the rest of his life (vv. 11–12). Indeed, one of the most intriguing differences between David and Saul is that Saul fears the loss of his own status while David trusts that God will protect and provide. Fear of others leads to an obsession with the self and the belief that nothing can provide sufficient protection (no matter how many bars on the windows, no matter how high the border fence), while generosity opens one to the gift of others. Fear shuts us off from one another and God; generosity opens the gates to life more abundant. Scott Bader-Saye writes, "Fear is not evil. It is not a vice. It is not wrong to fear, but excessive or disordered fear can tempt us to vices such as cowardice, sloth, rage, and violence. . . . While fear itself may not be evil, disordered fear can certainly create the opportunity and (apparent) justification for great evil."[19] Fear can wind up consuming life so that life is cut short.

Saul cannot bear having David in his chambers any more. His appointment of David as commander of the army can be interpreted variously: (1) as another attempt to have David killed, since such an

---

19. Scott Bader-Saye, *Following Jesus in a Culture of Fear* (Grand Rapids: Brazos, 2007), 26.

appointment sends the servant into the heat of battle; (2) as a cynical attempt to benefit from the people's acclaim for David (exploiting David's popularity in the hopes that Saul's status will also be bolstered); or (3) simply as a way to remove David from Saul's sight. None of these are particularly noble motives, and the result—contrary to any of these intentions—is even greater acclaim for David and a more difficult situation for Saul. David's every military undertaking is a success, for "the LORD was with him" (v. 14). Again, the narrator stresses David's achievements as the result of God's work and favor. In the face of this movement of the divine, Saul can only stand in awe of David, and the people of Israel come to love Jesse's son (vv. 15–16). There seems to be nothing that he does that does not kindle Israel's love, nothing that Saul can do to turn that love elsewhere. This section closes by remarking that David marches out and comes in leading Israel, leaving no mistake that the love of the people is with someone other than their king.

18:17–30

David Marries into Saul's Family

Saul had promised his daughter to the warrior who would slay Goliath (17:25). In this section, this promise gets fulfilled, albeit in a roundabout way. Saul's initial offer of Merab, his elder daughter, provides the typical resolution. Saul offers her to David with the stipulation that he continue to "be valiant for me and fight the LORD's battles." The king's thoughts, however, reveal his ulterior motives. Saul refuses to raise a hand against David but proposes to "let the Philistines deal with him" (18:17). If David is now to become more deeply intertwined in Saul's family by marrying Merab, the hope is that this family connection will not abide for long. David's response to the king, initially, is not to accept his promised reward. In a humble posture that has now become familiar, David contrasts his status with that of the king. "Who am I . . . that I should become son-in-law to the king?" (v. 18). Meanwhile, Merab is silent in these transactions. The narrator gives her no voice and we can only guess her thoughts (in contrast to the men of the story). The ways of kings and warriors, in so many ways, often ignore the voices of women or even fail to recognize that they have a voice. Then, in a surprising turn, Saul revokes his promise of Merab to David and gives her to Adriel the Meholathite (v. 19), a character who appears only one other time in Scripture, in an accounting of Saul's progeny (2 Sam. 21:8). Saul, apparently, cannot bear to make good on his promise.

If Merab is silenced, however, Saul's younger daughter, Michal, has a powerful voice. Readers, furthermore, are privy to her thoughts and emotions. She—like her brother Jonathan and like the people Israel—loves David, a love that pleases the king (v. 20). The king's pleasure, however, is not over the prospective happiness of his daughter but in the presumed role that her love might play in snaring David. The combination of a daughter's love and the Philistine threat may prove David's undoing. Saul intends to manipulate love to his advantage, first by flattering David with his love. Saul does not believe that Michal's love for David would ever conflict with his daughter's loyalty to her father. His daughter's love, instead, is something for him to toy with. David responds to Saul's offer of Michal's hand with customary humility, but this time he focuses on economic status: he is "poor and of no repute" (v. 23). The contrast between Saul and David is not only between fear for oneself and trust in the Lord; it is also between political power/economic privilege and relative poverty and powerlessness. Nonetheless, God's consistent action here, like that of Hannah's song, is to uplift the powerless and poor.

When David's words are reported to the king, Saul cynically takes into account David's professed poverty. David does not have the economic means to provide the typical marriage gift. (This is yet another mark of using women as a commodity of exchange. Even if Michal has voice in this narrative, she is not exempt from the practice of bride-price.) Saul tells his servants that no monetary means are necessary, only a gruesome symbol of military conquest: the foreskins of one hundred Philistines. Much is represented in this rather strange offering: (1) a vivid reminder of how the Philistines do not recognize the God of Israel, as they do not bear the mark of the covenant; (2) an act that is so rash that the king likely expects David to be killed in attempting it; and (3) an example of sexual humiliation and violence often present in war. In the frenzy of combat, soldiers commit atrocities against the enemy that are expressly forbidden by their own moral codes. Rape has been a "weapon" of war for millennia, witnessed in biblical times as well as present-day struggles. During the fall of the Libyan regime in 2011, for example, video captured an exultant fighter sodomizing Muammar Gaddafi with a stick or knife.[20] Christians who recall this story of Saul and David, as well as the examples of sexual violence rampant in contemporary warfare and social struggle ought to remember that the crucifixion might also be understood as an act of sexual violence. Jesus is stripped and scourged, abused and humiliated in a degrading form of public execution. David Tombs notes that "sexual abuse was not accidental or incidental to crucifixion as a form of torture and execution" and that there is "substantial evidence that other Roman prisoners suffered sexual violence of many different sorts."[21] Bearing witness to the crucifixion as an act of sexual violence does not mean that such actions (whether during the reign of Saul, Herod, or the age of American empire) are redemptive; rather, it points to God's solidarity with the victims of sexual violence and Christ's presence with them in agony, in outcry, and fundamentally in resistance to all that would maim, kill, humiliate, and destroy life. Saul's request is indeed horrific, but the experiences of the victims of such violence (whom we do not hear from in this story) are never forgotten in the life of God.

David's reaction to Saul's request is that he is "well-pleased to be the king's son-in-law" (v. 26). David accomplishes the gruesome task against insurmountable odds and brings the strange gift to the king. This time Saul cannot revoke his promise and presents Michal to David as wife. The plot to kill David is again foiled, a reminder again of how the Lord is with David. To add further to Saul's torment, Michal's love of David becomes even more apparent to the king. The result: Saul becomes even "more afraid of David," and becomes David's enemy (vv. 27–29). Within the span of one chapter, the servant to the king becomes the object of the king's anger, jealousy, fear, and ultimately an enemy. The spiral of suspicion has

---

20. http://www.globalpost.com/dispatch/news/regions/middle-east/111024/gaddafi-sodomized-video-gaddafi-sodomy.
21. David Tombs, "Sexual Ethics and the Scandal of the Cross," in *Theology in Service to the Church: Global and Ecumenical Perspectives*, ed. Allan Hugh Cole (Eugene, OR: Wipf and Stock Publishers, 2014), 127.

reached its zenith: Saul now considers David a threat who must be destroyed. The one who serves the king and is now part of the king's family by marriage is akin to the Philistines in the king's sight. But for David, the ongoing military engagements with the Philistines are further occasions for success, more "than all the servants of Saul" (v. 30). It is as if David cannot fail, on the battlefield, in friendship, in marriage. His fame grows in the people's sights. Even members of Saul's own family seem set against the king.

19:1–17
Further Conflicts in the Royal Family and a Flight from Saul

Family loyalties become more conflicted as time goes by and Jonathan and Michal increase their affection for David. Their affections stand out markedly from Saul's fear of David, which now borders on paranoia. If Saul's intentions toward David had been thinly disguised to others before, they are now revealed fully to his servants and to Jonathan: Saul intends to kill David. Jonathan, by contrast, takes "great delight in David" (v. 1). The bonds of friendship between the two are not simply ties of obligation but the source of pleasure. Indeed, the bonds between the two friends are markedly different than the bonds between father and son. Jonathan, in the end, does not forgo the ties of family (and eventually is killed in battle because of his loyalty to Saul), but the ties to his father are not cause for much delight. Jonathan sticks with his father because he has to. He sticks with David, at least in part, because the friendship brings happiness. One trait that distinguishes friendship from other kinds of human relationship is the mutuality of delight, the reciprocal nature of interaction. Friendship offers one model for the redeemed human community, where we delight in others simply because they are children of God. Perhaps this is why Jesus called his disciples friends at the Last Supper, offering a pattern for the redeemed community of the church. Jonathan, at this point, does not rebuke his father about his murderous intent; his thoughts are kept silent. But out of friendship he conveys a warning to David: for him to be on guard and to hide in a field as Jonathan attempts to learn more of his father's intent (vv. 2–3).

Jonathan speaks to his father directly, imploring the king not to sin against David because David has not sinned against him (v. 4). In many contexts the language of sin refers primarily to humanity's relationship with God. Sin is something committed against God. But in this instance, Jonathan's words remind the king (and us) that sin is also against one's neighbor, that one cannot be against one's neighbor and for God. Shirley Guthrie claims that "God becomes real to us only in and with and through our personal relationships with *other people*."[22] In this view, our responsibilities toward God and neighbor are *always* interrelated.

> [God] requires us to love our neighbor as ourselves, to show patience, peace, gentleness, mercy, and friendliness toward him, to prevent injury to him as much as we can, also to do good to our enemies.
>
> "The Heidelberg Catechism," in the *Book of Confessions*, 4.107.

By plotting David's murder, Saul is also rupturing relation with God. Jonathan further reminds Saul of David's service to the king: his defeat of Goliath, which entailed substantial risk to his own life. There can be no cause, even for a king, to kill this servant. The words, apparently, convince Saul, as he makes an oath, though he speaks in the passive voice. He does not directly state, "I will not strike David," but speaks indirectly: "As the LORD lives, he shall not be put to death" (v. 6). This passive voice effectively dampens Saul's responsibility. Nonetheless, an oath is an oath and Saul has sworn that David will not be killed. Jonathan then calls David from hiding, brings his friend to Saul, and restores the servant in his service to the king (v. 7). For a moment, it seems that Jonathan is loyal to both father and friend and that Saul has welcomed the servant back.

The servant returns to his standard role: military campaigns and their invariable success. The narrator relates no detail other than that David's attack against the Philistines is heavy and that the enemy flees. We can presume that his popularity among the Israelites continues to increase. But David's success leads again to Saul's fear. In words that echo the previous chapter, the Lord sends an evil spirit to torment Saul, a spirit that cannot be calmed

22. Shirley C. Guthrie, *Christian Doctrine*, revised edition (Louisville, KY: Westminster John Knox Press, 1994), 60, italics in original.

by David's music. At this moment, both God and family seem set against Saul, causing a rage bent on killing the musician (vv. 8–10). Almost as soon as Saul has made an oath to spare David, he breaks it in attempted murder. It is, after all, easier to violate an oath than keep it.

David escapes the king's chambers while Saul sends guards to keep watch over David so that he might be killed in the morning. But again, one of Saul's children protects David. Michal, whose love of David has already been attested, now finds her love put to the test. She warns David of her father's intent and concocts a scheme that will save his life. In a scene reminiscent of Israelite spies fleeing Jericho (Josh. 2:15), Michal, like Rahab before her, protects the fugitive by helping him escape through her window. Her subsequent ruse contains interesting details: laying an idol on their bed (complete with goats' hair and some clothes) and telling Saul's messengers that David is sick (vv. 12–14). The presence of an idol is somewhat odd, given that the word is used in other instances to connote idolatry and rejection of God's word (15:23). Is the presence of this object in Michal and David's chambers evidence of less than strict devotion to YHWH? Is it simply a household talisman common to the times? The story is relayed, however, without a hint of judgment against the idol, indicating an innocuous talisman or a stage in the progression from henotheism to strict monotheism in Israelite religion. At any rate, Michal surely cannot expect to deceive her father or his messengers for very long, only enough time to allow David to flee. When Saul displays his intentions yet again by telling his messengers to bring David to him "in the bed, that I may kill him" (v. 15), Michal's ruse is discovered. He suspects his daughter's duplicity and has apparently expected her cooperation in the killing. But for Michal, the ruse continues, as she covers her actions with a lie, claiming that David had threatened to kill her (vv. 16–17). The layers of deception are indeed more than Saul suspects, revealing again that when forced to choose between her husband and her father, Michal choses David, the beloved. Saul is now unaware of two secrets held by his own children: the depth of Michal's devotion to her husband and the bonds of Jonathan's friendship with the one Saul considers his enemy.

19:18–24

Saul and the Prophets

This next episode appears strange for a number of reasons. First, it contradicts the earlier assertion in 15:35 that Saul and Samuel would not see each other again before Samuel's death. Second, it repeats the proverb of Saul being among the prophets and an instance of prophetic fervor (10:9–16), albeit in a less flattering way. The story seems independent from the earlier material, and it is probably an editorial insertion that serves to further distinguish David, the anointed, from Saul, who experiences the loss of God's blessing. The episode begins by noting David's escape from death and his escape not to his homeland (Bethlehem) but to Samuel, the one who anointed him king. David finds Samuel, oddly, not in Ramathaim, Samuel's hometown, but in Ramah. The two settle at Naioth, another textual oddity that most likely means "encampments." David tells Samuel "all that Saul had done to him," but we hear no words from Samuel. Where Saul makes a vow not to harm David and immediately violates it, Samuel speaks no words but takes actions to protect the refugee. Saul finds out David's whereabouts and sends a succession of messengers to Ramah to take David. But the messengers encounter prophets gathered around Samuel and get caught up in their frenzy (vv. 18–21). Several details here are worth noting: Samuel stands "in charge of the prophets," indicating his ongoing stature; the spirit of God falls on Saul's messengers, which thwarts them from carrying out the king's command. Whereas Saul is earlier gripped by an evil spirit from God, the messengers are touched by a prophetic spirit that prevents them from committing evil.

Saul finally takes matters into his own hands, revealing his increasing desperation, and upon arrival in Ramah asks not simply for David, but for Samuel as well. Saul, likewise, falls to the fate that awaited his messengers: the spirit of God comes upon him and he falls into a frenzy. But the king's condition is related in greater detail, and the details are not particularly becoming. He strips off his clothes and lays naked all day and night (vv. 22–24), "a sign of his powerlessness."[23]

---

23. Johanna W. H. van Wijk-Bos, *Reading Samuel: A Literary and Theological Commentary* (Macon, GA: Smyth & Helwys Publishing, Inc., 2011), 109.

Here transformation is more dramatic than in chapter 10, focused on Saul in the grips of something beyond his control. A king who is naked long into the night does not inspire much devotion. The proverb of Saul being "among the prophets" in this instance sounds more like a byword than an acclamation. Even Saul's prophetic gifts now seem to be a shadow of their former self, leaving the king naked, vulnerable, and subject to scorn. On the other hand, *something* of Saul's prophetic gifts remain, and they are obvious to all who gather. Indeed, prophetic frenzy prevents Saul from seizing David. David, meanwhile, is also among the prophets but we hear no description of his behavior. In this instance again, he reveals himself as a different kind of king (and prophet) than Saul. Polzin sees in the episode yet another contrast between Saul and David: "Whereas it is God who seeks out David through the 'prophet,' it is rather Saul who seeks out God through the 'prophet.' Could it be that, for the Deuteronomist, God appropriately takes the initiative with prophets, but humans should not?"[24] If that is the case, Saul fails to grasp the meaning of kingship *and* prophecy.

20:1–42

The Devotion of Jonathan and David

Chapter 20 is pivotal in the saga of David, Jonathan, and Saul, for it illustrates the depth of the covenant between David and Jonathan and how their covenant is tested. It also provides a vivid account of Jonathan's conflicted loyalties and Saul's ongoing degeneration. The account begins by describing David's flight from Naioth back to the house of Saul and his beloved friend. He questions Jonathan pointedly, expressing bewilderment that Saul should seek his life when he is an innocent man. Upon hearing David's questions, Jonathan cannot believe them. His words to David are a defense of his father and a statement of his closeness to Saul. There is nothing, Jonathan claims, that his father does that is not disclosed to him, whether great or small. David turns on Jonathan's defense, however, by

---

24. Robert Polzin, *Samuel and the Deuteronomist* (San Francisco: Harper & Row, 1989), 184.

claiming that Saul knows "that you like me." This reminder of the covenant between them insinuates both Saul's jealousy and his fatherly
impulse to protect his son from knowledge that would disturb him.
David and Jonathan cannot harbor a secret from Saul, though Saul
can certainly keep Jonathan in the dark about some matters. Saul's
secret, David claims, brings David one step from death (vv. 1–3).
Faced with this claim, Jonathan makes a promise: "Whatever you
say, I will do for you" (v. 4). The transition is sudden: from disbelief of his friend's words to a promise to do *anything*, a promise that
stakes Jonathan's loyalty with his friend rather than with his father.

David forms the initial seeds of a plan: he will hide in a field while
Jonathan dines with Saul. Jonathan will lie to his father that David
has returned to his family in Bethlehem and Saul's reaction to this
news will reveal Saul's intent toward David. David then describes his
relationship with Jonathan as a "sacred covenant," or alternatively
rendered "covenant of the Lord." By offering his own life (David tells
Jonathan to kill him if he stands guilty), David also points to the risk
for Jonathan, because the covenant places him in conflict with his
father's house (vv. 5–8).

As the two friends journey to the field that will become David's
hiding place, Jonathan adds to the plan. His role will be to communicate his father's intentions (vv. 9–12). Jonathan expresses hope for
the Lord to protect and be with his friend "as he has been with my
father" (v. 13). Jonathan's use of the past tense is intriguing, either
indicating God's continued presence with Saul or Jonathan's real-
ization that the Lord is no longer with his father. His subsequent
request to David is to strengthen the covenant between them: if Jonathan lives, for David to show him the "faithful love of the LORD,"
and if he dies, for Jonathan's house never to be cut off from David's
love (vv. 14–15). Jonathan's words in reestablishing covenant with
David, "May the LORD seek out the enemies of David" (v. 16), may
have been softened. Some scholars have suggested that the original
version invoked a curse on David if Jonathan's heirs are cut off from
the house of David.[25] But however one interprets the covenant, it is

clearly marked by love, a love as strong as Jonathan's love for his own life (v. 17).

At this point a word on the nature of Jonathan and David's love for one another is in order. Their relationship has triggered the imagination of countless commentators. The way the narrator describes their friendship, furthermore, is almost unique in Scripture. Pledges of loyalty, of course, are fairly common in the Bible. But the degree to which the Deuteronomist describes the intimacy and affection between Jonathan and David certainly invites speculation. Recently, many commentaries have focused on a possible sexual relationship between the two men. After all, they embrace, kiss, and speak of their love akin to love of one's soul. David, furthermore, describes his love of Jonathan as "passing the love of women" (2 Sam. 1:26). The two men try to keep their relationship a secret; when it is fully discovered, Saul speaks about it in degrading terms (v. 30). And yet, the covenant between Jonathan and David abides, regardless of what others say or do. Tom Horner interprets this evidence (including Israel's "living in the shadow of the Philistine culture, which accepted homosexuality") by claiming that "we have every right to believe that a homosexual relationship existed" between Jonathan and David.[26] Indeed, the figures of David and Jonathan, for many LGBT persons, can serve as an icon for blessing same-sex marriages, as the promises they make to one another are meant to withstand even death. Others have argued that there are no reasons to view the relationship between Jonathan and David as sexual. The language that describes their covenant is more akin to political pledges or an avowed friendship.

Both interpretations, however, may be claiming a bit too much. It is perhaps most fair to the text to claim that there is nothing about

---

Lovers are normally face to face, absorbed in each other; friends, side by side, absorbed in some common interest.

C. S. Lewis, *The Four Loves* (New York: Harcourt, Brace & Co., 1960), 91.

---

26. Tom Horner, *Jonathan Loved David: Homosexuality in Biblical Times* (Philadelphia: Westminster Press, 1978), 28.

the narrative descriptions that either prove or disprove a homoerotic relationship between Jonathan and David. The fact that many LGBT persons in the churches find the relationship between the two to be a powerful sign of God's blessing of same-sex relationships is surely an example of how queer meanings can be found in ancient texts and a testament to the ongoing life of interpretation within communities of faith. Ancient stories keep giving rise to new meanings. But imposing a homoerotic relationship on Jonathan and David may also be problematic. Indeed, one of the tendencies in our day is to assume that an intensity of love must eventually become sexual, whether in Harry's words to Sally that men and women cannot be friends because sex always gets in the way (from the film *When Harry Met Sally*) or the suspicion of close friendships (If they are that close, they must be having sex, too.). Indeed, if the relationship between Jonathan and David is interpreted as not being sexual, it provides an icon for the power of friendship in the face of staggering odds, a testament to a different kind of love than sexual love. Perhaps the relationship between Jonathan and David was sexual, perhaps not. Much can be gained from either reading of the text, but hearing its multiple meanings does not depend on us understanding their relationship as sexual or not.

Jonathan agrees to communicate Saul's intent to David via secret symbols: arrows, which invoke Jonathan's status as a warrior (like David's), that he will shoot in the field where David is hiding and instruct a servant to gather. The words spoken to the servant will convey the truth. The plan has now been established with the contributions of both friends. To conclude their plan, Jonathan invokes the Lord as witness "between you and me forever" (vv. 18–23). Jonathan has made his vow. Unlike his father's, it is not mere words. He intends words to echo forth in action, regardless of what may come, even if it is death.

David hides; Jonathan stands while his father dines along with Abner. When Saul is in a pinch, Abner is always at hand. The night of the new moon does not raise Saul's suspicion. Saul has some thoughts that something is amiss with David (uncleanness?), but he does not give voice to them. On the second day, Saul asks his son about David's whereabouts and the secret plan unfolds. Yet the

lie about David's family obligations in Bethlehem provokes immediate anger (vv. 24–9). His first word to Jonathan is a vulgar insult
that Jonathan has "chosen the son of Jesse to your own shame" and
the "shame of your mother's nakedness" (v. 30). In a swift stroke,
Saul castigates his son for choosing David over him and claims that
Jonathan's mother's vagina has been defiled by giving birth to Jonathan. Jonathan's choice of David, furthermore, is to Jonathan's own
demise: "as long as the son of Jesse lives upon the earth, neither you
nor your kingdom will be established" (v. 31). By choosing David,
Jonathan relinquishes his claim to the throne. Saul vituperates that
David will die, and when Jonathan asks the question of what David
has done, his question incurs further wrath. The king now hurls a
spear at his son in an eerie recollection of Saul's previous attempts
to murder David (vv. 32–33). The break between father and son
reaches its climax as Jonathan leaves in anger, eating no more food.
Jonathan's refusal of food is both in lament for David and testament
to his disgust over the host of the feast. Where Saul can only mis-
guidedly call his son a disgrace, he actually disgraces himself by
hanging on to the throne at all costs, even through murder.

The plan unfolds further, with the fatal message being conveyed
to David through Jonathan's archery and a boy's retrieval of the
arrows. Their mode of communication is kept secret, even to the
boy, who "knew nothing" (vv. 35–39). Jonathan's command to
the boy to carry his weapon to the city does not arouse suspicion.
Furthermore, Jonathan's use of a "little boy" seems intentional, as a
youth might be least aware of the rift between Jonathan and Saul or
least suspicious of any ulterior motives. When the friends reunite, no
further words are necessary. But David's actions invoke worship: he
rises, prostrates himself, bows, kisses, and weeps. Jonathan responds
in kind, but David weeps more (vv. 40–41). The parting, perhaps, is
even more difficult for the son of Jesse than it is for the one who first
made covenant with him, even if they depart in peace. Essential to
worship, the blessing and greeting of peace (or in some traditions,
the kiss of peace) marks believers' claims on each other: to be instruments of God's peace for and with one another. The friends depart in
the name of the Lord, who has witnessed their covenant and blessed
it and who in Jonathan's words will be between "my descendants

and your descendants, forever" (v. 42). They depart promising each other that neither man walks away alone.

FURTHER REFLECTIONS
LGBT Theologies

Because Jonathan and David have proven iconic for many LGBT persons, it is important to survey the varied approaches within LGBT theologies and how they might help us interpret not only Jonathan and David, but other same-sex couples in Scripture. For the sake of simplifying a multifaceted movement, three phases represent the growth and continued flourishing of LGBT theologies.

The first phase might be described as an *apologetic* approach. In the face of active discrimination against LGBT persons in the various churches, many authors drew on contemporary insights in psychology and biblical studies to argue for the full inclusion of LGBT persons in church membership and leadership. Beginning in the 1960s, works such as John McNeill's *The Church and the Homosexual*[27] argued that homosexuality was a natural orientation (like heterosexuality) that did not require change or transformative therapy. The often espoused goal of this first period was for LGBT persons to gain a seat at the table, to be included in the deliberations of the church. In Daniel Spencer's words, "These authors argued that homosexual persons did not need to change to become heterosexual or remain celibate (as most Christian denominations demanded) to be either 'normal' or accepted by God, and they sought to answer dominant and anti-gay biblical and theological arguments with alternative, gay-affirming perspectives."[28] An apologetic approach to Jonathan and David might understand the two men as an icon for same-sex marriage and their pledges to each other as warrants for the church's recognition of such marriages.

A second phase in LGBT theologies might be described as

---

27. John McNeill, *The Church and the Homosexual* (Kansas City: Sheed Andrews and McMeel, 1976).
28. Daniel T. Spencer, "Lesbian and Gay Theologies," in *Handbook of U.S. Theologies of Liberation*, ed. Miguel A. De La Torre (St. Louis: Chalice, 2004), 266.

emancipatory/celebratory. The trend among these writers was to move beyond apologetics toward a fuller appreciation of LGBT experiences as liberating and sites of revelation. Carter Heyward represents one strand of this phase. Her work criticizes the traditional sexual teachings of the Christian churches and recovers neglected strands within it, such as the theme of divine and human eros. For Heyward, eros is the love that connects us to one another, opening us to the passionate love of God. In her theology, the body and its pleasures are one site of God's revelation to humanity.

Most exemplars of this phase stress the importance of *experience* for the knowledge of God; indeed, the experiences of LGBT persons can point to shortcomings within classic understandings of Scripture and tradition. In this approach, Jonathan and David are not merely icons for queer inclusion but are embodied celebrations of eros unjustly denied by tradition.

A more recent trajectory is *queer* theology. This movement is radical in its recovery of the revolutionary roots ("radix," Latin for "root") of early Christian understandings of gender, the body, and sex. Writers in this phase often refer to the work of literary theorist Judith Butler, who has argued that gender is less a fixed nature than it is a cultural "performance"[29] and who questions inherited readings of Christian classics. Gender-bending and queer sexuality, in this view, is part of the tradition itself. Gerard Loughlin, for example, sees gay marriage symbolized in the nuptial themes of Scripture and sexual intimacy in much eucharistic theology: "Certainly the Eucharist is as intimate as sex—taking another body into one's own—and just insofar as it unites men and women with Jesus, it is gay sex as well as straight sex, gay marriage as well as straight marriage."[30] Many queer theologians question the fixity of hetero- and homosexuality as well, arguing that our sexual identities ultimately pale in relation to the new identity given in baptism, the radical remaking of the person in Christ. All of our identities, thus, are fluid. Elizabeth Stuart writes, "For the church is the only community under a mandate

---

29. Judith Butler, *Gender Trouble: Feminism and the Subversion of Identity* (New York: Routledge, 1999), 33.
30. Gerard Loughlin, "Introduction: The End of Sex," in *Queer Theology: Rethinking the Western Body*, ed. Gerard Loughlin (Malden, MA: Blackwell, 2007), 6. See also p. 2.

to be queer and it is under such a mandate because its eschatological horizon teaches it that gender and sexual identity are not
of ultimate concern, thus opening the possibility for love."[31] In this
trajectory, the stories of Jonathan and David subvert fixed understandings of gender and sex and intimate the new—and queer—
creation of God's promised reign.

21:1–9
David and Ahimelech

After David's departure from Jonathan, he is a man on the run. The
bulk of the remaining narrative, until David is anointed king of all
Israel, depicts David in various stages of flight. He flees first to Nob,
which is near Saul's town of Gibeah but also not far from David's
ancestral home, Bethlehem. Again, it is intriguing how David
chooses not to flee to his home but to places that stand as symbolic
in other ways (here to a center of Israel's priestly life; subsequently
to Gath, the seat of Philistine power). By finding refuge in places
other than his hometown, David gradually cements the accoutre-
ments of kingly authority, even on the run. Nob is referred to later in
the narrative as the "city of priests" (22:19). Ahimelech is the great-
grandson of Eli, the descendant of the most prominent priestly
family. Thus, David meets here with the great-grandson of the man
who began this story (in chapter 1). At the middle of this story, the
future king is connected to the beginning. Though the family of Eli
was subject to an oracle of judgment, with the promise that it would
be "cut off" from the priesthood (2:31–6), this fate has not yet come
to pass. Ahimelech meets David, but his demeanor connotes fear,
as he is trembling (v. 1). He wonders, appropriately, why David is
alone, since a prominent servant of the king, especially a military
one, would likely arrive with an entourage. Ahimelech's fear may also
bear witness to his suspicion that David is a fugitive. Why else would
a prominent servant of the king arrive unarmed and unfed? David's
response to Ahimelech is hasty and rings hollow: a claim to be on an

31. Elizabeth Stuart, "Sacramental Flesh," in *Queer Theology*, ed. Loughlin, 65.

errand from the king, to meet up with "the young men for such and such a place," an errand that no one else is privy to (v. 2). David lies, and the lie is not a particularly good one, even if it accomplishes his intended aim. Ahimelech does not question David's response, but his subsequent actions may be just as much an attempt to get rid of a fugitive as they are a convincing demonstration that he believes David.

The first thing David addresses is his own hunger: David demands bread or "whatever is here" (v. 3). The only thing that Ahimelech has is holy bread. David's response illustrates, in this instance, a somewhat flexible attitude toward ritual protocol. Indeed, it separates him from some of Saul's attitudes. Saul, who at many times seems obsessed with following through on holy vows (14:24–46) and attempts to conduct proper sacrifices, even when he fails (13:8–15). David, on the other hand, is simply hungry. Though he claims that he may eat the bread because he has abstained from sexual relations "as always when I go on an expedition" and that the "vessels of the young men are holy" (v. 5), the law stipulates that the bread may only be consumed by Aaron and his descendants (Lev. 24:5–9). David's request is certainly not within the letter of the law and probably not within the spirit of it either. On the other hand, holy bread is the only bread available. Torah stresses hospitality, and David's request for food may entail an opportunity for showing hospitality to guests. Indeed, Jesus cites this episode when, out of hunger, he and his disciples pluck grain on the Sabbath (Matt. 12:3–4; Mark 2:25–26; Luke 6:3–4). Ahimelech is convinced enough to give David the bread.

In an abrupt transition, the narrator focuses attention briefly on Doeg, a servant of Saul. His appearance is sudden, yet he has been in Ahimelech's presence, "detained before the LORD" (v. 7), an odd phrase that is present nowhere else in the Hebrew Bible, perhaps indicating that he is among the priests as part of a ritual, present near the sanctuary that houses the bread of the Presence. His appearance is ominous, since it ensures that Saul will become aware of David's visit with Ahimelech. Indeed, it is doubly ominous, since Doeg will carry out one of Saul's most ruthless commands, the execution of the priests at Nob (22:6–23). Here we are introduced to a shadowy servant near the shrine who will eventually kill those entrusted with holy things. Even when he is on the run, David cannot escape Saul's trace.

Having received food, David now asks for arms. His words, again, are dubious: the king's business "required haste" and there was no time to gather weapons (v. 8). All that is present is a unique object held in a special place: the sword of Goliath, "wrapped in cloth behind the ephod," indicating that the sword held some ritual significance and was not designated for typical use. By receiving this sword, David recovers the weapon of the man who posed the greatest threat to Israel. (He had already taken Goliath's armor after their battle, cf. 17:54.) The slaying of Goliath has now come full circle, as David takes Goliath's sword on the verge of his flight to Philistia. David equips himself for the journey by taking two holy things from the center of priestly authority: food designated for YHWH and a sword held as a memory of Israel's defeat of Philistia. Ritual violation yields to the coming of a new king. In David's words, "There is none like it. Give it to me" (v. 9).

FURTHER REFLECTIONS
Theology and the Use of the Law

One question that David's consumption of holy bread raises is to what regard we are bound by law. This question is particularly vexing for Protestants, since the founders of that tradition reacted strongly against what they perceived as legalism within medieval Catholicism. In their strong insistence on justification by grace through faith, they sometimes distanced themselves from the commands of law, especially if those commands were dictated by ecclesial authorities. Martin Luther, and those who saw themselves as heirs to his movement, claimed that the law found in Scripture primarily served two functions: The first was to convict us of our sin. When we read or hear the law proclaimed (such as the Sermon on the Mount or the Ten Commandments), we realize that we cannot fulfill it because of our sin. The effect of the law, in other words, drives us to grace, where we alone find refuge and salvation. In the words of the Lutheran Formula of Concord, law serves "to bring people to a knowledge of their sin." The second use of the law is its restraining function. Because human beings are sinful, they need law to uphold some degree of order in the face of chaos. Again, the Formula of Concord states this function succinctly: "to maintain external discipline and decency against dissolute and disobedient people."[32] Law, in short, keeps us from grasping each other's throats. Both of these uses of law, it should be noted, are *negative* in the sense that they show us something that we cannot do or restrain us from doing something that we would do otherwise.

Some strands of the Lutheran tradition also emphasize a third, positive use of the law, but it is particularly the Reformed tradition that is responsible for this emphasis. In this view, law serves a "principal" function as a guide or teacher to a holier life. This use of the law is reserved for those who already know justification by grace. We can fulfill the requirements of the law, as outlined in the Scriptures, because we know salvation in Christ, by grace. For Calvin in particular, this use of law should not be seen as a burden or a demand, but as a gift from God. The law does not repel, but attracts us and kindles our desire with "the accompanying promise of grace, which alone sweetens what is bitter."[33] Serene Jones sees in Calvin's principal use of the law an aesthetic: "The people who accept [the law] find that it is so beautiful they cannot help but adore it and seek to live within it. . . . We should follow the law because it entices and compels us!"[34] Regardless of how one understands the function of law in Christian life, it is important that the church not suggest that Jesus Christ stands in contrast to the law. When the church does so, the depiction of Christ and law sound foreign to the one who claimed that he came not to abolish the law, but to fulfill it (Matt. 5:17), and it risks understanding Judaism only as a foil to Christianity and not as the soil out of which the church grew. Viewed in this light, David's consumption of holy bread is less an

---

32. "The Formula of Concord," in *The Book of Concord: The Confessions of the Evangelical Lutheran Church,* ed. Theodore G. Tappert (Philadelphia: Fortress, 1959), 563.

33. John Calvin, *Institutes of the Christian Religion,* ed. John T. McNeill, trans. Ford Lewis Battles, LCC (Philadelphia: Westminster Press, 1960), 361.

34. Serene Jones, "Glorious Creation, Beautiful Law," in *Feminist and Womanist Essays in Reformed Dogmatics,* ed. Amy Plantinga Pauw and Serene Jones (Louisville, KY: Westminster John Knox Press, 2006), 43.

abrogation of Jewish law and more a recognition that law is for the sake of human flourishing.

21:10–15
David and King Achish of Gath

David's next stop is a strange place to seek refuge: Gath, the center of Philistine power, Goliath's hometown. As Saul's servant, David has been engaged in nearly constant combat with the Philistines, and his success against them has been great. David's decision to flee to Gath conveys desperation, and it foreshadows his eventual service to King Achish (chap. 27). At this point in the narrative, it is unclear—beyond Jonathan—who David's friends really are. He is alone in the presence of Israel's enemies. If David expects to be incognito, King Achish's servants recognize him at once. They even know the song that commemorates David's killing of Philistines. Furthermore, they refer to David as "king of the land," an intriguing title (vv. 10–11). Is their name for him a mistake (the military man who is assumed to be king by the enemy) or recognition of David's true identity? It would fall in line with a common scriptural pattern if the Philistines first recognize David before his compatriots. The lips of "outsiders" often convey the truth about someone's identity. It is the Roman centurion—not the disciples, not anyone in Jesus' inner circle—in the Gospel of Mark (a consummate outsider, a representative of Roman imperial authority) who first proclaims Jesus as God's Son (Mark 15:39); it is Ruth, a Moabite, who aligns herself with her mother-in-law and becomes one of the covenant people, an ancestor of David (Ruth 1:16; 4:13–17). The Bible continually shifts our understanding of who is "inside" the drama of salvation history and who is "outside" it. Those on the margins are uplifted, while those who occupy prominent positions are laid low.

> The entire Bible, beginning with the story of Cain and Abel, mirrors God's predilection for the weak and abused of human history.
>
> Gustavo Gutiérrez, *A Theology of Liberation,* trans. Caridad Inda and John Eagleson (Maryknoll, NY: Orbis, 1988), xxvii.

Perhaps it should come as no surprise that David seeks refuge among those who are so far outside the covenant that they attack the people of God.

But if David seeks refuge among the Philistines, it is not without fear. Indeed, fear of King Achish compels him to "change his behavior before them" and feign madness (vv. 12–13). Here is another intriguing contrast between David and Saul. Saul, who earlier is possessed by a maddening spirit of the living God, is prevented from nabbing David in Ramah (19:18–24). Now David, who feigns possession by madness, escapes death at the hands of his enemies. Apparently his performance is convincing. King Achish wonders why the madman has been brought to him, that there are plenty of madmen already in his presence. Or is it convincing? Achish also wonders why his servants "have brought this fellow to play the madman in my presence" (vv. 14–15). Though Achish does not welcome David into his house, the "madman" will soon find a home nearby.

22:1–5

David on the Run

David leaves the land of Israel's enemy to seek refuge in his homeland. While David is on the lam, both desperation and hope gather around him. He first finds refuge in the cave of Adullam, to the southwest of Bethlehem. A cave, to be sure, is not a particularly noble accommodation; it is better suited for hiding than hospitality. Fugitives and vagabonds, not kings, seek shelter in caves. But the text is also ambiguous. Later on in this episode, David's shelter in Adullam is described as a stronghold, suggesting a fortress or other structure more fitting for would-be kings. Both cave and fortress, however, capture something significant about the once and future king: he is a man on the run, who has to find shelter in out-of-the-way places; and he is also an effective military commander who amasses a squad of loyalists. David's family, who does not play a large role in the story thus far (or subsequently), goes to Adullam to be with him. Tossed out of Saul's house, David finds refuge with his family, even away from his ancestral home. But David also finds a family in the growing band that gathers around him. The narrator takes pains to note the economic and social circumstances of this growing army: they are in debt, in discontent, in arrears (vv. 1–2). David, the outcast, becomes captain of a band of outcasts, reminding readers both of his desperate situation and of a mark of David's leadership. This king, at the outset, is a champion of the oppressed.

From Adullam, David travels to the east, Moab, where he also finds refuge. David's presence here recalls that his own great-grandmother, Ruth, was a Moabite. His request to the Moabite king to harbor his parents reveals both his connection to the Moabites by blood and his concern that his own kin are at risk because he is a fugitive. But if David finds refuge for his family among the Moabites and for himself in Adullam, it is not for long. The prophet Gad, who will subsequently invoke God's judgment on David's reign (2 Sam. 24:11–19), suddenly appears to warn David to leave Adullam and go to Judah. Without further dialogue, David obeys (vv. 3–5). This is a king who heeds the voice of prophets, even when it drives him out of relative safety into danger.

22:6–23

Saul Orders the Priests Killed

David hearkens the word of prophets, while in this next episode Saul slaughters priests. The contrast between a fugitive would-be king who heeds another's voice and a king holding desperately to power could not be greater. The story begins with Saul in regal pose: in his hometown, atop a hill, sitting under a tamarisk tree with a spear in his hand, conversing with servants who stand around him. He bears the symbol of military might in a posture evocative of wisdom and judgment. He sits in comfort while his servants stand, ready to do his bidding. This is the way a king should look, according to the nations. From this position of power, Saul has heard of David's whereabouts. But unlike a king secure in power, Saul's words to his servants evoke tribal rivalry and increasing paranoia. Calling his followers Benjaminites, he questions whether David, the son of Jesse, a Judahite, will give them fields, vineyards, or positions in the military. The message is clear: stick with me and you will get your just reward; betray me and you will wind up at the mercy of someone outside your tribe. Leaders throughout the centuries have manipulated tribal rivalries for personal gain. Ethnic and religious struggles in Iraq and Afghanistan, as well as heated rhetoric surrounding "illegal" immigrants in the United States, merely draw from the same page as Saul. As he speaks to his servants, moreover, Saul begins to question whom he can trust, even members of his own tribe. He uses language of conspiracy to describe those standing around him and charge that they have hid Jonathan's alliance with David from him (vv. 6–8). For Saul, the world seems set against him, a conspiracy that now encompasses his family and servants.

A foreigner, Doeg the Edomite, shows himself to be most loyal, at least on Saul's terms. Consumed by suspicion of those closest to him, Saul now finds a kindred spirit in a foreign mercenary who shows himself ready to commit a heinous act on behalf of the king. But first, Doeg divulges Ahimelech's hospitality toward David. This news causes Saul to send for Ahimelech, his entire house, and all the priests at Nob. The king confronts Ahimelech, questioning why he has "conspired" against Saul. He furthermore charges Ahimelech with "inquiring of God" for David (vv. 9–13). Intriguingly, this detail of David's time with Ahimelech is not reported earlier, as David gets provisions and Goliath's sword. Doeg has added a bit of drama to the story, knowing that religious aura heightens the sense of betrayal. Thus informed, Saul is now a picture of rage.

Ahimelech's response to Saul is honest: he believes David to be a loyal servant of the king, he is the king's son-in-law, and this is not the first time he has inquired of God for David. To suggest otherwise, Ahimelech claims, is to impute something false to David and his house. But such words only add to Saul's fury. His retort is brief: Ahimelech, and all his father's house, shall die. They are conspirators and conspirators shall be killed. But Saul's power, apparently, is not absolute. Even those who are closest to Saul, the servants who surround him, cannot follow through on his order. They sense the sacrilege of the order, the violation of the covenant that this slaughter would entail. When Saul turns to Doeg to carry out his command, he turns to one "outside," who not only follows the order but amplifies it, for Doeg kills not only the priests but also men and women, children and infants, and livestock (vv. 14–19). The scene is insane violence. Raging obsession with loyalty leads to mass murder. Not only is there horror in this story, as Wijk-Bos notes, but irony as well: slaughtering innocents "while earlier Saul had been incapable of completing such an action on an enemy (1 Sam. 15)."[35] An oracle uttered against the house of Eli (2:22–36) has now been fulfilled, in the hands of a ruthless foreign mercenary commanded by a desperate and increasingly ruthless leader. It would sound like fiction if it were not so familiar to human history.

For the Deuteronomist, history unfolds according to God's providence: what God has decreed will come to pass. But this story is told without glorifying "God's plan" or glibly claiming that the slaughter of these innocents was "according to God's plan." Indeed, God's plan is not even mentioned. Readers who look to this story to find every detail unfolding from the inexorable hand of God—the slaughter of babies and their mothers—look in vain. God reveals Godself in history and human beings act in history, often in direct opposition to the will of God. This ugly tale illustrates both the horror of human behavior and the mysterious presence of God in the midst of horror. As we read it, we should not simply accept the events that occurred but protest against them, whether we see them as coming from the hand of humanity or God. That protest, after all, is for the sake of the life of God's people.

Only one member of Eli's house escapes: Abiathar, who flees to David and brings him the awful news. This slim remnant, David promises, will find refuge with him, a promise that David fulfills by installing Abiathar to the high priesthood (2 Sam. 20:25). But rather than put blame on Saul or Doeg, David takes responsibility for the slaughter (vv. 20–23). David knows that if he had not lied to Ahimelech, then Ahimelech may not have harbored him and given him provisions. David knows that his lie may have been the flutter of the butterfly's wing that spawned the thunderstorm thousands of miles away. Even if David was unaware of the potential consequences, he put Ahimelech in danger, especially since he saw Doeg

35. Wijk-Bos, *Reading Samuel*, 121.

in the presence of the priests. David's words and gesture of responsibility are more than required, but they are precisely the words that presage an auspicious reign. Good leaders know the extent of their power and the consequences of their actions, and they accept the responsibilities that come with that knowledge.

23:1–14
David Defends Keilah

This story offers a contrast between a fugitive who rescues an Israelite city from the Philistines (a king's responsibility) and a king consumed by a personal vendetta against the fugitive. David learns the Philistines are raiding Keilah, a city not far from Philistia, south of his stronghold in Adullam. David's response to this news illustrates both his religious integrity and his recent promise to Abiathar: he inquires of the Lord whether to attack the Philistines. Though later in this episode David will make use of the priest, at this point he inquires directly and individually. God answers this prayer by saying David should attack and "save Keilah" (vv. 1–2). The incident shows the intimacy between YHWH and David, even the ease of communication between them: David asks God, God responds, and David follows through by acting according to God's command. The pattern reveals David's absolute trust in God to accomplish God's purposes and his willingness to be a participant in those purposes for the sake of his people.

The army of outlaws that has gathered around David, however, are afraid to engage in battle. As men on the run from their own kinsmen, why should they further risk themselves by fighting a superiorly equipped foreign army? David's second petition, which yields the same answer as the first, seems for the sake of his army rather than himself, yet it is also the mark of an effective leader. Before David embarks on the battle, he wants to assure his followers of their promised success: a "heavy defeat" of the Philistines, plenty of captured livestock, and the rescue of Keilah (vv. 3–5).

Abiathar appears on the scene with an ephod, a symbol of priestly authority. This instrument is referred to elsewhere as a garment

(22:18; Exod. 28:4), but here it appears as a tool of divination. David's previous petitions show that he has personal access to God's answers; here he defers to a priest as intermediary. Saul, meanwhile, has become consumed with pursuing his foe. When he finds out David is in Keilah, he boldly asserts that God has given David to him. Again the contrast is strong: a fugitive who inquires of God and a king who assumes to know what God had done without consulting YHWH. The king's summons of all people to war smacks of hyperbole, but it also illustrates the strength of Saul's army in relation to David's (vv. 6–8). When David instructs Abiathar to bring the ephod, it is David, intriguingly, who inquires of God. Here David not only shows deference to the priesthood; he also plays a priestly role. The episode offers further demonstration that David is close to YHWH's heart: what may otherwise seem like presumption is relayed here without a hint of disapproval, from the narrator or Abiathar. Furthermore, David refers to himself as God's servant, hardly a presumptuous title. David's inquiries yield divine answers that protect the fugitive and his army: he finds out that Saul will come to Keilah to seek him and that the people of Keilah will hand their rescuer over to the king if he stays (vv. 9–12).

The action David must take is obvious: leave town. The narrator states that his army "wandered wherever they could go" (v. 13), a description that evokes drifting from place to place. Having just saved an Israelite city, David's army finds itself in desperate straits again. But Saul gives up finding them, at least for the moment. David finds refuge in the wilderness, far from the important cities. Intriguingly, the wilderness has provided refuge for other characters on the run in the drama of Scripture. One prominent example is Hagar, who, expelled from Abraham's house, haunted by Sarah, finds refuge with her son Ishmael in the wilderness (Gen. 21:8–21). God answers Hagar's cries in the wilderness, where she finds new life. Though the wilderness often appears threatening, it can also spur reliance on God. Indeed, David's closeness to God is echoed in the final sentence of the episode: "Saul sought [David] every day, but the LORD did not give him into his hand" (v. 14). The struggle is not only between Saul and David, but between Saul and the living God. In that struggle, Saul does not have a chance.

23:15–29
Adventure in the Wilderness

The wilderness offers refuge for David while it also offers him the space to find out about Saul's advances. David receives news that Saul continues to seek his life, news that is not at all surprising given previous events.

> Jesus call you. Go in de wilderness, / Go in de wilderness, go in de wilderness. / Jesus call you. Go in de wilderness / To wait upon de Lord.
>
> Thomas Wentworth Higginson, "Slave Songs and Spirituals," in *Afro-American Religious History*, ed. Milton C. Sernett (Durham: Duke University Press, 1985), 123.

Jonathan seeks him as well, but in the name of friendship and allegiance. His visit is described with an interesting phrase: "he strengthened [David's] hand through the LORD" (v. 16). Much is implied in this: a vow of allegiance, encouragement, an appeal to God on David's behalf, and some kind of material or personal support. Furthermore, Jonathan states overtly what his earlier actions toward David implied: "You shall be king over Israel; and I shall be second to you" (v. 17). What had been whispered in secret is now proclaimed loudly and openly. Jonathan's vow to be "second" is both a pledge of allegiance and an expectation for a post in the new king's court. The political implications of his statements are enormous: Jonathan is surrendering his claim to the throne and placing himself in direct opposition to his father. Furthermore, Jonathan claims that his father knows all of these things. If there were secrets kept from Saul before, they are secrets no more. The interchange between David and Jonathan concludes with yet another description of their covenant (v. 18). This is now the third time the Deuteronomist has used this language (cf. 18:3; 20:8, 16). Some versions of the David saga may have first mentioned the covenant at this point in the drama; its narrative repetition in its present form indicates the depth of Jonathan's commitment to David, despite the risks.

The wilderness is not without inhabitants. Ziphites are aware of David's presence and journey to the king, divulging David's location and offering to surrender him to Saul. We do not know why the

Ziphites have concocted this plan, but it is hard to imagine that they do not expect something in return (vv. 19–21). It is often good for local politics and economies to do favors for the leader who resides elsewhere. Saul, however, does not immediately muster the troops to descend on David. Perhaps he is not sure whether the Ziphites are being truthful. He also describes David as being "cunning," betraying slight suspicion of the Ziphites as well. Could they be venturing to Saul at David's bidding? At any rate, he wants to be sure and only assembles the troops after sending the Ziphites back as scouts, to return with "sure information" (vv. 22–23).

David journeys to hiding places in the hill country and eludes Saul until he seems surrounded on all sides. From the opposite side of the mountain, the king's troops are descending on him. But at the last possible moment, Saul gets word of Philistine raids (vv. 24–27). The shift is dramatic: Saul's army turns to battle a now-familiar foe. The place where the tide turned may be alternately read as "Rock of Escape" or "Rock of Division" (v. 28), connoting David's escape from the king and the rift between David and Saul. The ironies here are compounded: The Philistines, who have threatened Israel throughout the narrative, now provide unwitting liberation for David; David, who had sought refuge with the Philistines but did not find it, now finds indirect refuge by the mere threat of them; and Saul, who is in the midst of pursuing his son-in-law, gets detained from a personal conflict by the urgent national business of dealing with a foreign threat. It is more becoming for the king to fight the Philistines than deal with David, even if the king would rather do the latter. The effect of this episode, however, drives David further into the wild hills, to En-gedi, near the Dead Sea. There he finds another stronghold (v. 29), more remote than the last.

24:1–22

David Spares Saul

The drama turns to the most memorable instance of David's sojourn in the wilderness, relayed with suspense and humor, displaying David's integrity and Saul's momentary change of heart. It begins

with Saul's renewed pursuit of his son-in-law. The urgent matter of
national security—the Philistine invasion—has only merited a brief
aside. There are no descriptions of battles, only a pithy statement
that Saul has returned. Clearly, Saul is more consumed by his own
personal struggle, as he amasses three thousand men to seek David
(vv. 1–2). If David's troops number four hundred (22:2), then the
odds are certainly stacked against the fugitive.

Here the story takes a humorous turn, as Saul enters the cave to
relieve himself, the very cave where David's troops are hiding. The
king, obviously, is in a compromising position. David's soldiers urge
him to kill Saul, claiming that this is the day the Lord has promised
to give David his enemy. No promise is found elsewhere in the narrative, suggesting that the soldiers are pasting a religious veneer on
an opportunity that cannot be spurned. Humor and embarrassment
abound, for as the king exposes his nakedness, David is near and cuts
the corner of Saul's cloak. David Gunn has suggested that the cutting
renders Saul even more vulnerable, that the cloak symbolizes the
king's penis, and that by cutting Saul in this way David castrates Saul,
cutting off his seed.[36] Whatever the case, the incident is not cause for
rejoicing. As David returns to those who have egged him on, he is
stricken with remorse and disgust at the suggestion that he should
kill the king, referring explicitly to Saul as the Lord's anointed and
his own allegiance to the king. If a change in kingship is to occur, it
will not be because of David's hand; nor will it come from David's
men (vv. 3–7). But as this incident and others that follow indicate,
it is really David who is pursuing Saul, rather than vice versa.[37] Saul
cannot find David, but David consistently finds Saul.

After Saul leaves, David goes out of the cave and calls to the king.
Their interchange is arresting: David first shows his allegiance to Saul
by referring to him as lord and bowing down before him. He secondly appeals to his family connection with Saul by calling to him as
father. He holds the corner of Saul's cloak in his hand, illustrating his
restraint, loyalty, and innocence. By invoking the Lord's judgment,
moreover, David takes the struggle out of the interpersonal realm.

36. David M. Gunn, *The Fate of King Saul: An Interpretation of a Biblical Story* (Sheffield, UK:
    Journal for the Study of the Old Testament Press, 1980), 94–95.
37. Green, *Saul's Asking*, 91.

In effect, David is saying that this is the Lord's fight, not his. David invokes a proverb that implicates Saul in wickedness. But none of this changes David's obeisance to the king and his innocence before him. He has made clear that he stands blameless before Saul and even disparages himself hyperbolically as a dead dog and a flea (vv. 8–14). The position of the king, in this regard, is ludicrous—assembling thousands to pursue an insignificant foe. But to the reader this comparison rings a bit hollow. For in this much, Saul is right: David is a significant foe, one who has already snatched the allegiance of Saul's own family members.

Saul's response to these words is poignant. His first words to David are familial: my son. The narrator describes a change in Saul's heart and appearance: Saul weeps, expresses astonishment at David's blameless behavior, and acknowledges his own evil in the face of David's good actions (vv. 16–17). These are the words that typically accompany a conversion. And, for the moment, they are true. Saul even hopes for David's reward at the hand of God "for what you have done to me this day" (v. 19). But more astonishing still is Saul's acclamation of David as king. The very thing that Saul had feared, the idea that spurred him to pursue his foe at all costs, is now the thing that he proclaims boldly in the face of his own troops: "Now I know that you shall surely be king, and that the kingdom of Israel shall be established in your hand" (v. 20). The story seems to have come full circle and reached its resolution. But in the face of Saul's knowledge that his family will no longer occupy the throne, he makes one last request: for David not to cut off Saul's descendants or wipe out his name. Saul has already experienced David cutting off his garment; he knows well the power of kings in regard to life and death. This last appeal is for David to remind himself that he, too, is a part of the family of Saul. In a certain respect, Saul is echoing Jonathan's own covenant with David. In a concluding display of loyalty and integrity, David swears this promise. And that is enough to send Saul home and David back to his stronghold in the wilderness (vv. 21–22).

Whatever transformation occurs in this incident is rather short-lived. Soon after arriving home, Saul resumes pursuit of David. Saul's "conversion" demands that we inquire about the nature of conversions in general and how they are measured as being genuine or not. The Christian church, historically, has made conversion a significant theme in its theology. Baptismal vows speak to a turning from sin and a turning to Christ, who will transform the heart of the most hardened sinner. Conversion, in this sense, is the hope of every life: the far horizon of our transformed life at the end of days and the intimation of that transformation as we live renewed lives today. If we measure Saul's conversion solely by his words, it is hard to imagine a more radical conversion. For his words literally turn him around from pursuit of David to the abandonment of pursuit. But however lofty his words are, they are soon forgotten. Saul's subsequent actions bear witness not to transformation but to the same old king.

But if the episode makes us rush to judge Saul, we ought to pause. For Saul's actions reveal much about the human condition, how it is easier to speak of transformation than to live it. We are creatures who are often captivated and moved by experiences, religious and otherwise. We make resolutions in light of them, vow to live differently from this day forward, pledge to act more charitably, to harbor fewer grudges. But our vows and resolutions are often short-lived. If we are honest about ourselves, we are more often like Saul than David: sticking to the same ruts, trapped in patterns that are often self-destructive, living in ways that do not reflect the love of God or neighbor. What is so intriguing about Saul is that he captures both the tendency to become mired in destructive patterns *and* promise of a transformed life. If we begin to understand him, we begin to understand ourselves better.

25:1

Samuel Dies

The story of Saul and David is interrupted briefly by an obituary announcing Samuel's death. Though there are no reports of David or Saul gathering for funeral rites, the narrator may include them by reporting that "all Israel assembled and mourned" for Samuel. He is buried at home, Ramah. This succinct obituary is fitting for an old guard that is passing away quietly. If Samuel played the critical transitional role in Israel's embrace of kingship, he disappears from the scene imperceptibly. We hear nothing of David's or Saul's reaction to the death of the one who anointed each man king. This lack of reaction, perhaps, is further judgment on kingship itself, reminding readers that God compromises with Israel in granting the people a king. The new order rapidly causes people to forget the old, even if they mourn the old order for a time. David, in the meantime, advances further into the "wilderness of Paran," a rather odd claim, since that is located in Sinai, at a vast distance from prior and subsequent events in the narrative. Many scholars, therefore, suggest "wilderness of Maon" as a more likely alternative.

25:2–44

Hospitality and Inhospitality: David, Nabal, and Abigail

The fabric of ancient Mediterranean societies, perhaps more than our own, was premised on hospitality. Offering food and drink to neighbors, and even strangers in need, was not chiefly an act of charity but a basic human obligation. For the Deuteronomist, hospitality toward strangers is also found at the heart of covenant: "For the LORD your God is God of gods and Lord of lords, the great God, mighty and awesome, who is not partial and takes no bribe, who executes justice for the orphan and the widow, and who loves the strangers, providing them food and clothing. You shall also love the stranger, for you were strangers in the land of Egypt" (Deut. 10:17–19). To deny another hospitality is not simply to spurn a guest, but to turn from God.

> Do not neglect to show hospitality to strangers, for by doing that some have entertained angels without knowing it.
>
> Hebrews 13:2

This story of hospitality and inhospitality begins by describing a rich man who lives near where David and his men are staying. It is sheep-shearing time, a time to celebrate the bounty of his vast holdings. His name, Nabal, or "fool," reveals much of his character, but his wife, Abigail, is a complete contrast: she is "clever and beautiful" while he is "surly and mean" (v. 3). David's party has offered protection to Nabal's shepherds while they were tending his flocks. David sends some of his men to Nabal with a salutation of peace and report of the good treatment his shepherds have received in David's company (vv. 4–7). David wishes prosperity and peace on Nabal's house, yet he also has a request for Nabal: to "give whatever you have at hand to your servants and to your son David" (v. 8). The request is hardly unreasonable; indeed, it speaks of the circle of hospitality that keeps society civil. Furthermore, this is a time of feasting, when food and drink will be flowing abundantly. David refers to himself as "your son" to Nabal as further demonstration of his deference and good intent.

Nabal, in response, grossly violates the basic expectations of hospitality. He questions who David is and suspects him of betraying his master. At this time of feasting, furthermore, Nabal hoards for himself instead of sharing his abundance. He insults David's men and accuses them of criminal behavior, sending them away empty-handed. Since the incident occurs as a dream-like sequence between two stories of David sparing Saul's life, Green suggests an analogy: "Nabal is Saul at his most churlish and isolated."[38] Shown inhospitality by his king and would-be host, David vows to avenge the insult, as he summons four hundred men to attack Nabal's house (vv. 9–13).

Abigail learns of Nabal's behavior from a servant, who describes the protection Nabal's shepherds received from David's men. The present situation, furthermore, has now become dangerous, since "evil has been decided against" Nabal's house and Nabal is so "ill-natured that no one can speak to him." Abigail then takes matters into her own hands, sending her servants to David laden with provisions and gifts (vv. 14–19). The plan illustrates her generosity of spirit, willingness to contravene her husband, and an independence that is willing to take risks in order to do what is right. In a patriarchal society, Abigail averts disaster and bloodshed between men.

When David meets Abigail's party, however, he vows to kill all the men of Nabal's house (vv. 20–22). Yet David breaks this vow, forgetting it once he hears Abigail's voice. If David is the agent of

38. Ibid., 100.

Saul's transformation in the previous chapter, here Abigail transforms David. Her first words convey service and courtesy: she begs
for a word with David by taking guilt upon herself if the conversation should lead to greater injury. She refers to David as "my lord,"
bows down before him, and makes light of her husband's name. But
beneath these words of courtesy and allegiance is a reprimand of
David—to restrain from incurring bloodguilt by taking vengeance
on Nabal. These are not the pleas of an abject servant; they convey
a determined woman's shrewd plan to change David's mind. Her
words also convey the Deuteronomistic view of David: that he is
God's anointed, that he will prosper, that he fights the battles of the
Lord, and that evil shall not fall on him (vv. 22–28). Her words are
remarkable in their content: she apologizes for her husband's behavior, invokes a blessing on the future king, turns David away from warring madness, and offers gifts for the future king's party. Her words
also restore the cycle of hospitality that Nabal has broken: "If anyone
should rise up to pursue you and to seek your life, the life of my lord
shall be bound in the bundle of the living under the care of the Lord
your God; but the lives of your enemies he shall sling out as from
the hollow of a sling" (v. 29). She captures much in these words:
David's protection from enemies, David's name in a divine register
(cf. Ps. 69:28, "book of the living," and Dan. 12:1, "book of life"), and
judgment against those who would harm him. As she concludes her
address, she invokes God's blessing and urges David to remember her
(vv. 30–31). Wijk-Bos also indicates that Abigail's words are meant
to instruct David on characteristics of a good ruler: "one who is not
out for personal vengeance, for that issue is up to the Holy God."[39]
Indeed, her words change the future king. David's first response is to
bless God and Abigail. He further recognizes Abigail's words as the
Lord's. God has sent Abigail to him; God has restrained David from
harming Abigail and Nabal's house. He receives the gifts from Abigail
and sends her home with an offering of peace (vv. 32–35).

The story concludes with humor and tragedy. During Abigail's absence, Nabal has been enjoying the bounty of the feast
and the fruit of the vine. The drunken man is left to his revelry

39. Wijk-Bos, *Reading Samuel*, 135.

until his morning hangover. The next morning, as Abigail reports her journey, his demeanor—unlike David's—does not change, evoke thanks, or express the new life she has given him by saving it. Instead, it conveys death: "His heart died within him; he became like a stone" (v. 37). For David, Abigail's words result in praise and a new lease on life; for Nabal, they bring death when the Lord strikes Nabal (v. 38). Nabal's response to the truth is to deny his own guilt in refusing David hospitality, refusing to acknowledge Abigail as the one who saved his life. His inability to accept this truth leads to his death. His posture recalls the ways in which human beings are tempted to live lies instead of the truth. Karl Barth claimed that sin represents the falsity of living without God: "Man is not without, but with God. . . . To be in sin, in godlessness, is a mode of being contrary to our humanity. . . . If he denies God, he denies himself."[40] Sin is reflected in the various lies we tell ourselves. (I'm a self-made man. I don't owe anything to anybody. Deep down, I'm nothing. I'm *not* a child of God.) Both the willful arrogation of oneself, the refusal to acknowledge others *and* the abject denial of ourselves as children of God are manifestations of sin. Nabal chooses to live the former lie, while Abigail brings truth that can set us free to be with others (cf. John 8:32).

David's reaction to Nabal's death is testimony that vengeance does not belong to human beings, but to God. But almost as soon as David praises God, his attention turns to Abigail, as he seeks and woos her to become his wife (vv. 39–40). Their marriage, apparently, involved more than David's command. It required a little convincing, a little romance. But the marriage also evokes David's royal status, as Abigail bows down and expresses her servanthood, with five maids in attendance. The narrator further notes David's marriage to Ahinoam; with many wives, David is now behaving like a king. If Saul has annulled David's marriage to Michal (vv. 41–43), his attempt to strip David of a claim to the throne contrasts with the growing recognition of David as king by others. Indeed, some scholars have surmised that David's marriage to Ahinoam is a subsequent marriage to Saul's own wife (cf. 14:50; 2 Sam. 12:8).

---

40. Barth, *Church Dogmatics* III/2, 136.

26:1–25

Sparing Saul's Life Again

This episode mirrors chapter 24, with a remarkably similar narrative sequence: Saul learns of David's hideout and pursues him only to have David sneak upon him and spare his life. The strong similarities between these chapters suggest different narrative renditions of the same event. Their repetition within a relatively brief span of space is dramatic, reinforcing David's blamelessness and Saul's obsession. The story also points to the ephemeral nature of Saul's conversion. What he proclaimed loudly in front of David and his army is quickly forgotten in the heat of pursuit.

The episode begins with Ziphites divulging David's location (identical to the earlier narrative, cf. 23:19). The details of Saul's pursuit, moreover, sound familiar: Saul's camp is on the side of the hill where David is supposedly hiding, with David's troops ensconced in the wilderness. This time, however, David and his army play a more active role: he sends spies to discern Saul's presence, and his troops stealthily advance. As they arrive at Saul's camp, Saul is lying down while his army and the commander Abner surround him (vv. 1–5).

Abner's presence with Saul is mirrored by David's own loyalist, Abishai, who is Joab's brother and the son of David's sister, Zeruiah. These blood ties are powerful, since David's nephews, especially Joab, remain staunch supporters of David throughout the course of his reign, even in the midst of rebellion. But there is also a loyalist who is a foreigner: Ahimelech the Hittite, who only appears here in the story. David's band has as well gathered mercenaries and people who come from other lands. Abishai's willingness to accompany David in the infiltration of Saul's camp indicates the depth of his loyalty. When they descend on Saul, the opportunity seems golden: the entire army is sleeping and Saul's spear lies stuck in the ground next to his head (vv. 6-7). Abishai interprets the opportunity as a gift from the Lord and offers to kill Saul, thereby offering a loophole for David to avoid bloodguilt. If David has scruples, he will not have blood on his hands, at least in a direct way. Abishai promises to do the deed quickly, with one stroke. But David is not satisfied with loopholes. His first words to Abishai mirror the letter of the law and are quite specific: "Do not destroy him," which prohibits mutilation. But his subsequent words are more comprehensive in their meaning: "Who can raise his hand against the LORD's anointed and be guiltless?" (vv. 8–9). David's words imply that *any* attempt on the king's life is a form of mutilation. It radicalizes the commandment not to kill and places high regard for the sanctity of kingship. Regicide cannot be tolerated in any form. David interprets Abishai's offer to kill Saul as a direct violation of the law: "The LORD forbid that I should raise my hand against the LORD's anointed." Given the golden opportunity, David ignores the counsel of his military and instead grabs tokens that demonstrate his restraint: Saul's spear and water jar. This opportunity, furthermore, has come from God's hand: the camp will not awake because of a "deep sleep from the LORD" (v. 12).

David's subsequent words mirror those of chapter 24. But unlike that version of the story, David's first address is to Saul's commander, Abner. Calling to Saul's army from a distance, David's words sound like a taunt, but they are also a call to Abner's responsibility for the king. He accuses Abner of not keeping watch over Saul, says that he deserves death for his negligence, and asks where Saul's spear and water jug are (vv. 13–16). Barbara Green sees in this incident, and in David's earlier "sparing" of Saul's life in the cave, not gestures of David's graciousness but "powerful, double-voiced assaults on Saul's person/position."[41] David's words might be expected to arouse wrath in Saul's camp, yet they have the opposite effect. No words fall from Abner's mouth, and instead Saul responds, using words of family bond: "Is this your voice, my son David?" (v. 17). David responds, again, with terms of (feigned?) loyalty, indicating his servanthood and acknowledgment of Saul as king. He claims his innocence, but his words go beyond those of chapter 24. In asking who has compelled Saul to pursue him, David offers two possibilities. If God has initiated the search, David is willing to present an offering to the Lord. But if mortals have done it, David makes a serious charge: those who have encouraged Saul to pursue David, and even Saul himself, are then guilty of encouraging David to practice

41. Green, *Saul's Asking*, 98.

idolatry. By keeping him on the lam, Saul's troops are preventing David from making offerings to the Lord and worshipping according to the commandments. In charging those who pursue him with encouraging idolatry, David is suggesting that they are—indirectly at least—idolators themselves and cursed people. David's charge gets to the heart of Deuteronomistic history and its regard for David. The pursuit of an innocent, God's anointed, is tantamount to violating the commandments and pursuing other gods. He also compares the killing of him to an illegitimate sacrifice, where blood would fall far from God's presence. Killing David, in other words, would amount to sacrilege. David finally likens himself to a flea or a partridge in the mountains, with the second animal being particularly apt since its dwelling place is the same as David's current hideout (vv. 18–20).

Saul responds with a confession: he has done wrong and he will never harm David again. They echo the response of chapter 24 but are more comprehensive and self-deprecating. By calling himself a fool, Saul reveals the extent to which he has failed in his role as king. David shows further regard for the king's life by not keeping the king's items as bounty but by giving them back. And he invokes the Deuteronomistic view of history once again: since David has held Saul's life as precious, his own life will be precious to God. The analogy here is that life is an offering and that David's life is entrusted and offered to the Lord. If David has been kept from worshiping God according to the commandments while on the lam, his righteous behavior has constituted a kind of worship. It is fitting that the final words uttered in this episode are ritual, as Saul blesses David (vv. 21–25). Again, Saul suspends his pursuit of David by turning back home while David goes his own way. A hint of another conversion lingers, but not for long.

27:1–28:2

David Finds Refuge with the King of Gath

This interlude expresses both David's desperation in the face of Saul's pursuit and a strong theological claim: the God of Israel is not a tribal god who only looks after the affairs of the covenant people.

Rather, God guides and uses people outside the covenant to accomplish God's purposes in history. The Philistines appear in this story not simply as strangers or enemies but as agents who help ensure the rise of David to the throne, even if they are unaware of this purpose.

David voices his fear of Saul and senses an "out" if he flees to Philistia. Though David has sought refuge in Philistia before (21:10–15), he did not find it there. His return to the same place—and the same king—intensifies the desperate nature of his plight. Arriving in King Achish's court, expressing the appropriate courtesies toward the king, David proposes a military alliance. David also suggests that he be granted residence in a country town, indicating that his presence in the royal city is somewhat unbecoming. Here David shows himself a shrewd dealmaker (or in Saul's words, "cunning," cf. 23:22): in exchange for his courtesy and service as mercenary, David will be granted a residence at some distance from Gath. Achish agrees to the proposal in terms more generous than David proposes: he gives David Ziklag, a border town of some dispute between Philistia and Judah. (It is listed as a Judahite city in Josh. 15:31.) This is no brief sojourn for David's entourage, as they remain in Philistia for one year and four months (vv. 1–7).

The military alliance, however, is decidedly on David's terms. He attacks a series of somewhat insignificant neighbors in the south. Apart from the Amalekites (Exod. 17:8–13; 1 Sam. 15:1–9), these neighbors do not loom large in the trajectory of Deuteronomistic history. David's defeat of these tribes is nothing less than total, offering further evidence of his military prowess. As he brings tribute to Achish, David's words are less than truthful. When the king asks David about his exploits, David indicates that he has battled Judahites in the southern reaches. This is why the king claims that David has been made abhorrent to Israel and assumes his perpetual loyalty. The term that describes Achish's regard, moreover, is strong: "Achish trusted David" (vv. 8–12). This is a dramatic shift from David's first journey to Gath and testament to a strange alliance. When the king announces war against Israel, Achish instructs David and his men to go out with the Philistines. David agrees, albeit in indirect terms: "You shall know what your servant can do," whereupon Achish makes David his bodyguard "for life" (28:1–2). The interplay between truth, trust, lies, and half-truths is intriguing. Achish takes David at his word, while David plays with words. David seeks refuge and finds it but never gives Achish his loyalty. Though Achish provides David refuge, David also experiences refuge on his own terms. Through it all, God uses surprising people, such as Achish, as instruments for carrying out God's promises to Israel.

28:3–25

Saul and the Medium of Endor

Saul, meanwhile, has become so desperate in his pursuit of David that he is isolated and on the verge of self-destruction. The story begins retrospectively, by recalling Samuel's death and Saul's prior expulsion of mediums and wizards (Hebrew *ob* and *yiddehonei*, which also mean "bottle" and "one who has a familiar spirit"). More broadly, these terms indicate necromancy (v. 3), but their connotations also indicate the fluid boundary between the realm of the living and the dead in Israelite religion of this time. One who conjures spirits is like a "bottle" that can contain and bring up familiar spirits. Such conjuring, however, is explicitly forbidden by Mosaic law. Leviticus both disallows Israel from consulting mediums, since such practices defile (Lev. 19:31), and endorses stoning those who engage in necromancy (20:27). According to the law, necromancy is evidence of idolatry, but Saul's expulsion of these mediums and wizards also indicates benign toleration of them throughout periods of Israel's history and some latitude in treating those who practice these mysterious arts. (They were present, obviously, before Saul's edict of expulsion.) The realm of the dead, not only for ancient Israel but today as well, has generated much conjecture and speculation. Contemporary euphemisms for death, such as "passing away," convey much about our attitude toward death, that the boundary between life and death is not rigid and impermeable but a more fluid passing from one state to another. To connect with that other state is a common longing, especially when a loved one has died.

As soon as the narrator mentions the mediums the Philistines appear again, encamped at Shunem, ready to attack the Israelites who are at Gilboa. These geographical locations move the story north, far from David's wilderness wanderings, distant from Philistine territory. Perhaps this new location indicates the expansive nature of the Philistine threat: the battle with Philistia is no longer restricted to the borderlands but moves into the heart of Israelite territory. When Saul sees the Philistine army, he is afraid (vv. 4–5), a fear that is less the "fear of the LORD" that "is the beginning of knowledge" (Prov. 1:7) and more a fear for himself. So much that has transpired over the previous chapters was the result of Saul's inordinate fear: his pursuit of David, his murder of priests. Now this fear is extended to Israel's consummate enemy. Whereas Saul defeated the Philistines earlier (chap. 14), now he is paralyzed by fear, surrounded by enemies on every side.

Saul's turn to the Lord is fruitless, whether by his own petition, ritual objects, or prophets. Everything is now failing him, and God will not answer his cries. The people and the living God have abandoned the king. Alone with a few servants, Saul turns to them and seeks the only available means of answering his cries: a medium. Saul's request is highly unusual given his edict of expulsion. In effect, Saul is violating Mosaic law and his own decree. Consulting the medium in Endor places Saul northeast of the Philistine camp, even closer to his perpetual enemies (vv. 6–7).

Saul's disguise as he approaches Endor at night conveys the shame of a king at wit's end, a shadow of his former confidence and courage, resorting to measures expressly forbidden by law. But the disguise also conveys self-interest. He does not want to reveal to others (even to the medium) his true identity. Traveling by night incognito offers some degree of safety from the Philistines who are close at hand. The medium, who does not recognize Saul at first, responds to Saul's request with dismay. She notes that Saul has "cut off" (a significant phrase, since it also recalls that the kingdom itself will be cut off from Saul) mediums from the land. If she agrees to Saul's request, moreover, her life is in danger. Indeed, death surrounds this entire scene: Saul, whose grip on the kingship is near death, consults the realm of the dead through a medium who fears for her life. Inordinate fear of death often paves the path to destruction. Søren Kierkegaard claimed that for the Christian, however, physical death is not to be feared, for "death itself is a passing into life."[42] The death that should be feared is a spiritual death manifested in despair, or in Kierkegaard's words, "*before God . . . in despair not to will to be oneself, or in despair to will to be oneself.* Thus sin is intensified weakness or intensified defiance: sin is the intensification of despair."[43] Both forms of despair are evident in Saul's life.

> A self that has no possibility is in despair, and likewise a self that has no necessity.
>
> Søren Kierkegaard, *The Sickness unto Death*, 35.

He swears, however, that no harm will come upon the medium (vv. 8–10). Irony, indeed, to swear upon the Lord as he engages in a practice forbidden by law. Saul is manipulating various forms of piety here, appealing to higher ground in his desperate attempts to find answers to his fears. Invoking God, after all, is often an effective way to cajole people into seeing things your way, whether in political speeches or matters of war. But such tactics invariably run into idolatry. During the heady growth of American influence on the global stage, Reinhold Niebuhr consistently warned against the tendency among religious leaders to assert "that the will of God was being fulfilled in the policy of their state." Patriotism, he wrote, "is a form of piety which exists partly through the limitation of the imagination."[44] Where imagination is lacking, one becomes only concerned with oneself and one's compatriots.

Saul requests that Samuel be brought up. When Samuel appears, the medium recognizes Saul and cries out that he has deceived her. Indeed, the deception has been great: Saul has not only disguised himself, but he also has endorsed a practice that he had sought to extirpate in Israel. Saul comforts the woman not to fear and asks about the spirit which has arisen. The description is intriguing, "a divine being coming up out of the ground," an old man clothed in a robe (vv. 11–14). The term is "elohim," typically translated as "god" or "gods," the plural form of one of the chief ways of referring to God

---

42. Søren Kierkegaard, *The Sickness unto Death: A Christian Psychological Exposition for Upbuilding and Awakening*, ed. Howard V. Hong and Edna H. Hong (Princeton, NJ: Princeton University Press, 1980), 17.
43. Ibid., 77, italics in original.
44. Reinhold Niebuhr, *Moral Man and Immoral Society: A Study in Ethics and Politics* (Louisville, KY: Westminster John Knox Press, 2001), 66.

in the Hebrew Bible. Its usage here in reference to the spirit of the departed stands out. Perhaps it stands, in part, as further judgment against what Saul is doing, a form of idolatry and longing for other gods, once the God of Israel refuses to answer him. In his ghostly appearance, Samuel wears a robe, marking his role as a priest as Saul bows down before him. This obeisance, however, looks like a parody: Saul is making an explicit show of deference in ways that he did not always display when Samuel was living. Furthermore, Samuel does not want to be disturbed from his rest. Undeterred, Saul tells Samuel that his distress is great, chiefly at two things: the Philistine army and the fact that God has "turned away from me and answers me no more" (v. 15). He conspicuously does not mention his chief fear: David. This holding back says much about the practice of confession: we are often hesitant to admit our deepest fears, particularly when we know them to be so misguided. Saul's unwillingness to voice his major fear mirrors our own inability to make full confession much of the time.

Samuel's words to Saul are not a comfort; they are not an absolution; and they do not point to divine or human help. Instead, they reiterate the judgment that he had already pronounced upon Saul (15:10–35) and make the case even stronger. Now God has become an "enemy" to Saul, tearing his kingdom from him and giving it to his neighbor, David. Saul's failure to follow through on God's commands regarding the Amalekites, again, is ostensibly the reason. The prophecy becomes even more ominous, however: tomorrow Saul and his sons will die, and the Philistines will vanquish Israel (vv. 16–19). This illicit journey to a medium, in short, has resulted in confirming Saul's worst fears.

If Saul experienced isolation prior to his encounter with the spirit of Samuel, now he is alone, exhausted, and terrified. His fasting (presumably as preparation for encountering Samuel's spirit) has left him utterly spent. Yet here, near the end of his life, Saul also experiences the hospitality of cakes and a fatted calf. Steussy remarks how the medium's kindness, cooking, and offer to feed Saul "stands in sharp contrast to Lord's abandonment and Samuel's bitterness."[45]

45. Marti J. Steussy, *Samuel and His God* (Columbia, SC: The University of South Carolina Press, 2010), 93.

Saul is compromised here—he can do nothing—but he is also the recipient of grace from a woman he had earlier banished from the kingdom. In the end, it is a most unlikely figure—a woman on the fringe of religious propriety (often referred to as a "witch")—who "breaks through Saul's isolation and unrelatedness."[46] Green even suggests that the meal provides a "moment of reconciliation with God, an opportunity to hear God's voice not simply from the scolding Samuel but also from the bracing witch who gave him the strength needed for his final and answerable deed."[47] Here, like in other strands of biblical narrative, it is the outsider who shows readers the hospitality of God. At his servants' urging, Saul eats and leaves to face the Philistines and his own foreseen death.

29:1–11

David Is Dismissed by the Philistine Army

While Saul unravels, this short chapter provides absolution for David: first it absolves him of betraying his own people; second, it absolves him of lying outright to King Achish. Indeed, the story offers a stirring and humorous example of the power of words and the difference between how words are spoken and how they are received. David and his men are toward the rear of the Philistine army, nearest the king, indicating his favor in Achish's sight. The Philistine commanders note David's presence with skepticism, referring to his men by their ethnicity: "What are these Hebrews doing here?" Ethnic rivalries often loom large in military conflicts; the Philistine commanders may be stirring up their troops with these words, hammering home the message that "they" are not like "us." Achish responds to their query by identifying David as Saul's servant, noting David's presence with them for "days and years" as a man without fault. Even if Achish claims David as Saul's servant, he assumes that David has now become *his* servant. This assumption has allowed David to deceive Achish and will prove pivotal in further deception. The words of the king, however, do not satisfy; the

46. Green, *Saul's Asking*, 117.
47. Ibid., 125.

commanders urge that the king send David back to Ziklag, suspecting that if he stays, he will become their adversary. To add fuel to the
fire, the commanders quote the song touting David's military success against Philistia (vv. 1–5).

Achish relents to his commanders but exonerates David with his
words. His exoneration is remarkable because he invokes the name
of YHWH, one of the few occasions in Scripture that the name
comes from the lips of a non-Israelite. The uniqueness of this reference is increased, moreover, because Achish speaks it like a devotee
of YHWH: "As the LORD lives, you have been honest . . ." (v. 6).
There are several ways of interpreting these words: Achish is playing with words, pretending devotion to YHWH, to curry favor with
David; alternatively, his words may be as a gesture of respect to
David and his God; or David's conduct with Achish has convinced
Achish of YHWH's power and guidance. Achish further proclaims
David's innocence, but in his remarks, Achish only sees what he
believes to be true. Achish tells David to return peacefully and "do
nothing to displease the lords of the Philistines" (v. 7). Acceding to
the demands of his military commanders, Achish also expresses his
wish that David be able to march with them into battle.

David's reply to the king displays mastery of verbal manipulation.
He offers a further profession of his own innocence by questioning
what he has ever done to deserve such treatment, especially given his
record of military service. When Achish hears "my lord," he assumes
that David is speaking of him (not Saul). But the "enemies of my
lord" that David is pledged to fight are the enemies of Israel, not Philistia. Achish's dismissal of David from the army of the Philistines
thus allows David to engage in doublespeak. The Philistine king
marches off to battle convinced that David is one of his own, despite
the suspicion of his military commanders and despite David's own
carefully-chosen words. Achish's exoneration of David is complete
when he compares David's blamelessness to "an angel of God" (vv.
8–9). High praise, indeed.

This entire exchange prompts one to consider the broader nature
of truth telling. What does it mean to tell the truth? Should one tell
the truth in all circumstances? Does one lie or manipulate the truth in
order to protect oneself or others? And if so, how far are we justified

in twisting words and truths? Does the commandment against bearing false witness against one's neighbor (Exod. 20:16) prohibit deceitful words in all cases? Most ethical treatments of these questions note degrees. Lying on a job application (in order to gain privilege for oneself) is different from lying to the Gestapo that one is not hiding Jews in one's house. Philosopher Robert Kane, echoing Immanuel Kant, claims that we ought to "treat every person in every situation as an end and never as a means (to your or someone else's ends),"[48] which would imply that lying is *never* justified. But Kane also recognizes that the moral sphere often breaks down, as people treat others as means to their ends: criminals steal and commit acts of violence, Gestapo send Jews to concentration camps. In such cases, our actions ought to seek to thwart the abuser's intentions and protect the victims of abuse. Lying to the Gestapo, in other words, can prevent murder from happening. Kane thus modifies the ends principle by stating that we should "treat every person as an end and not as a means . . . whenever possible. When it is not possible, strive to sustain this ideal to the degree possible, by choosing those actions that will best restore and preserve moral spheres (in which everyone can be treated as an end)."[49] David's words to Achish present an interesting case: they are not self-serving lies (although they do display some degree of self-interest); nor are they spoken solely to protect someone else. But the fact that the narrator relates this story without a hint of judgment against David suggests that his words, however deceptive, are justified, if for no other reason than to ensure that God's will be done: that David's life be spared and that he be enthroned as king of Israel. David both protects himself and the people Israel in his deceptive words to the Philistine king. Sometimes a lie is just a lie; sometimes one lies in the name of a greater truth. Part of the artistry of moral living is discerning between these two kinds of lies, carefully choosing our own words so that our lives reflect truth rather than falsehood. Having uttered these words to one another, the two men go their separate ways: one to battle, one back to the land of the Philistines (vv. 10–11). Though David knows the true

---

48. Robert Kane, *Through the Moral Maze: Searching for Absolute Values in a Pluralistic World* (Armonk, NY: North Castle Books, 1996), 21.
49. Ibid., 26.

meaning of his words, Achish is still ignorant of them. The Philistine commanders have perceived David more truthfully than Achish has.

30:1–31
David the Military Avenger

The return to Ziklag is neither triumph nor relief. Instead, it yields devastation, an ugly scene of a burned-out city devoid of inhabitants. It is like countless scenes reenacted throughout human history, displaying the brutality of the victors who smash the enemy. Call it what one will—"shock and awe," "preemptive war," "revenge," "psychological operations"—the result is the same: the obliteration of homes, the humiliation of a people, pummeling resistance. In the heat of battle, troops wreak devastation on the innocent. This is the work of the Amalekites, the tribe that has figured into the narrative at other pivotal points. Saul's failure to follow through on God's command to utterly destroy them (sparing the king and much livestock) led to his rejection by YHWH(15:1–9). David, moreover, has recently been engaged in battle with the Amalekites (27:8), and the Amalekite raid on Ziklag is most likely an act of revenge on David. The narrator mentions that no people were killed and that all the women and children were taken captive but gives no indication that David knows these facts. His troops' initial glimpse of the destroyed city most certainly would have led them to suspect the worst possible carnage. The only thing they can do is weep until they have no more strength. The scene reverses the typical homecoming for troops. Instead of soldiers arriving home in the embrace of loved ones (and mourning for those who have not returned), these soldiers return home to mourn. There are no exceptions, down to David's own family. The soldiers he has led during this sojourn in Philistia now turn against him and speak of stoning him. How soon grief has turned to anger; the experience of loss leads the soldiers to seek someone to blame: Who else but David? David's response to their anger offers further demonstration of his leadership: he turns to YHWH for strength (vv. 1–6). This trust in YHWH sets him apart. His response to a threat on his life is not primarily to fear for it (as Saul does in chapter 28) but to turn to God for help. Whatever David's faults, his undeniable asset is that he trusts in the Lord completely.

As in chapter 23, David calls for Abiathar and consults the ephod for guidance, emphasizing his deference to the priesthood and close relationship with YHWH. His question is direct: whether to pursue or overtake the band who has destroyed Ziklag. God's answer, however, exceeds the bounds of David's question. Not only should David pursue and overtake the band, he shall "surely rescue." David will not only avenge the attack on Ziklag but also save those who have been captured. The band journeys out and comes to the Wadi Besor: those who have been exhausted by the journey stay at this spot, while the remaining troops venture on (vv. 7–10). This detail is telling: the travels over the past days have taken their toll. A full one-third of the troops are so tired they can no longer walk.

The army encounters an Egyptian servant to the Amalekites who is similarly exhausted. The army's response to him illustrates some of the basic guidelines for hospitality in Torah. Indeed, David's treatment of this Egyptian (and his treatment of the exhausted faction of his army) contrasts starkly with the Amalekites. In the Amalekite army, the weak are left behind to fend for themselves, while under David's provision, the exhausted are protected, fed, and strengthened. After the Egyptian is strengthened by David's army, they learn that the Amalekites destroyed Ziklag. David's request that the Egyptian lead him to the Amalekites is met by a counter-request: only if David's army will not kill the Egyptian or hand him over to his master (vv. 11–15). This is an intriguing exchange, revealing the agency of both parties. The Egyptian is not a passive actor in the affairs that unfold; he is not the mere receiver of hospitality from David; rather, he strikes a bargain that spares his life. Without him, there would be no recovery of the captured women and children. The carrying out of God's intent for Israel, the establishment of David on the throne, also depends on this wandering Egyptian, far from his home, who has been serving for some time in another foreign land. This "outsider" to much of the biblical drama is in fact a rather key "insider" to the unfolding of Israel's subsequent history.

A bargain is struck and David's troops approach a jubilant—even bacchanalian—Amalekite camp. David's troops attack relentlessly, either (depending on translation) from dawn until evening or from twilight until the evening of the next day. The success of the onslaught may be a bit exaggerated, but whatever people and livestock had been lost are now recovered; indeed, David's troops have now gained more than they have lost, and David, too, has his spoil (vv. 16–20).

The returning victors meet the two hundred left behind at the Wadi Besor, but the encounter is hardly paternalistic. David first salutes those who were too exhausted to go on. What transpires next offers another example of hospitality and sharing within the covenant community. Many who had fought the Amalekites suggest that the spoils of war should only go to the combatants. Their suggestion is to recognize degrees of responsibility for the victory: to those who engaged most intensely in battle, who risked life and limb, should go the greater share of the booty. Those who have earned the spoil, in other words, most deserve it. The assumption is similar to that encountered in contemporary American society. People deserve whatever financial blessing they get. Those who work hardest deserve the greatest share. Those whose jobs are the most important ought to be paid the most. According to this logic, software engineers are more important than janitors; soldiers on the front line are more important than mechanics at the rear; a professional basketball player is worth more than a homeless person. But the narrator offers a different assumption and describes the soldiers who make such suggestions as "corrupt and worthless" (v. 22). David's words to them suggest that they have not earned the spoil in the first place; rather, the Lord has given the victory to them by preserving them and "handing over to us the raiding party that attacked us" (v. 23). This is not a philosophy of "to each his own" or "each deserves what she gets," but "all that has been given to us ought to be shared" and "in thanksgiving to God all get to partake in the bounty." Or, in David's words, "They shall share alike" (v. 24). David does not assume scarcity, that whatever is gained must be hoarded by those who "deserve" it, but abundance, that there is always more than enough to go around. Assumptions make all the difference in behavior; the assumption that David makes becomes a statute and ordinance for Israel down to the present (v. 25).

When David returns to Ziklag, he begins to act as a king. Indeed,

what happens next plays a key transitional role in the drama that follows. Like a benevolent lord, David shares the spoil with his friends,
sending portions of the bounty to many different cities and rulers in
Judah (vv. 26–31). The gifts are both a form of thanks for the ways in
which these various settlements have aided his own journey on the
lam from Saul and a sign that a new sheriff is in town who must be
reckoned with. The gifts express thanks, but they also say, "stick with
me and you, too, will benefit." The once and future king is beginning
to gather allies and consolidate his realm.

31:1–13

Saul's Sons Die in Battle, Saul Kills Himself

Saul's reign now comes to its foreseen, inglorious end. The king,
who had distinguished himself as a military leader and had dealt
effectively with the Philistines at nearly every previous turn, now is
unable to lead his troops to victory. The battle is narrated tersely—
almost embarrassingly—without detail. Israel flees before the Philistines while many fall on Mount Gilboa. The narrator relates these
details as if they are best forgotten, except for the most important
part: the death of the king and all three of his sons. Jonathan's death
fighting at his father's side shows that, despite his bond with David,
he does not betray Saul.[50] As the Philistines converge on Saul, he is
battered but not yet defeated, wounded but not dead (vv. 1–3). But
the king detects no hope for victory this time. In desperation, Saul
tells his armor-bearer (a position, ironically, that David once held, cf.
16:21) to kill him with Saul's own sword. This servant refuses, most
likely out of recognition of the ritual holiness of the king's body:
to commit such an act would be to defile God's anointed. So Saul
commits the act himself, falling on his own sword, followed by the
servant who can see no way out. Saul's suicide can be understood
in multiple ways: Ostensibly, Saul kills himself out of concern for
ritual purity, "so that these uncircumcised may not come and thrust
me through, and make sport of me" (v. 4). Green has a somewhat

---

50. Exum, *Tragedy*, 80.

charitable interpretation of Saul's death, claiming that, in the end, "Saul dies well."[51] His suicide represents the termination of a kingship that "had been moribund for some time already."[52] But we can also interpret it as an act of fear, of Saul's unwillingness to face his destiny. It may even be understood as a final act of pride and desperation. Exum interprets Saul's death more along these lines: "Saul's suicide functions as his last desperate attempt to wrest from his destiny its final meaning." For Exum, this makes Saul an ultimately tragic character who experiences death "in isolation from YHWH."[53]

Saul's death also has implications beyond the sphere of individual action and accountability. Polzin claims Saul's violent death as a metaphor for Israel's experience with monarchy. "Kingship, despite all its glories, constituted for Israel communal suicide." Consistent with his character in the preceding narrative, Saul "refuses to let the Lord's providence run its course and takes matters into his own hands by ending his life."[54] In this interpretation, Saul resists the flight of YHWH's spirit from him until the end, kills himself, and thus points to the nation's own downfall and culpability in its demise.

However one interprets Saul's death, suicide is not what one typically expects of leaders. During the closing days of the Third Reich, many Nazi leaders killed themselves rather than face accountability for their genocidal actions. Suicide, in those circumstances, was an act of hubris. But most suicides do not resemble those of Hitler and Goebbels. Far more often, suicides result from despair, hopelessness, and self-abnegation more than overweening self-pride. The Christian tradition, accordingly, has had conflicting interpretations of suicide. Thomas Aquinas considered it a mortal sin that jeopardizes one's salvation. For Thomas, suicide is contrary to natural law and charity; it "injures the community" of persons and is a sin against God, because it takes away life, which God has given to each person.[55] More recently, Christian ethicist James Gustafson has reexamined

51. Green, *Saul's Asking*, 117.
52. Ibid., 122.
53. Exum, *Tragedy*, 25.
54. Polzin, *Samuel*, 224.
55. Thomas Aquinas, *Summa Theologica*, vol. 3, trans. Fathers of the English Dominican Province (New York: Benziger Bros., 1948), 1463.

many of the traditional interpretations of suicide and found them lacking. Some suicides, tragically and mournfully, can be justified.

In most cases, suicide deserves not judgment but compassion for the victim, consolation for those who mourn, and efforts to alleviate those in similar circumstances of despair before they take the final exit. Saul's suicide seems a combination of many influences: some pride, some despair, some sense of maintaining ritual purity. But in the end, his act reflects poorly on his status as king. It seems more a desperate evasion than a courageous facing of destiny.

Saul and Jonathan's deaths presage the total defeat of the Israelite army; when those beyond the Jordan hear of the defeat and death, they, too, flee from their towns while the Philistines occupy them. The tide has turned dramatically. The uncircumcised now have conquered Israelite towns, even those far from the scenes of battle. To add to the indignity, the Philistines commit sacrilege on Saul's body, dismembering it while his armor hangs in the temple of a goddess, his body nailed to a wall (vv. 7–10).

Yet a remnant of the Israelites, the people of Jabesh-gilead, recognizes the sacrilege and goes to recover the bodies of Saul and his sons. They journey through the night, apparently without skirmish, and as an act of tribute and thanks, they commit the bodies to decent cremation and burial, fasting as an act of reverence in the face of enormous indignity (vv. 11–13). These people, who were earlier recipients of Saul's military aid (11:9–13), are the first to mourn, the only act that is fitting.

2 SAMUEL

1:1–27

David Learns of the Deaths and Mourns

David learns of Saul and Jonathan's death in Ziklag, three days after he has returned from his rout of the Amalekites. His lament over the destruction of the town that has provided him refuge for more than a year soon pales to the public lament that follows. A man from Saul's company approaches David in the typical appearance of mourning—torn clothes and dirt on his head—though they may also be indications of the terrible battle. His actions toward David are of a subject toward his king, as he falls to the ground and does obeisance. From the moment of his arrival, this man makes an elaborate display of (false?) allegiance to David. When David learns that the man has escaped from Israel's camp, David inquires about the battle. The man, however, reports events differently from the previous chapter, indicating that he has ulterior motives. The man relays the facts accurately: the Israelites have been defeated, the army has fled, and Saul and Jonathan have died. When David asks how the man knows of these tragedies, he claims that he was on Mount Gilboa, the site of Saul's death, and that he came upon a wounded Saul as the Philistines were closing in. At this point, the man reveals his identity to Saul (and to David in the telling of the story) as an Amalekite (vv. 1–8). This detail is telling: David has just returned from avenging Ziklag against the Amalekites; the Amalekites are the very people against whom Saul did not carry out YHWH's command. Readers learn subsequently that this man, if he is being truthful about his identity, is a resident alien (v. 13), which accords him the privileges of an Israelite but also the responsibilities and expectations of Torah. The hospitality Israel extends to resident aliens is reciprocated as aliens act in accordance with Mosaic law.

According to this report, Saul asked the Amalekite to kill him out of mercy (v. 9). But unlike the armor-bearer of the previous chapter, the Amalekite is willing to kill the king. He does it swiftly and adds a significant detail: "I took the crown that was on his head and the armlet that was on his arm and I have brought them here to my lord" (v. 10). The Amalekite seems to expect reward as the first to pay homage to the new king. But his calculations have been wrong.

Instead of expressing thanks or exultation, David mourns. And this act of mourning, unlike the Amalekite's tale, is ingenuous. He tears his clothes, as do "all the men who were with him." They weep, mourn, and fast: for Saul, for Jonathan, for the army of the Lord, and for Israel (vv. 11–12). This is a lament not simply for a king or for a friend but for the entire people of God. David recognizes the loss that the Amalekite does not. He further recognizes the sacrilege that the Amalekite should have seen, questioning why he was not afraid to lift his hand "to destroy the LORD's anointed" (v. 14). David's use of the term "destroy" indicates that the man is not only guilty of regicide but of desecrating Saul's body. For this offense, David claims, the Amalekite must die. Here the opportunist meets an ugly end. David commands one of his men to strike the man down; he has testified against himself and shown his guilt: "Your blood be on your head" (v. 16). Almost as soon as the Amalekite appears on the scene, he is gone.

From this pivotal scene, the story moves to a more public act of mourning, expressed in verse. From the lips of David come one of the most ancient pieces of poetry contained in the Hebrew Bible, a song of lamentation for Saul and Jonathan. It is a song, purportedly, that David ordered taught to "the people of Judah" (v. 18), an expression of David's grief and the mourning of a nation. With it, David fulfills an expectation that the new leader mark the king's death with decorum. It expresses both political calculation—for it expresses magnanimity toward his rival, Saul[56]—and personal loss.

The hymn opens by stating that Israel's glory "lies slain upon your high places," contrasting Israel's grief and the desire to prevent the exultation of the "uncircumcised" of Philistia. The place of Saul's death, moreover, is cursed. The mountains of Gilboa will not experience bounty but drought (vv. 19–21), representing what has been lost. The land here is not incidental. Israel concerns not simply a people, but a land, or better stated, a people who live closely on the land given them by God. Much of Torah includes regulations concerning land: how to plant, how to sow, when to harvest, when to let the land lie fallow. Indeed, the Hebrew Scriptures themselves can

---

56. Robert Polzin, *David and the Deuteronomist* (Bloomington: Indiana University Press, 1993), 13.

be understood through an "agrarian reading," reflecting the biblical authors' attention to land, landscape, and place. Ellen Davis offers one such reading:

> The biblical writers attend to the physical means of human existence, the chief of those being arable land. . . . The Scriptures of ancient Israel know where they come from. They reflect the narrow and precariously balanced ecological niche that is the hill country of ancient Judah and Samaria. . . . The Israelite farmers knew that they survived in that steep and semiarid land by the grace of God and their own wise practices.[57]

In ancient Israel, the destiny of a people and the destiny of the land are inextricably intertwined.

If Jonathan's bow and Saul's sword slew the mighty in blood and fat, they and their weapons were not able to return. Instead, they lay beside their bearers in death. As father and son are united now in death, David sings that "in life and death they were not divided" (vv. 22–23). The reader of this history, of course, knows of rifts between the two: a son's covenant that places him at odds with his father; a father's insult to his son, cursing the loins of his wife, Jonathan's mother. Whatever poetic hyperbole the hymn expresses, however, Jonathan does not abandon Saul in the heat of battle or join David's men. The division between Jonathan and Saul in life, perhaps, is overcome in their death. The song pays further tribute to Saul's wealth, how the daughters of Israel ought to lament Saul who "clothed you with crimson, in luxury" (v. 24). If part of Israel's desire for a king was in order to become more like the nations, then that desire has been fulfilled in the material prosperity that benefitted some people in the land.

The hymn's conclusion is the most stirring, for there we glimpse David's heart. Jonathan is slain and David is "distressed" (bound, tied up) for Jonathan. David's life has become constricted because of his beloved friend's death. Love echoes throughout the penultimate verse, as David, the beloved, also calls Jonathan his beloved. If readers hear more of Jonathan's love of David in previous episodes (cf. 18:3), they now understand how love shapes David's regard for

---

57. Ellen F. Davis, *Scripture, Culture, and Agriculture: An Agrarian Reading of the Bible* (Cambridge: Cambridge University Press, 2009), 26.

Jonathan. Their covenant was not Jonathan's one-sided pledge of loyalty to the future king; rather, it was a pledge of intimate friends, an expression of love that passed "the love of women" (vv. 25–26). The language, indeed, evokes marriage, or a promise of intimacy, friendship, and loyalty. To lose one's partner in such a covenant is also to lose a part of oneself. In a letter composed in a prison cell on Christmas Eve, 1943, Dietrich Bonhoeffer wrote,

> There is nothing that can replace the absence of someone dear to us, and one should not even attempt to do so; one must simply persevere and endure it. At first that sounds very hard, but at the same time it is a great comfort, for one remains connected to the other person through the emptiness to the extent it truly remains unfilled. It is wrong to say that God fills the emptiness; God in no way fills it but rather keeps it empty and thus helps us preserve—even if in pain—our authentic communion.[58]

This is the heart of David's personal grief, now expressed for all Israel to hear.

2:1–11
Rival Kings

David's public display of national and personal grief now yields to private devotion. After mourning Saul and Jonathan, David petitions YHWH. Amid tumult and calm, David has consistently relied on the Lord and sought God's wisdom. This time he asks whether he should return to Judah after his exile. God responds by telling David to go to Hebron, the chief city of Judah. This means that David will not go first to his ancestral home of Bethlehem, but to the center of political life. The meaning is unmistakable: he returns to Judah as a king-in-the-making, to the public affirmation of what had been quietly proclaimed long ago, when David was anointed by Samuel (1 Sam. 16:13). David's entourage returns—wives, household, and the

---

58. Dietrich Bonhoeffer, *Letters and Papers from Prison*, ed. John W. de Gruchy (Minneapolis: Fortress, 2009), 238.

men who have accompanied him in exile—to settle "in the towns of Hebron," indicating a disperse settlement throughout the region. The settlement is completed by David's anointing as king over Judah (vv. 1–4). David's kinfolk thus first recognize him as king.

As soon as he is anointed, David makes strategic alliances with other tribes. He sends a blessing to Jabesh-gilead, recognizing their piety and decorum in giving Saul proper burial, promising reward for their deed. In this message, David combines religious thanksgiving and an overture of political alliance. He knows that these loyalists of Saul could potentially prove troublesome in subsequent struggles. His remarks to them are both a sincere expression of thanks and flattery designed to influence and win over potential adversaries. What is intriguing about David's tactics, however, is that they do not conflict with one another. David's actions are not a crass act of partisan double-speak, saying one thing and meaning another. Rather, his piety and his political strategy are in line with the will of YHWH. They make sense because of his earlier discernment of the Lord's instruction. David wishes for the continued strength and valiance of the inhabitants of Jabesh-gilead but reminds them their lord Saul is dead and that David is now king of Judah (vv. 5–7). It is an implicit invitation for them to recognize him as king as well.

At the same time, however, another king has arisen in the land. Whereas David's kingship was recognized and established by the people of Judah, this kingship is established by one kingmaker, Abner, who takes Saul's sole surviving son, Ishbaal, across the Jordan to Mahanaim and there establishes him as king. The location of this coronation in the Transjordan is significant, for it is far from the Philistine threat. Ishbaal thus sits in a position of relative safety, though he is distant from Saul's ancestral home in Benjamin. The new king's name, "man of Baal," is striking and somewhat problematic, since Baal is a Canaanite deity who often appears as a chief example of idolatry in Israel. But as P. Kyle McCarter Jr. has noted, the name can also mean "man of lord" or "man of master," and may have been "an acceptable way of referring to the God of Israel in Saul's day."[59] The narrator enumerates several places that comprise Ishbaal's kingdom,

59. P. Kyle McCarter Jr., textual notes for 1 and 2 Samuel in *The HarperCollins Study Bible,* ed. Wayne A. Meeks (New York: HarperCollins, 1993), 468.

including Transjordan regions, areas in the north and Samaria, as well as Saul's ancestral home. It also includes a puzzling mention of the Ashurites, likely Assyrians, whose presence at this point in the narrative is anomalous. The net result, however, is clear: there are now two kings in the land. What follows is the result of that division, and the difference between a king propped up by a military strategist and a king anointed by God.

2:12–32

The Battle of Gibeon

The consequences of that division now unfold in bloodshed. Troops led by Abner and troops led by Joab gather in Gibeon, a border region between Judah and Israel, northwest of Jerusalem. No explicit reason is given for this battle, though the overture David makes to Jabesh-gilead is a strong possibility. Abner and Joab, who each represent the military support of their rival kings, engage in dialogue as their respective troops face each other. Abner proposes a proxy battle, with a few young men engaging in a contest before the assembled armies. Joab agrees. The twelve men from each army symbolize the twelve tribes of Israel. The fact that these men and tribes are now engaged in a fight to the death pronounces judgment on the battle and the subsequent struggles that culminate in David's kingship over Israel. The Deuteronomist does not glorify the war that ensues; instead, this battle and subsequent ones are narrated with graphic realism. This new chapter of Israel's history begins with kin fighting kin and the unnecessary spilling of blood. Twelve men from each side march out to face each other and die together. As twenty-four young soldiers die, a greater battle erupts with extensive loss. If Joab's troops win the battle, it is at the expense of disarray among the covenant people (vv. 12–17).

Attention shifts to David's three nephews—Joab, Abishai, and Asahel—who are fierce partisans, eager to avenge any slight to their king. Asahel is a fast runner, "a wild gazelle" (v. 18). He is also single-minded in his pursuit of the man whom he deems the power behind the rival king, Abner. Abner recognizes the man pursuing him and calls him by name, personalizing their confrontation. By calling out to Asahel, Abner is trying to stop the pursuit. His offer of one of his servants is either an offer to sacrifice one of his own or a clever ruse to divert Asahel's attention in order that Abner might kill Asahel himself. But Abner's remark that he does not want to kill Asahel indicates some desire to stop fighting. Asahel, by contrast, does not call Abner by name. His pursuit of his foe is relentless but eventually fails as Abner impales Asahel in the stomach, forcing the spear through his body. There is no glory here; only the sickening sight of kinsmen slaughtering each other. The combatants know each other by name, and this recognition does not stop the killing. The sight is enough to make all who came to the place where Asahel died stand still (vv. 18–23).

Spurred no doubt by the indignity visited upon their brother, Joab and Abishai continue the pursuit of Abner toward the east as the day is ending. But the retreating army has also gathered together, forming a unified band at the top of a hill, an easier place to defend. Abner calls his pursuers (chiefly Joab) with prophetic words, appealing to Joab to turn away from bloodshed, warning of a bitter end if the slaughter continues. For a loyalist to Saul, these are stirring words. The story is not simply of a "good" party fighting a "bad" one. Even if David is God's anointed, the struggle that precedes his kingship of all Israel documents the inhumanity of interfamilial fights. The battles between Judah and Israel are hardly a righteous crusade. Even in the defense of a divinely anointed king, the battles that ensue are more tragic than justified, more unnecessary than a just cause. Joab, the staunch loyalist of David, heeds Abner's words, claiming that if Abner had not spoken, the heedless slaughter would have continued. The trumpet sounds and the battle stops (vv. 24–28).

Abner's men return to the Transjordan, journeying through the night while Joab ventures toward Hebron. The armies move back to their respective seats of power. Though the casualties are great— twenty of Joab's troops and 360 of Abner's—Asahel's death is most significant, for he represents the heart of David's loyalists. Even if the numbers favor Judah, Abner strikes the most decisive blow. Asahel, appropriately, is given honorary burial in the tomb of his father in

Bethlehem, David's ancestral city (vv. 29–32). It is a death that many will want to avenge.

3:1–5

David's Wives and Sons

As war continues, David's troops strengthen. So, too, does David's own house. This list not only provides an interlude to the ceaseless battles but also evidence that David is now acting as king. David gathers wives as he consolidates wealth and power. Sons are born who will ensure the family line. Some of the wives and sons are only mentioned here or in Chronicles and play minor roles (such as sons Chileab and Ithream; wives Haggith, Abital, and Eglah). Others have already played significant roles (such as Abigail) or will soon play tragic roles (such as Amnon and Absalom). The list, therefore, is also foreboding, since one of these children will die tragically, as the result of David's complicity in the murder of one of his servants, and another one will rebel against his father, usurping the throne. The Deuteronomist has already made clear that David has YHWH's blessing. The impact of this blessing on David's family, however, is decidedly mixed.

3:6–39

Abner Proposes an Alliance with David and Is Killed

If Saul's house is experiencing its demise (v. 1), Abner, the king-maker, "was making himself strong in the house of Saul" (v. 6). His concern, it seems, is chiefly for himself; he may even have his eyes on the throne, as his seizure of Saul's concubine, Rizpah, suggests. Indeed, Rizpah's prominence in mourning Saul's sons and grandsons later in the narrative (21:10–14) indicates her significance. Ishbaal, meanwhile, functions as a puppet, barely speaking or acting on his own. But Ishbaal does ask Abner a pivotal question: "Why have you gone in to my father's concubine?" (v. 7). The question arouses Abner's immediate indignation: he implies that he is being treated as a "dog's head," a clear insult. He insists that he has been loyal to Saul's house and that he has protected Ishbaal from David, though he could have easily betrayed him. He even denies Ishbaal's charge: he does not admit to taking Rizpah and refuses to speak her name: "you charge me now with a crime concerning this woman" (v. 8). It is a common tactic throughout the ages: when confronted with a sexual indiscretion or infidelity, the man in power refuses to acknowledge the woman's existence. "I do not know her." Such words deny responsibility and deny the woman's personhood. Abner's message to Ishbaal is clear: Ishbaal's very position on the throne depends on Abner's loyalty. Because Ishbaal has insulted the kingmaker, Abner's words suddenly and drastically turn against the house of Saul, parroting the Deuteronomist as they cite the inevitability of David's reign. Indeed, Abner claims that he will play the pivotal role in transferring power to the house of David. Faced with these words, Ishbaal cannot say a word and is reduced to fear (vv. 9–11).

Acting as the seat of power in Saul's house, Abner sends messengers to David proposing an alliance, a covenant. But the covenant that Abner suggests is not based on friendship and loyalty (as Jonathan's was) but on political expediency and the desire to consolidate power. His question to David, "To whom does the land belong?" implies that it really belongs to Abner, not Ishbaal. If David wants to become king over Israel, he needs to reckon with Abner. It is a bold claim, indeed; in effect, Abner is playing the role of kingmaker again. David recognizes his need for Abner's support, agrees to a covenant, yet meets Abner's overture with a counter-request: the return of Michal, whose marriage to David Saul had annulled. Subtle maneuvering among Abner, Ishbaal, and David ensues. David sends notice to Ishbaal (who is still king, even if it is in name only), and it is Ishbaal who takes Michal from her husband Paltiel (vv. 12–15). By relying not simply on Abner, David both goes over Abner's head to the monarch and makes an overture to Ishbaal. His demand for the return of his former wife indicates to Ishbaal that David is a king to be reckoned with and that he is not maneuvering behind Ishbaal's back by communicating only with Abner. It is an astute political move, enabling David to play both men to his advantage.

The return of Michal is also striking, accompanied as it is by

Paltiel's grief and Abner's admonition for him to return home (v. 16). The scene conveys both the lament of a spouse and the power of a kingmaker. Readers, however, hear nothing of Michal's reaction. This is a conspicuous silence indeed, since her devotion to David led her to deceive her father Saul and plot David's escape (1 Sam. 19:11–17). Perhaps there is erasure here of a woman's voice yet again; perhaps it foreshadows Michal's disapproval of David's subsequent behavior as the ark arrives in Jerusalem (6:20–23).

Abner resumes his role as kingmaker by contacting the leaders of various regions and tribes. His message to them is overtly political and somewhat unexpected: "For some time past you have been seeking David as king over you" (v. 17). If this is indeed the case, readers have not heard of it prior to now. His message, then, either reflects the spirit of the leaders or is shrewdly designed to convince them to support David as king. The second half of the message freights the political with the sacred: David is the one promised by God and through David the people will be saved from the Philistines. The elders, Abner claims, are enjoined to "bring it about" (v. 18). If Abner plays the role of kingmaker, he appeals to the elders to behave as kingmakers themselves. Abner also pays special attention to the Benjaminites, the tribe of Saul, in his overtures. Apparently, the overture is successful, as Abner reports that the "whole house of Benjamin" (v. 19) is ready for the new king. Abner thus emerges as a mixture of self-preservation, self-interest, and an instrument of transition between monarchies. He is neither craven nor without blemish.

David recognizes his need for Abner and fetes their alliance upon Abner's return. But Abner's words to David also play on the king's self-interest: "you may reign over all that your heart desires" (v. 21). We have heard rather little of David's desires thus far in the narrative. His ascent to kingship, instead, is marked by his submission to God's desires. Thus far, the journey to the throne has been marked less by David's grasping for power and more by his faithfulness to God's promises. Abner's words to David foreshadow desires that eventually prove destructive, for when David attempts to seize what his heart desires, the kingdom starts to crumble. The reach of David's kingdom will indeed be great, but the greatness of his realm will come at enormous cost to him personally.

Suddenly Joab reenters the story in his customary role: returning from a raid with treasure. If David needs Abner to ensure his rise to the throne, he also needs Joab as the one who does the dirty work to consolidate David's reign. Most leaders need men like Joab, even when they disavow them. If Ronald Reagan expressed dismay with Oliver North, if Harry S. Truman dismissed General MacArthur from duties, both of these U.S. presidents, in putting distance between themselves and their military men, also acknowledged their dependence on them. Joab is astonished that David has been meeting with Abner, suspecting espionage of Saul's right hand man (vv. 22–25).

David does not respond to Joab's accusation but perhaps considers it. Like many henchmen, Joab does not wait for word from his commander, but brings Abner back to Hebron without David's knowledge and murders him. Joab kills not for the sake of David's kingdom, but to avenge Abner's killing of Joab's brother, Asahel (vv. 26–27). For Joab, personal vendetta trumps the king's desire and command, a further example of Joab's impulsiveness, even if he thinks he is serving the king well.

David finds out about the killing and immediately proclaims his own innocence. Yet there is duplicity in David's voice, as Exum notes: "Abner, it seems, would have given David authority over the northern tribes without a struggle. Yet in spite of appearances, Abner's death benefits David. David will not owe his kingdom to the hot-headed general who has already betrayed one king, and Abner will not live to cause problems for David in the future."[60] Joab's guilt, by contrast, will be revisited for as long as his house endures (vv. 28-9). This theology speaks less to divine vengeance and more to the profoundly social implications of sin. The rupture caused by sin is not simply between one human being and God (or between one human being and another). Rather, the wounds of sin invariably ripple outward in multiple directions, affecting present and future relationships. One impulsive act—even if it benefits the king—can leave scars generations hence. The narrator indicates, furthermore, that Joab's brother Abishai is also complicit in Abner's murder (v.

60. J. Cheryl Exum, *Tragedy and Biblical Narrative: Arrows of the Almighty* (Cambridge: Cambridge University Press, 1992), 105.

30). This contradicts verse 27, where Joab kills Abner "privately," but it also attests to the brothers' interconnected lives and how both are motivated by a desire to avenge their brother's death.

After pronouncing a curse on Joab's house, David makes another important political move: a public act of mourning for a fallen soldier. Joab, who believes he has saved David from peril, is also ordered to mourn. Joab, without a word, accedes to the humiliating request. Abner is given the trappings of a military funeral, heralded with honor, and buried in Hebron (a sign of David's favor). The king mourns and fasts, expressing remorse and allying himself with the house of Saul. By distancing himself from Joab's behavior, David also shows that he owes much to Joab. The murder has made David look even more pleasing in Israel's sight, making him seem a man above pettiness and violence: "All the people took notice of it, and it pleased them; just as everything the king did pleased all the people" (v. 36). David, the beloved, becomes more beloved by the nation. He is exonerated, blameless, and above it all, even when he depends on men who are "too violent" for him (vv. 37–39). The episode is narrated without varnish, testament to the Deuteronomist's suspicion of kingship. From the beginning, kingship was a compromise that has yielded ambiguous results. More killing is yet to come.

4:1–12
The Killing of Ishbaal

One final act of violence leads to David's kingship over all Israel. In this case, like so many others in this narrative history, *Realpolitik* and the ways of God stand in opposition to one another at the same time that they are intertwined. When Abner is murdered, Ishbaal is fully exposed as impotent: His courage fails "and all Israel was dismayed" (v. 1). Two of Ishbaal's captains, Baanah and Rechab, capture the spirit of the people. They hail from Beeroth, a town assigned historically to the tribe of Benjamin but that also was a Gibeonite city: a town composed of non-Israelites (cf. Josh. 9).

The introduction of these two captains, who intend to assassinate the puppet king, is interrupted briefly by the presence of

Jonathan's son, Mephibosheth. The effect is to recall David's covenant with Jonathan in the midst of bloodshed and power struggles. The narrator moves backward in time, to news of Saul and Jonathan's death. During the chaos that accompanied this devastating news, Mephibosheth falls from his nurse's arms and becomes crippled (v. 4). If his introduction here is brief and reminiscent of solemn pledges between friends, he will pose a challenge to kingship later (19:24–30).

Rechab and Baanah set out in the "heat of the day" (and, correspondingly, in the heat of their passion and frustration with the king) to Ishbaal's house. During this customary time of rest, they feign as though they are taking wheat and strike Ishbaal in the stomach, the organ where wheat is digested. The murder is gruesome: it happens while the king is in his bedroom lying on his couch, while the king is most vulnerable. After killing him, they cut off his head and escape across the Jordan, heading toward Hebron and the house of David (vv. 5–7).

The two Benjaminites, upon presenting Ishbaal's head to David, expect to be rewarded for dispensing with the final obstacle to the throne. They claim that Ishbaal has sought David's life (for which there is no evidence in previous text). They see their act as vengeance on an enemy, but it is hard not to see these two as opportunists. Dismayed at the unraveling of Ishbaal's kingship, they attempt to curry favor with the next leader. David's response to them recalls his words in the wake of Saul and Jonathan's deaths. Those deaths, at least, occurred during war with the Philistines. Ishbaal's death, however, was committed by "wicked men" on a "righteous man on his bed in his own house." Rechab and Baanah have incurred bloodguilt and they will be destroyed "from the earth" (v. 11). David's orders are swift: he commands some of his servants to kill, and they dismember the bodies. They are deprived proper burial and hung in public beside a pool. The message is unmistakable: these men have acted sacrilegiously and their bodies will be treated as such. The supposed trophy of Ishbaal's head, by contrast, is given proper burial in a place of honor: in the tomb of Abner (v. 12).

The stage is now set for David's anointing as king over all Israel. It has come through God's promise but also through the actions of violent and unpredictable men. War has pitted Israelite against Israelite. Much blood lies on the ground; much guilt surrounds those who have committed unspeakable deeds. The Deuteronomist does not glorify the affairs of war or the machinations of power-hungry men.

Cure Thy children's warring madness / Bend our pride to Thy control / Shame our wanton selfish gladness / Rich in things and poor in soul. / Grant us wisdom, grant us courage, / Lest we miss Thy kingdom's goal, / Lest we miss Thy kingdom's goal.

Harry Emerson Fosdick, "God of Grace and God of Glory," in *Glory to God* (Louisville, KY: Westminster John Knox Press, 2013), #307.

But somehow, underneath it all is the perceptible hand of God's promise that God will not let go of the people Israel and that God has chosen David to lead that people. Despite the blood that surrounds him, David, thus far, remains blameless, wholly trusting in the Lord. As he prepares to assume the throne, the signs look promising. But David, as we will see, does not always make good on his promise. As he assumes the throne, promises are fulfilled and promises are reneged.

2 Samuel 5:1–12:31

The Reign of David

The reign of David brings increased security and prosperity in Israel. This king of Israel's longing is hardly the subject of hagiography but is one of the most complex characters in all of Scripture. In these pivotal chapters, David experiences blessing and tragedy, shows piety and sin, fullness of faith and lack of faith. These chapters also contain one of the most stunning affirmations in the entire Bible: the prophet Nathan's oracle that declares David's kingdom will endure forever. Blessings overflow, almost from the moment that David is anointed king over all Israel, and there is an intimacy between YHWH and David that is nearly unprecedented in Scripture. David is the blessed child, the one for whom God is father. But if King David is God's anointed, he is not a monarch who does whatever he wants; he submits himself to the law and the covenant. Indeed, the prosperity and health of the kingdom depends, in large part, on the faithfulness of the king.

These chapters chart an increase in David's power and growth in Israel's territory. Even the Philistines disappear from the story for a while as David forges an empire that extends north. As David leads the nation in this increase in wealth and land, he experiences the privilege and perquisites of being king. He has come a long way from Bethlehem, and with the establishment of a capital in Jerusalem, he embraces the trappings of royal power. But these chapters also show David at his most ignoble. The power of the kingship also yields to abuse, narrated most vividly in his act of adultery with Bathsheba and subsequent orchestration of the death of her husband, Uriah. Here the narrator displays a king who has become accustomed to power, who spawns tragedy by his own abuse of power. If the Davidic kingdom is established "forever," this does not leave David off the hook when he acts contrary to the law. The result of these pivotal chapters is an unforgettable depiction of kingship, warts and all, and of a God who works with warts to demonstrate continued faithfulness to God's people.

5:1–5

David, King of All Israel

The transition between one regime and the next has been painful and bloody, but it has not resulted in partisan jubilation. David has tried to act not only with his own tribe in mind but also with the well-being of the entire people Israel. His time of anointing has come. The narrator claims that all tribes come to the seat of David's power in Hebron, with words that express intimacy and family ties: "Look, we are your bone and flesh" (v. 1). This greeting evokes Adam's cry to Eve (Gen. 1:23) and Laban's words to Jacob (Gen. 29:14). The tribes come to David and acknowledge him as one of their own. They also recognize David's past service to Saul: Their claim that David "led out Israel and brought us in" (v. 2) refers chiefly to David's position as military commander (cf. 1 Sam. 18:13, 16). But they also suggest a greater role that David has inhabited all the while, that David in fact *led* Israel before he became king. This secondary meaning to the phrase is reinforced by the tribes' report of YHWH's words to David, that he will be shepherd and ruler to the people Israel. These two images, shepherd and ruler, describe both David's past and future. He is the shepherd youth who slayed the warrior Goliath and he is to serve as shepherd to Israel, guiding and protecting his people. He is the ruler who has been chosen by God to submit to God and wield power on behalf of the covenant people. The effect of this speech is to show that Israel has also chosen David as king; indeed, God's anointing is confirmed by the people. David responds to their words by making a covenant with the people who have come to him. Monarchy in Israel is different: it binds a king to God and to his people. The king, in other words, stands under the promises he makes and the commandments that God gives. Who anoints David as king? In this episode it is not a single person and it is not even God alone. Rather, the tribes anoint David, confirming the choice God has already made. This auspicious moment concludes with chronological and geographical markers of David's reign. He will reign long and move the capital from Hebron to Jerusalem (vv. 3–5), a city that will play a prominent role in events yet to unfold.

5:6–16

Jerusalem, David's City

The new king's reign begins with a military expedition that in some ways completes the Exodus. Jerusalem has long been surrounded by Israelites, but ever since the conquest of Canaan, it has remained a Jebusite city (cf. Josh. 15:63). Readers do not hear much from these indigenous residents of Jerusalem in prior chapters of the Deuteronomistic History, other than occasional benign references (cf. Judg. 1:21). But here the Jebusites taunt David's advancing army, warning him that "even the blind and the lame will turn you back" (v. 6). The point is clear: this army on the march will be defeated by those who cannot see or walk. The taunt, however, is met with a decisive display of force. David's troops capture the stronghold of Zion, probably the most important military position in the city, as David responds to the Jebusite taunt: "Whoever would strike down the Jebusites, let him get up the water shaft to attack the lame and the blind, those whom David hates" (v. 8). The force of these words is shocking, even if it is difficult to interpret them. The difficulty increases when one considers alternate textual readings (such as "those who hate David"). But the very suggestion of attacking those whose physical disability renders them most vulnerable ought to arouse questions in any reader.

What is going on here? The first half of the sentence is perhaps more quickly resolved: David offers a military strategy, perhaps a strategic attack on the city's water supply or a clandestine route to other defended parts of the city. But the second half is potentially horrifying: attacking the blind and lame, whom David hates? The worst renderings of this story promote prejudice (or worse yet, violence) against disabled persons. Here David, the valiant preserver of purity, kills those whose bodies represent impurity. (Indeed, the law stipulates that those whose bodies are blemished by various disabilities are not to serve as priests. Cf. Lev. 21:16–23.) Such readings, which have an ostensible anchor in Levitical holiness codes, however, run against the privilege that Torah grants the vulnerable (cf. Deut. 24:17–22; 27:19). Indeed, the text can become a text of terror for disabled persons, much like analogous texts have been used against women and LGBT persons (Lev. 20:13; Judg. 19:22–30; 1 Cor. 14:34–35). It is perhaps more consistent with the story thus far to interpret David's remarks as a retort to the Jebusites: if the Jebusites say that the blind and lame will turn David away, David will kill them. David's hatred here is directed less against a particular class of people—the blind and the lame—and more against the taunt itself. But this interpretation does not really make the problem of the text—violence against disabled persons—disappear. Neither do some Christian interpretations of the story that see this episode as a foil to Jesus' subsequent healing of the blind and lame: "In the old Jerusalem of this text, the blind and lame are excluded and despised. In the new Jerusalem envisioned by the gospel, all are welcomed, and the blind and lame are transformed into full, welcome participants."[1] To claim as much risks relegating this text to a relic that is "overcome" in the ministry of Jesus. Perhaps there are elements of many of these interpretations in the story: a Levitical recognition of the sanctity of the body and concern with honoring the body in light of God's holiness and David's rather dramatic response to an insult. If so, then the conquest of Jerusalem, however central, is also marked by ambiguity. Like in so many other cases, the Deuteronomist does not gloss over the ugly parts of the story: even King David is not immune from acts that appear senseless. Perhaps it is best if we continue to struggle with this text, working against interpretations that stigmatize and marginalize disabled persons.

David conquers Jerusalem by occupying the stronghold. He

---

1. Bruggeman, *First and Second Samuel*, 241. Brueggeman is also critical of this tendency to use David's words as a foil to the Gospel in many Christian interpretations of this story.

rebuilds it and names it after himself, a common practice in ancient Mediterranean warfare. Indeed, the king and the city almost become inseparable after this victory, as David becomes "greater and greater" thanks to God's presence (vv. 9–10).

An interlude refers to David's alliance with King Hiram of Tyre, who provides cedars and skilled workers for the construction of David's house. Leaders from other lands have begun to take notice and curry favor with him. David perceives this growth in his power, however, as the work of God. David, who has just conquered a city that has eluded Israel for centuries, who has received gifts from another king, is remarkably humble in his demeanor, attributing little to himself. If the 2012 U.S. presidential election fostered a debate over the question of "who built this?"—me, by myself? or with the help of others?—David's answer to the question suggests that there is nothing we do on our own, completely by ourselves. Indeed, we are never far from the work of God in our lives or the collaboration of others. The kingship of David, we have already noted, is different: Kings do not make themselves; they are established by YHWH and the nation. They serve not themselves but serve for "the sake of [the] people Israel" (vv. 11–12). If the nature of kingship in Israel is different, however, David's appearance sometimes resembles kings of the nations. He takes concubines and wives and becomes the father of many children (vv. 13–16). Those mentioned in this conclusion are children born in Jerusalem. Among them, Solomon will play the most prominent role as the builder of the temple, YHWH's house. David looks and acts very much like a king. In much of what follows, his fate and Israel's fate will depend on whether he acts like a king of the nations or as a king who submits to the living God.

FURTHER REFLECTIONS
Theology and Disability

Because the conquest of Jerusalem, particularly David's injunction to strike down those whom he hates, has been linked to prejudice against disabled persons, it is important to survey the Christian tradition's ambiguous understandings of disability. Some strands of the New Testament—even those connected with Jesus' ministry—seem to correlate physical disability and sin. The well-known episode of Jesus' healing of the paralytic includes these words: "When Jesus perceived their questionings, he answered them, 'Why do you raise such questions in your hearts? Which is easier, to say, "Your sins are forgiven you," or to say, "Stand up and walk"?'" (Luke 5:22–23). But on other occasions, Jesus emphatically rejects the correlation between disability and sin. In John's narration of Jesus' gift of sight to a man born blind, "His disciples asked him, 'Rabbi, who sinned, this man or his parents, that he has been born blind?' Jesus answered, 'Neither this man nor his parents sinned; he was born blind so that God's works might be revealed in him'" (John 9:2–3).

In many quarters of the ancient Mediterranean world, the practice of infant exposure—the abandonment of babies born with physical disabilities—was common. Many of the church fathers and mothers, however, argued vociferously against this practice. Lactantius, for example, states, "It is always wrong to kill a man whom God has intended to be a sacrosanct creature. Let no one, then, think that it is to be conceded even, that newly born children may be done away with, an especially great impiety! God breathes souls into them for life, not for death."[2] The broad consensus among these early theologians was that the value of persons was not their physical appearance or mental condition but their reflection of the *imago Dei*, endowed with a body that is good, regardless of physical impediment, and a soul that is sacred.[3]

In the Middle Ages, Thomas Aquinas asked whether persons with mental disabilities and illnesses (in his language, "imbeciles" and "madmen") ought to partake in the central sacraments of the Christian church, Eucharist and baptism. In response to those who would deny their participation in these rites, Thomas answers with an emphatic "yes." Despite his insistence that reason is one of the chief markers of personhood, Thomas holds that "those lacking the use of reason can have devotion towards the sacrament; actual devotion in some cases,

2. Lactantius, *The Divine Institutes,* trans. Mary Francis McDonald, O.P. Fathers of the Church, vol. 49. (Washington, DC: Catholic University of America Press, 1964), 452.

3. See Almut Caspary, "The Patristic Era: Early Christian Attitudes toward the Disfigured Outcast," in *Disability in the Christian Tradition: A Reader* ed. Brian Brock and John Swinton, 26–28 (Grand Rapids: Eerdmans, 2012).

and past in others."[4] In this view, those who have physical and mental disabilities are no less a part of the church as the body of Christ.

For much of the tradition, however, physical or mental disability has been understood as a "lack" or "deficiency." Recent theologies have questioned this assumption. Jürgen Moltmann takes a pneumatological approach toward disability, where he considers handicapped life a charisma of the Spirit: *"Every handicap is an endowment, too.* The strength of Christ is also powerful in the disablement."[5] Each person in the community is a gift to the others: there is diaconal ministry of the non-disabled to the disabled *and* of the disabled to the nondisabled. Nancy Eiesland considers disability in relation to Christology. In the incarnation, crucifixion, and resurrection, she claims, Jesus Christ reveals a disabled God. In the resurrection, for example, Jesus reveals his wounds:

> In presenting his impaired hands and feet to his startled friends, the resurrected Jesus is revealed as the disabled God. Jesus, the resurrected Savior, calls for his frightened companions to recognize in the marks of impairment their own connection with God, their own salvation. In so doing, this disabled God is also the revealer of a new humanity. The disabled God is not only the One from heaven but the revelation of true personhood, underscoring the reality that full personhood is fully compatible with the experience of disability.[6]

Jesus, the disabled God, in other words, reveals the fullness of humanity (and the fullness of God) *in* his disability.

Other recent work has focused on intellectual disability. Molly Haslam, a theologian and physical therapist who has worked with persons with profound intellectual disabilities, questions the legacy of interpretations of humanity (such as Thomas Aquinas's) that focus on rationality and offers a vision of the person characterized by responsiveness and relationship: Those with profound intellectual disabilities "image God not because of some intellectual capacity

4. Thomas Aquinas, *Summa Theologica*, 2491.
5. Jürgen Moltmann, *The Spirit of Life: A Universal Affirmation.* trans. Margaret Kohl (Minneapolis: Fortress, 1992), 193, italics in original.
6. Nancy L. Eiesland, *The Disabled God: Toward a Liberatory Theology of Disability* (Nashville: Abingdon, 1994), 100.

they possess, but because their participation as responders in relationships is expressive of the longing that God is."[7] In a similar vein,
Amos Yong, a Pentecostal theologian whose brother has Down syndrome, reconceives theological anthropology along relational lines:
"The more severely or profoundly disabled express and manifest their
self-identity precisely in and through their relationships of interde-
pendence with others."[8] Each of these recent voices helps the church
look toward its eschatological horizon, where all persons are recognized not for their supposed deficiencies but for their fulfillment in
the image of God, their relationships to others and to the God who
gives life: an image that is not diminished, but revealed in disability.

5:17–25
More Battles with the Philistines

David's kingship is beginning to look different from his predecessor's,
but he also has many of the same tasks that consumed Saul. Chief
among them is dealing with the Philistine threat, a task in which he is
even more successful than Saul. This relatively brief excursus supplies
details of two battles with David as Israel's commander and indicates
how quickly his circumstances have changed. David, who had spent
more than a year in refuge with the Philistines (and who had been
on the verge of marching against Saul's army) now leads the Israelites against Philistia. The Philistines hear that David is the new king
and go up in search of him. This is clearly not a search for a strategic alliance, since David heads to his stronghold when he hears the
news. Since the Philistines are gathering in the valley of Rephaim,
southwest of Jerusalem, Adullam seems to be David's likely location.
Before engaging in battle, David inquires of God, a petition consistent with David's behavior thus far. He has asked this question before
(1 Sam. 30:8), and again David listens to YHWH's promise of a swift
victory. The location of the battle, Baal-perazim—"Lord of Bursting

7. Molly C. Haslam, *A Constructive Theology of Intellectual Disability: Human Being as Mutuality
and Response* (New York: Fordham, 2012), 110.
8. Amos Yong, *Theology and Down Syndrome: Reimagining Disability in Late Modernity* (Waco,
TX: Baylor, 2007), 185.

Forth"—reflects David's interpretation of events. But the most telling detail of this first battle is the Philistines' abandonment of their idols (vv. 17–21). As David's army carries them away, the earlier Philistine capture of the ark is effectively reversed. As David prepares to bring the ark to Jerusalem, his people now hold foreign gods as captives. By ending with this detail, the narrator indicates that the battle between Israel and Philistia is not just a battle between rival peoples in the Mediterranean world, but a clash between deities. The struggle is as much theological as it is political.

The second battle with Philistia occurs on the same battleground, where David again inquires of the Lord. But God's response this time differs: David should not go up against the Philistines, but around to the rear. This change in tactics adds an element of surprise to the Israelite attack, but it also indicates one of the few times in 1 and 2 Samuel that YHWH acts directly without human mediation. God tells David to wait at the rear, to listen to "the sound of marching in the tops of the balsam trees," which indicates that the "LORD has gone out before you to strike down the army of the Philistines" (vv. 22–24). Whereas in most of the stories thus far, God acts behind the scenes as orchestrator or guider of events, here God goes out in front of David. David's devotion to God that has consistently interpreted each victory and blessing as the work of YHWH now in this scene achieves external confirmation as David waits on the Lord. The God who acts through human persons also acts directly on human events. David does what the Lord commands, and again victory is assured. But intriguingly, as he waits on the Lord, the narrator also claims that David "struck down the Philistines from Geba all the way to Gezer" (v. 25), an extensive swath of territory. David waits on the Lord, but David also acts. Even in the most explicit narration of God's direct activity, David also plays a role in the final result.

6:1–23

The Ark Journeys to Jerusalem

With David's military prowess effectively demonstrated, attention now turns to Israel's cultic life. This memorable vignette effectively demonstrates the convergence of David's devotional life and the liturgy of the nation. These two aspects coalesce in the new capital city, where the ark finds its permanent home. The episode begins with David's calling of some thirty thousand, an exaggerated number that symbolizes the gathering of a nation around its most revered object: the ark, the physical manifestation of God's presence with the people. Though many of the details of this story may seem remote from the liturgies of contemporary Judaism and Christianity, the central conviction is shared across time: God makes a home among mortals. The God of the ark, the God of the synagogue, the God of Jesus Christ does not remain remote from humanity but enters in to human life by drawing near, in word, in deed, in law, in grace.

David retrieves the ark from its temporary home in Baale-judah (perhaps another name for Kiriath-jearim, cf. 1 Sam. 7:2). A new cart has been built for the journey to Jerusalem, sanctified for this holy purpose. Two of Abinadab's sons, Uzzah and Ahio, accompany the ark on its journey (vv. 1–4). Readers have not encountered them previously, since earlier another of Abinadab's sons, Eleazar, tended the ark (cf. 1 Sam. 7:1). The procession is festive, with David and the large crowd "dancing before the LORD with all their might," accompanied by instruments and singing (v. 5). This dancing has elicited countless comments over the centuries. On the one hand, David's dancing seems on the fringe of religious decorum, as indicated by his wife Michal's subsequent reprimand.

> Dance, then, wherever you may be; / I am the Lord of the Dance, said He. . . .
>
> American Shaker melody, Sydney Carter.

When one is caught up in the movement of a crowd, it is possible to lose oneself in dance, and this is precisely what seems to happen. Ecstasy is not too strong a word. The question, of course, is the source of ecstasy. For David, it is a dance before the Lord.

In the midst of the frenzy and commotion, the ark becomes unstable. The text states that the "oxen shook it" (v. 6), but it is easy to imagine that the oxen are moved by the dancing crowd. In an understandable gesture, Uzzah—probably unwittingly—reaches out to steady the ark. But this act proves fatal, since it represents an unprepared encounter with holiness. The ark, which represents God's dwelling among the people, is holy *and* dangerous. If one reads this story and considers it merely as a remnant of primitive religion, we need only recall the highly charged nature of holy objects in our day—be they ones of civil religion (such as the U.S. flag) or sacred ones (such as the cross). The use (and abuse) of these objects often elicits strong reactions. To handle them, one must prepare oneself. Uzzah's reason for touching the ark is admittedly "good," to prevent the ark from falling to the ground. But he is also unprepared for his encounter with the holy. In another example of YHWH's direct action (falling close on the heels of the Lord's defeat of the Philistines), YHWH's anger is kindled against Uzzah, striking him dead. To encounter the holy casually, in short, is to risk death. David, who accepts many previous events as coming from the hand of the Lord, has a strong reaction to the incident. He does not passively accept Uzzah's death but becomes angry and struggles with God. His response shows us that anger can also be a mark of piety, even—and perhaps especially—when directed to God. The psalms, which tradition ascribes to David, also illustrate this, as they mark the full range of religious emotion—from praise to lament, from jubilation to anger—all addressed to the same God. David's anger does not slacken his piety; it puts it on a different course.

The full range of religious emotions is further evident in David's fear of YHWH. Witnessing what has happened to Uzzah, he asks how the ark can be entrusted to his care. The king seems to stop in his tracks at the holiness and power of God, as the procession stops and takes an unexpected detour to the house of Obed-edom the Gittite, where it remains for three months. Obed-edom's presence is intriguing, as he is a former inhabitant of the Philistine city Gath. The ark thus finds a home with another outsider who is not a part of Israel by blood. Scholars have conjectured that Obed-edom was a man who became loyal to David during his sojourn in Philistia and follows him to Israelite territory after David is dismissed from the Philistine army. It is impossible to determine his precise identity, but his connection with Gath is certainly significant, indicating that YHWH is not only the God of Israel, but the God of all creation.

Just as the ark has a drastic impact during its time in Philistia (cf. 1 Sam. 5), it now makes its presence known with the Gittite, as Obed-edom's household receives the Lord's blessing (vv. 9–11). Here, in an ironic reversal of Uzzah's encounter with the ark, the Gittite, who was unprepared to receive the ark, receives the unexpected gift of God's blessing. Both incidents underscore the often surprising nature of God's encounter with humanity, for which we are never fully prepared.

David learns of this blessing, which prompts the resumption of the ark's journey to Jerusalem. This second half of the journey is like the first, but it becomes even more festive and elaborate as it enters the royal city. "When those who bore the ark of the Lord had gone six paces, [David] sacrificed an ox and a fatling" (v. 13), phrasing that may indicate repeated sacrifices every six paces during the ark's procession. Religious frenzy, preparation, and purification accompany the ark as the people prepare a new home for it. David's dancing is described in greater detail here: he is clothed in a linen garment (perhaps with little hidden from the eye). There is shouting and the playing of the trumpet. There is order and there is chaos, or better said, order teetering on chaos. For one of the inhabitants who sees David—his wife Michal—it is all too much. She spies David in the midst of the chaos and "despised him in her heart" (vv. 14–16). Her reaction is certainly understandable, as David's behavior seems unbecoming to a king. Earlier in the narrative, a window signals freedom for a man when Michal lowers David to freedom (1 Sam. 19:12). Here, a window expresses confinement for a woman who witnesses David's dance from afar.[9] Michal's reaction, however, is about more than the king's attire. As her words to her husband will later indicate, the main issue is "David's taking the kingship from the house of Saul."[10]

The entire procession evokes extravagance: a procession, burnt offerings, and choice foods offered to everyone gathered. Everyone present is fed (vv. 17–19). David, after all, dances before a God who

---

9. J. Cheryl Exum, *Tragedy and Biblical Narrative: Arrows of the Almighty* (Cambridge: Cambridge University Press, 1992), 89.

10. J. Cheryl Exum, *Fragmented Women: Feminist (Sub)versions of Biblical Narratives* (Valley Forge, PA: Trinity Press International, 1993), 25.

does extravagant things: making a home among mortals and choosing Israel as God's own; bringing people into a land flowing with milk and honey; embracing the world in the flesh of Jesus Christ. David's dance, the feast, and the sacrifices made are all thankful responses to God's extravagance. Sometimes extravagance is the veneer for greed: celebrity homes keep getting bigger, the largest paychecks keep getting fatter. But the extravagance of this procession is different. Here the *entire* people of God take part in a feast; here all give praise as God's anointed king embodies their praise in dance. After taking part in this extravagance that celebrates the extravagant gift of the ark, the people and the king return home.

> The liturgy is never a mere meeting of a group of people. . . . Heaven is torn open here, and we are incorporated in the great chorus of praise. . . . And we know that we are not alone, that we are joining in, that the barrier between earth and heaven has truly been torn open.
>
> Joseph Cardinal Ratzinger, *God and the World,* trans. Henry Taylor (San Francisco: Ignatius, 2002), 412.

David returns to bless his home but instead encounters a reprimand. Michal, who is repeatedly referred to in this narrative as Saul's daughter—an indication of rivalry between royal houses—scolds David for "uncovering" himself before his servants' maids (v. 20). The accusation suggests David's nakedness or at least near-nakedness in the frenzy of dance. If so, one can easily see how David's actions might be seen as a loss of control or unbridled sensuality. Her words, as Exum interprets them, are also "an act of self-assertion." But whatever assertion she expresses is quickly dispensed by the narrator and David's reaction: "Such boldness on her part cannot be tolerated; the narrator lets her protest but robs her of voice at the critical moment, allowing her no reply to David and no further speech."[11] David responds to Michal's accusations with overt hostility, as he taunts Michal that God "chose me *in place of your father*" and promises to make himself "yet more contemptible than this" (vv. 21–22). Exum observes that David seems to have no feelings for Michal (if he ever did), whom he now makes the object of political

11. Ibid., 37.

venom: "We see in David's response to Michal what was so neatly concealed in his relationship to Jonathan and resolved by Jonathan's death: David's taking the kingship from Saul's house. . . . The hostility one would have expected David to express toward Saul, who sought his life, and toward Jonathan, who as heir to the throne stood in David's way, is directed toward Michal, where it offers less of a threat."[12] The final narrative blow to Michal is the remark that this "daughter of Saul" remains childless until death (v. 23), again cutting off the house of Saul from the monarchy. Exum remarks that David ceases "to have sexual relations with Michal, by putting aside the woman who earlier saved his life," though it may also be the case that Michal "refuses to have sexual relations with David," which would not be out of character.[13] Whatever the case, this ensures that Michal will have no heir; in a patriarchal world, this status amounts to a woman's narrative erasure.[14]

Michal's barrenness may also have wider implications, as Polzin observes. In this reading, the journey of the ark has been nothing short of disastrous, despite the abundant celebrations that surround it. Here, David seems to be using the ark for political gain: "The glory somehow departs from Israel when the ark of God is taken up in behalf of kingship. Michal's childlessness may represent the Deuteronomist's hope that the glory would one day return to Israel, and that Israel, like Michal, would remain kingless before the Lord to the day of her death."[15] Because David's kingship is beset with tragedy almost as soon as it is established, this interpretation is certainly plausible. The journey of the ark to Jerusalem is thus marked by fruitfulness and abundance, rivalry and political calculation. David's participation in the dance is both an expression of praise to YHWH and a taunt of his wife's house. Michal refuses to partake in it, for good reason.

---

12. Exum, *Tragedy*, 87.
13. Ibid., 88.
14. One reading of 2 Sam. 21 is that David ensures that five sons of Michal are killed, yet further evidence of his determination to rid Israel of the remnants of the house of Saul.
15. Robert Polzin, *David and the Deuteronomist* (Bloomington: Indiana University Press, 1993), 71.

7:1–29

Nathan's Oracle, David's Response

The ark is now in David's royal city; the king is "settled in his house" (v. 1) constructed with cedar from a faraway land. At last, David can rest from his enemies, because the Lord has delivered him from them. At the beginning of his reign, the outlook is very good. But the image is not of a king luxuriating in prosperity and favor. Instead, David's mind is on the contrast between his own cedar house and the ark, which lies in a tent. Nathan, whom the reader first encounters here, is a pivotal character. He is both David's subject and the king's teacher; a bearer of God's blessing and judgment. In the king's court, Nathan has a large degree of power, even when he says things that are disturbing and disruptive. Indeed, Nathan represents one of the pivotal checks on David's royal prerogative. David listens to Nathan, even when the message comes at personal cost, because Nathan represents God's word to the king, reminding David that the king and the people always stand under the Lord. David, who is keenly aware that YHWH has placed him on the throne, is motivated to build a house for the ark, a symbolic house for the Lord. Nathan's first words to the king are for him to do all he has in mind (vv. 2–3). The meaning seems clear enough: David shall also build a house for the ark.

Prophets in Israel, however, wait for a word from God. The word that Nathan receives that evening directly opposes David's desire. Nathan reports YHWH's question to David: "Are you the one to build me a house to live in?" (v. 5). The God of Israel, since the exodus, has been a God on the move: dynamic, transformative, bringing a people out of slavery into the promised land, making covenant with a people, anointing a king to serve the people. This is a God who has "not lived in a house" but moves "about in a tent and a tabernacle." The Lord has not required any leader in Israel to build a house for the ark (v. 7). Indeed, the impression from these verses is that a house for the Lord is antithetical to God's actions in history. To build a house for the Lord would represent a vain attempt to contain God's spirit or domesticate God's presence. In Nathan's report to David, God resists the idea of a house. The God that Nathan proclaims is not a God that we make a home for; rather, that God is always ahead of us, calling and summoning us to renewed life. As soon as we think we have made a home for God, we risk not being surprised by the movement of God. For that God, a moveable tent and tabernacle seem more suitable than four fixed walls.

This question of whether there is a home for God ought to lead us to question some of our own intense desires for home. For, if God is the very one who resists a home, and if Jesus Christ, for Christians, is the one who has no place to lay his head (Luke 9:58), there is a primacy of homelessness in the Christian tradition. The longing for a home, like anything else, can become idolatrous. Christianity, in many senses, is strange in that it recognizes not any one place in the world as the "home" of its religious life. (In this respect, it is different from Judaism's emphasis on the land of Israel and Jerusalem and Islam's focus on Mecca.) In the Christian sacred landscape, any place can become holy. There is not one primary sacred pilgrimage in Christianity (à la Mecca), but multiple pilgrimages and holy sites. There is not one ancestral home of the faith; that home is found whenever and wherever two or three are gathered in Jesus' name.

The God of the tabernacle and tent is a God on the move, resisting a home until all find a home.

> Thus says the LORD: Heaven is my throne and the earth is my footstool; what is the house that you would build for me, and what is my resting place?
>
> Isaiah 66:1

The Son of Man has no place to lay his head because he is always on the move, inviting others to follow him. And for those who take up that invitation, there is also the possibility that they will lose their sense of home and family in the process (Luke 14:26). This does not mean that home is not important; it means that home is not *ultimately* important, that there are times when one must leave home to find one's true home in the new life that God is offering right here, right now. The God of tabernacle is both a warning against our attempts to domesticate God and our tendency to become supremely content with our own homes, especially when others lack a place to call home.

Instead of acceding to David's desire to build a house for the Lord,

YHWH (via Nathan) reminds David of God's mighty deeds. This God has made David who he is, turning him from a shepherd who follows sheep into a prince who leads a people. YHWH is the one who has cut off Israel's enemies and who will make David's name great, "like the name of the great ones of the earth" (vv. 8-9). This phrase is interesting. If one of Israel's desires in wishing for a king was to become like the nations, this wish has now been granted in spades. YHWH, the one whose name cannot be spoken, will make David's name known far and wide. From God's earlier disavowal of a home, however, there appears a slight shift. After speaking of David's name, God speaks of "a place for my people Israel" where "they may be disturbed no more" (v. 10). The referent here is fluid. This "place" may refer to the land that Israel has already been inhabiting, with Jerusalem as its capital. If so, YHWH's words here are the confirmation of the mighty acts already enumerated. But this "place" may also refer to a permanent place of worship, the house that YHWH had seemingly disavowed earlier. If this is the case, the subsequently mentioned "evildoers," who will no longer afflict Israel, may refer to corrupt priests. But these evildoers may also refer more generally to the enemies that surround Israel, those from whom God will give David rest. In either case, however, the "home" where God plants Israel and YHWH's "home" are tightly interwoven. Nathan's speech to David then makes another reversal. This king, who seeks to build the Lord a house, instead finds himself the recipient of a house built by the living God. There is a double-referent here: God will preserve and protect both the physical space that David now occupies and the people of David's family. New life will come out of David's death as God promises abundant offspring (vv. 11–12).

The oracle then turns to one of the most stunning affirmations in all of Scripture: the establishment of the house for God's name and the kingdom of David "forever" (v. 13). David's offspring will build the house that David desires for the ark, a house not to confine but to revere God's name. Here is a subtle reversal of God's earlier disclaimer against a house. But even more astonishing is this notion of "forever" in relation to David's house. Readers have heard an intimation of this before, in the rejection of Saul, as the kingdom is torn from him and given to another (1 Sam. 15:28). But here God is making an irrevocable promise: that the kingdom will not be taken away from David or his heirs. On one level, this is a political state-ment that identifies the house of David with the nation Israel. We know, of course, that this kingdom does not endure over time or even for very long. Israel becomes divided, kings fall as the land is occupied by a succession of foreign powers, and eventually there is diaspora, persecution, and the Holocaust. The promise of "forever" seems to fly in the face of the brutal facts of Jewish history. The Chris-tian church has tended to spiritualize the rather concrete promises made here, claiming that the kingdom God promises is a spiritual one that is consummated in Jesus Christ, who is of the house and lineage of David. The kingdom of Christ, in this view, is not of this world. But the Christian read of this promise can become over-spiritualized and betray the deep incarnationalism of both Chris-tian and Jewish traditions: that God makes specific promises to people of this world, in this world right here, right now. The most stunning dimension of this promise is that God will be with God's people, no matter what: that God will not abandon or turn God's back on God's anointed. This is a radical statement about the kind of God that YHWH is: a God who binds God's very self to God's people forever, and that means that the people will endure, what-ever comes. The statement is both a claim about a covenant-making God and the tenacity of a people. Indeed, it shows that a people's tenacity arises out of God's faithfulness. This is why the analogy of father to son is so appropriate (v. 14), for the closest thing that we have in our human experience to the kinds of ties that are promised here are the bonds of family. Our parents are always our parents, no matter what we or they do; our children are our children, no matter what we or they do. If Jesus is heralded as the one who called God "Abba," or "father," this name and this claim have deep roots within Israel's tradition. The king will be a son to God, who will experience punishment when he commits sin. But nothing will take away God's steadfast love. No more will a blessing be lost (vv. 14–17). It could hardly be clearer. No greater promise can be made.

How can one respond to such astonishing claims? After hearing Nathan's oracle, David goes in and sits "before the LORD" (v. 18), indicating that he is alone in the tent and the presence of the ark.

David is near YHWH in a way that fringes on danger. Touching the ark can lead to death (6:7); no one can behold the face of God and live (Exod 33:20). At this time in Israel's history, sitting is not the customary position for prayer.[16] Thus, the scene portrays an intimacy between David and God that is almost without parallel in Scripture. David's response to the oracle is humility. His question to God suggests that he has not deserved any blessing or promise. On the heels of the most astonishing promise, David directs attention not to himself, but to the living God, and considers the great thing that has happened to him and his house as a "small thing" in God's eyes. This small thing, moreover, is according to God's own heart, the one who is like no other (vv. 19–22).

> **Wonder of wonders, here revealed: / God's covenant with us is sealed, / and long before we know or pray, / God's love enfolds us every day.**
>
> Jane Parker Huber, "Wonder of Wonders, Here Revealed," in *Glory to God* (Louisville, KY: Westminster John Knox Press, 2013), #489.

David then turns his praise from God's actions toward his house to God's election of Israel, expanding and amplifying his prayer. What is happening with the house of David has already been witnessed in God's unique behavior toward Israel. David's prayer here is classic salvation history, enumerating the mighty deeds of God: covenanting with a people, driving out enemies, adopting a people as God's own. In prayer, David presents himself as YHWH's servant, asking God to confirm God's promises, desiring that God's name be magnified forever (vv. 23–26). The word "forever" echoes throughout this chapter, occurring three times in Nathan's oracle and five times in David's prayer. It is tempting to consider such language hyperbolic, especially when experience teaches us that nothing lasts forever. But David's prayer is not pious hyperbole; it is not the prayer of a person confident in the righteous endurance of his nation; it is not even a testament to a nation with a "divine purpose." These kinds of prayers are often voiced on political stages. As citizens of the superpower of the age, Americans have been prone to see their material blessings and economic prowess as a sign of God's favor.

---

16. P. Kyle McCarter Jr., "2 Samuel," textual notes in *The HarperCollins Study Bible*, ed. Wayne A. Meeks (New York: HarperCollins, 1993), 478.

American exceptionalism became a prominent chord in the 2012 American presidential campaign: that we are a unique nation on earth, entrusted with a sacred mission that God will reward. But such prayers move in the opposite trajectory of David's prayer. God's election of Israel does not stem from something that Israel has done, earned, or even needs to prove. David's prayer does not assume God's blessing but asks for it. It begins not with the confidence that David's house or the nation is on God's side but in humility asks "Who am I?" and "What is my house?" The prayer, furthermore, expresses confidence not in the nation, but confidence in God, whose "words are true" (v. 28), who will continue to bless. Only with that blessing can anything endure. The "forever" that is spoken here is a mark, first and foremost, of God's faithfulness, which will not disappear, whatever may come.

8:1–14

Military Ventures

The narrative moves rather swiftly from devotional praise to the cold, hard realities of military campaigns. Indeed, this shift demonstrates two prongs of David's complex personality. He is the humble servant of YHWH, who attributes all that he has gained to God *and* the imposing commander of a conquering army. He seems equally at home in the tent housing the ark and on the battlefield. Indeed, in either location, he is never far from God's presence. In this section, David expands Israel's footprint, but first he must deal with the ever-present Philistines. David subdues them (v. 1) and they will not resurface until the end of his reign (21:15–17). David thus proves himself superior to Saul in dealing with this ubiquitous foe.

David's skirmish with the Moabites, however, is more perplexing, since David's parents found refuge in Moab during David's time in the wilderness (1 Sam. 22:3–4). It is not clear why David would go to war with a people whose king had provided hospitality for David's family. Perhaps the only explanation is that this is a king with empire on his mind. Wijk-Bos remarks, "For the first time, battles are not fought on a defensive or semi-defensive basis, or because of provocation on the part of an enemy. At this turn David, as a king who is also a military leader, wages battles of aggression and expansion."[17] What is even more haunting about this war with Moab is the random, even sadistic nature of the violence. As David forces the vanquished to lie down and measures off lengths of a cord to determine who will live and who will die (v. 2), we recall the grim "death-camp selections under the Nazi regime."[18] As those who once showed David hospitality now come to him bearing tribute, the portrait of the new king becomes increasingly violent.

The events of verses 3–14 occur oddly at this point in the narrative. Many have suggested that this material belongs chronologically at the conclusion to chapter 10, which narrates David's war with the Arameans. The change in location is abrupt, far to the north, even to the river Euphrates. In striking down King Hadadezer of Zobah, David conquers territory in modern-day Syria. The reference to the "monument" at the river Euphrates (v. 3) is ambiguous: it could refer to Hadadezer's monument or to David's. If it is the latter, then David falls in line with his predecessor on the throne (cf. 1 Sam. 15:12). In short order, David has become a king to be reckoned with, even when far from Jerusalem. David captures a great number of Hadadezer's troops, hamstrings his horses, and defeats Arameans who come to the Zobahites' aid. The end result is Israelite troops in Damascus. David's kingdom is now taking on the appearance of an occupying foreign power. Other peoples are becoming servants to this king and paying tribute. And, in Deuteronomistic fashion, these advances are interpreted as coming from the hand of God. He returns to Jerusalem bearing trophies of his success: gold shields borne by his conquered leaders. With an increase in territory also comes an increase in wealth and symbolic tokens, most notably the large holdings of bronze that represent the latest military technology (vv. 4–8).

The king who conquers is also the king who makes strategic alliances. King Toi of Hamath, who had battled with Hadadezer, finds out about David's victories and sends his son to congratulate (and

---

17. Johanna W. H. van Wijk-Bos, *Reading Samuel: A Literary and Theological Commentary* (Macon, GA: Smyth & Helwys Publishing, Inc., 2011), 182.
18. Ibid., 184.

ingratiate himself to) David. In a classic example of how the enemy of my enemy becomes my friend, Toi showers David with gifts, further increasing the royal treasury. Joram, the name of Toi's son, is striking, meaning "YHWH is exalted." This name may be an honorific, representing the extent of Toi's loyalty to David. And, since no wars with Hamath occur during David's reign, Toi's gesture may have iced the deal between the two kings. As soldier and diplomat, David is a consummate success; on all sides of Judah, he expands Israel's territory (vv. 9–12).

This is the king who "won a name for himself" (v. 13). If God has given David the kingdom, the king has also shown himself ready to make decisive use of his powers. On the way home, the Israelites kill eighteen thousand Edomites and establish military stations in the land. If these military victories come from the Lord (v. 14), they also raise questions about this expanding empire. How will territorial growth affect David, the servant of YHWH? Will it compromise the people and the covenant in any way? Will the one who was anointed king become like the kings of the nations that surround Israel? What happens, in other words, when the benefits of the Lord's favor become greater than anything a people or a king have expected? What happens to the power that has accumulated? What happens when a people turns from being conquered to being the conqueror? These are age-old questions, borne out in the history of most nations and peoples. Here, at the height of a king's power, his political and military actions seem beyond reproach. But will it continue?

The wars conclude with a list of administrative servants. A growing empire requires delegation of responsibilities. David rules, according to the narrator, by administering "justice and equity to all his people" (v. 15), including, it would seem, the peoples whom David has conquered. David's appointment of servants in some way reflects the ideals of justice. Joab is named first, who commands the army. He has proven himself steadfastly loyal during David's exile. David's appointment of him reflects his high estimation of Joab despite his earlier reservations (2 Sam. 3:39). Or perhaps it reflects David's recognition that it is better to have Joab on his side than otherwise. David's appointment of two priests, Zadok and Ahimelech, is anomalous, since that role has previously been filled by one person. There is also textual discrepancy about "Ahimelech son of Abiathar" (v. 17) on two levels: first, because earlier in the narrative Abiathar is the *son* of Ahimelech (cf. 1 Sam. 22:20; 23:6; and 30:7); secondly, because later in the narrative *Abiathar* serves as David's priest (cf. 17:15). Finally, the indication that David's sons serve as priests is also puzzling, since David's family is not from the tribe of Levi. The mention of David's sons as priests may either be a later editorial addition that ascribes further honor to David's house or refer to a practice during David's reign that the priesthood was not restricted to Levites. The net effect of these appointments is a king amassing power, prestige, and favor with his own people, and even inviting loyalty from those far away. Nathan's oracle seems to have been fulfilled already.

9:1–13

David and Mephibosheth

The narrative now turns from the consolidation of power and land to David's act of personal obligation toward Jonathan's son, Mephibosheth. But the episode is not only personal, it is also political: in offering hospitality and honor to Mephibosheth, David also is reckoning with the house of Saul, the chief rival to the throne.

It begins with David's question of whether anyone is left of the house of Saul. David's question implies that he does not know whether there are any surviving heirs. But it also shows his intent to honor his covenant with Jonathan, "to show kindness for Jonathan's sake." Death does not break the covenant, and in some ways it intensifies it. David summons Ziba, a servant in the house of Saul. He will serve as an important ally to David during Absalom's revolt (16:1–4). Ziba's words to David offer a foreshadowing of that strategic presence: "At your service." David learns from Ziba of Mephibosheth, whose disability is mentioned again (vv. 1–3). Mephibosheth's condition seems to add to the responsibility that David promised Jonathan during their last meeting. It also contrasts with David's conquest of Jerusalem, where those who cannot walk experience a different fate (5:8–9). There, the blind and lame do not enter the house; here, the lame gets a place of honor at the table of the king. Such details portray some of the complexity of David: he both protects those on the margins and conquers the marginalized. Indeed, in David's behavior toward others, readers sense some of the grandeur and abjection of the human person, how the same person can both uplift and afflict their fellow human beings.

Mephibosheth resides in Lo-debar, a town in the Transjordan, the region of Saul's staunchest support (cf. 1 Sam. 10:27–11:11). He is residing in the house of Machir, a man who will also serve as an ally to David during Absalom's rebellion (17:27–28). In David's behavior toward Machir, Ziba, and Mephibosheth, we see how potential foes become strategic allies. David summons Mephibosheth, who upon arrival in the king's court proclaims his loyalty and obeisance (vv. 4–6). The encounter betrays some of Mephibosheth's fear, however, since David enjoins him not to be afraid. Such fear is easy to imagine, since Jonathan's son is standing before a man who fought against his grandfather. Again, David reiterates his desire to do kindness "for the sake of your father Jonathan" (v. 7). What is more, David promises to restore all of Saul's land to Mephibosheth and invites him to dine at David's table perpetually.

With these gestures David restores what had been lost to Saul's house and promises Mephibosheth security. But these gestures may not be magnanimous: David may simply want to keep this member of Saul's house close, under his watch. With self-deprecation, Mephibosheth compares himself to a "dead dog" (v. 8) but accepts David's gifts. If Mephibosheth's claim to the throne is somewhat remote, by presenting himself as David's servant he effectively relinquishes that claim.

> There is no such thing as "my" bread. All bread is ours and given to me, to others through me, and to me through others.
>
> Attributed to Meister Eckhart, quoted in Chrissy Post and Callista Brown, "A Foretaste of the Feast to Come," *Holden Village News* 41 (winter 2002): 14.

The episode concludes as David summons Ziba once again. Ziba, his sons, and his servants shall tend the land and reap the harvest, all in order that Mephibosheth shall "have food to eat," both from the bounty of the land and at the king's table. The promises are upheld on all sides; Ziba presents himself as

David's servant and Mephibosheth becomes like a son to David. The act of generosity and political astuteness, in effect, has widened the circle of family. It echoes a familiar theme throughout these chapters: family is not simply about blood but about the promises people make to one another. Yet the blood line of Saul also continues in Mephibosheth's son, Mica (v. 12). As the family circle expands, the old ties also remain. As David promised Saul, his name will not be wiped out from his father's house (1 Sam. 24:21–22). David remains true to his word by honoring this remnant of the old king, even to the point of including them in his own household and family in the royal city that David has established (vv. 9–13).

10:1–19

Aramean and Ammonite War

The story of Mephibosheth is sandwiched between two accounts of similar (or perhaps identical) descriptions of wars against Arameans. Making sense of the placement of this narrative is difficult. Most interpretations of this chapter place it chronologically before 8:3–14. In its present form, however, it sounds as if David engages in two wars with the Arameans: one ignited by their alliance with the Ammonites (chap. 10); another as David advances to increase his empire to the north (chap. 8). But 10:15–19 seem to narrate the same battle as chapter 8. Whatever the case chronologically, the narrative repetition of these battles adds drama to David's expansion of the kingdom.

The king of the Transjordan kingdom of Ammon has died. David speaks fondly of the deceased king, Nahash, though his claim that Nahash "dealt loyally with me" (v. 2) is surprising, since there is no prior reference to any alliance between David and Nahash. Readers know that the Ammonites were enemies of Saul and Israel, whom Saul defeated soundly (1 Sam. 10:27–11:15). Readers also know, subsequently, of a small act of assistance that Shobi son of Nahash provides David during the time of Absalom's rebellion (2 Sam. 17:27–29). It is hard to imagine a staunch enemy of Israel becoming allied with David (though it may have been possible during David's time as a fugitive).

Whatever the reasons for these words of homage, David decides to send envoys to Nahash's son, Hanun, to console and to pay tribute. Ammonite princes, however, receive David's words with skepticism, telling Hanun that David is sending spies. Hanun then humiliates the envoys by cutting their beards and cutting their clothes so that their legs and groins are exposed. The gesture is unmistakable: a ritual stripping of the visitors by cutting off their garments at mid-hip, removing facial hair and clothing so that they appear "naked" before all (v. 4). Hanun spurns David's gesture of sympathy and sends the messengers away naked and empty handed. Upon their return home, they are "greatly ashamed" (v. 5). The Ammonites take a page out of military psych-ops: to humiliate and dehumanize the opponent by removing what is most sacred on their body. Recalling the scandals of Abu Ghraib, we can understand the significance of these actions. There, too, American soldiers stripped and degraded the "enemy." Acts of sacrilege and desecration can often prove more destructive than combat or at least ignite more outrage. The more Westerners have become accustomed to hearing stories about Qur'an burnings, urination on corpses, or films that denigrate Muhammad, the more hatred these acts provoke in the Islamic world. We live amid the haunting aftereffects of actions not unlike the Ammonites' humiliation of David's emissaries. David, sensitive to his servants' condition, orders the emissaries to stay at Jericho (and not return to Jerusalem), until their beards have grown back.

The Ammonites know how their actions will be interpreted. The text uses strong language, that "they had become odious to David" (v. 6). Expecting some form of retaliation, the Ammonites forge a coalition with powers to the north: Arameans (in present-day Syria) as well as with the king of Maacah (northeast of the Sea of Galilee) and the inhabitants of Tob (southeast of the Sea of Galilee). A formidable army has now amassed against Israel. Joab, who will seemingly undertake anything for the king's sake, leads the Israelites into battle. The enemy has a strategy that, at first, seems unshakable. The Ammonites will remain at the gates of their city (most likely Rabbah), while the other armies will gather in the open country outside the city, which will surround Joab's troops as they approach Rabbah. Joab recognizes his peril, as the battle comes at him from the front and the rear. But he also reveals his acumen as a military strategist by dividing the army, so that both prongs can be engaged and each side can come to the assistance of the other, if needed (vv. 7–11). Joab's brother Abishai will command the other half of the divided troops. These sons of Zeruiah have already revealed their violent, impulsive ways. In the heat of battle it will serve them well. If David has expressed reservations about these loyal servants' behavior, Joab's words at the pivotal moment sound like they could have come from David's mouth: to be courageous for the sake of the people and the cities of God in order that the Lord "do what seems good to him" (v. 12). Joab exhorts the troops and reminds them to whom they belong, conveying a trust in YHWH that we have not yet adequately glimpsed in his character. No further details of the battle emerge other than the fleeing of each party: the Ammonites to the safety of their city, the Aramean coalition to the north. Joab does not capture territory at this point but returns to Jerusalem (vv. 13–14). Mission accomplished.

The sequel to this battle may be a repetition of 8:3–8. The Arameans regroup, gathering fellow tribespeople from the far north, beyond the Euphrates. These reassembled troops gather at Helam (a site unknown but which is ostensibly in the Transjordan, cf. v. 17). In this battle, unlike the skirmish outside Rabbah and like the battle narrated in chapter 8, David is directly involved as leader of the troops. Whereas the earlier battle does not result in the conquest of territory or the loyalty of peoples, this war produces substantial carnage, including forty thousand horsemen and the death of the Aramean commander, Shobach. The humiliation is total; the alternatives few for those who have been defeated. Again, the narrator makes sweeping statements: all the allied kings see the failure of their troops, make peace with Israel, and become subject to them (vv. 15–19). The ritual humiliation of David's servants has resulted in the military humiliation of the surrounding nations. David is not to be taken lightly. His wars result in an expansion of land, growing alliances, and subjection of peoples who stand against him. This is the closest the narrative comes to military hagiography. But if it is a form of hagiography, it is strange indeed, especially as it is succeeded by the most heinous abuse of royal power contained in the entire David cycle. If David is a hero on the battlefield, he fails in his personal life and tries to disguise his sin by orchestrating the death of one of his most loyal and capable soldiers.

11:1–13

David Seizes Bathsheba

Other than the story of David and Goliath, this episode may be the most widely known event in the entire span of 1 and 2 Samuel. It is full of contrasts: between a king at rest and his servants at war; between an Israelite king who transgresses the law rather flagrantly and a Hittite soldier who upholds the law beyond what might be expected of him; between a king who seizes whatever he wants and a woman who is the object of his seizing. The episode gives an indication of David at the height of his power, where power has gone to his head. And yet, when faced with the consequences of his own abuse of power, he initially appears powerless to cover up his offenses. The fact that this story has been preserved throughout history, furthermore, gives readers an indication of the understanding of kingship in Israel's tradition, for here we see David at his worst. As Israel remembers its kings, it does not construct unblemished biographies. If David is a hero in the history of Israel, he is a different kind of hero who succumbs to the depths of human behavior and tries to escape the consequences of that behavior, even to the point of denying it. The story, then, also displays the extent of David's power and his powerlessness, revealed in a singular tragic act that leads to even more horrific actions as he attempts to undo the results of his behavior.

The story begins by depicting a king who is becoming distant from his subjects, both in physical location and in ethos. It is spring, a time of new beginnings and fecundity. Thoughts wander in spring as layers of clothes come off: David is no exception. But David is safely at home, in his royal house, while his army is engaged in battle. Earlier in this narrative, David was commanding troops and distinguishing himself as a military leader. Now he has given those duties to his loyal servant Joab while David rests far from the battlefield.

The troops are engaging the Ammonites by besieging Rabbah (v. 1), which indicates that this story takes place during the battles narrated in the previous chapter. While the king's thoughts wander, his subjects risk their lives for his sake and for the sake of the people Israel.

Late in the afternoon the king rises from a nap and walks on his roof. The imagery here is purposefully luxurious: of someone who has sufficient leisure who, upon rising, surveys the royal city. And he sees something that entices him: a woman bathing, "the woman was very beautiful" (v. 2). The language is direct and unadorned. The king sees the woman, though there is no indication that she sees him. Exum notes how the narrator here controls our gaze akin to pornography: "A woman is touching herself and a man is watching. The viewing is one-sided, giving him the advantage and the position of power. . . . And if Bathsheba is purifying herself after her menstrual period, we can guess where she is touching. Readers of this text are watching a man watching a woman touch herself."[19] Aroused by what he sees, the king wants her at once. But before he can carry out his desire, he inquires about the woman. To find out who she is, David must delegate. The language here is evocative of kingly power: the person who finds out about the woman does not have a name but is simply another servant of the king. The king "sends" this person, a verb that repeats itself over and again in this episode. David is the one who sends others; they obey, and he gets what he wants, whether it is information or another human being. The picture is of a king who objectifies others, both the objects of his desire (Bathsheba) and the subjects who are at his command. The king finds out (note the passive voice, "It was reported," v. 3) the woman has a name, a heritage, and a husband: Bathsheba, daughter of Eliam, wife of Uriah the Hittite. Uriah's identity as a Hittite is critical here, either denoting his status as a resident alien who serves in David's army or designating him as an Israelite who is descended from Hittites. Marking him as a Hittite may imply some degree of distance from the law and covenant, even if he is David's loyal servant. There is

19. Exum, *Fragmented Women*, 174–75. The sexual objectification of Bathsheba has continued throughout history. Given the voyeurism that inaugurates the story, Exum remarks "it is little wonder Bathsheba has become the quintessential object of the gaze in literature and art through the ages. Her 'punishment' for being desired is to be forever visualized as the sensual woman who enflames male lust." Ibid., 195.

further critical information conveyed in these words to the king: the object of David's desire, Bathsheba, is married to one of the king's trusted, elite military warriors (23:39). Uriah is no ordinary subject but comes from a close circle of David's protectors.

The critical information does nothing to dampen David's desires. Unrelentingly, he seizes the woman who has become an object to him. There is no seduction here, no romance, no reciprocity between man and woman. The entire "affair" (and that is a dubious word to use in this case) is carried out bluntly, forcefully, with David as the subject of the action. He sends messengers "to get her," Bathsheba comes, and David lays with her (v. 4). There is no lingering or afterglow, just a king who summons a subject who has no choice but to obey and submit to the king's desire. The language that conveys the episode is more akin to rape than seduction.

> The same body that connects us with spouse and child can be reduced in a moment to the object of another's cruelties.
>
> Stephanie Paulsell, *Honoring the Body* (San Francisco: Jossey-Bass, 2002), 22.

Gerald West, in a study of Southern African women's reception of 1 and 2 Samuel, remarks, "Although there is considerable scholarly debate about whether Bathsheba was raped by David, with some scholars arguing that there are indications in the text that Bathsheba was a willing participant, most African women readers are adamant—Bathsheba was raped. David is the subject of the verbs in 11:1–4. . . . Bathsheba is the object here."[20] The king wants this woman and gets what he wants by seizing her, first through delegates and then with his own hands. After it has happened, Bathsheba does the only thing she can do: return home. The narrator adds further detail to the story by indicating that Bathsheba was "purifying herself after her period" (v. 4), indicating her fertility. But if David is the one who is the subject of the verbs that narrate the seizing of Bathsheba, Bathsheba becomes the subject of the consequences: she conceives and sends word to the king that she is pregnant (v. 5). Faced with an ignominious condition (becoming

---

20. Gerald West, "1 and 2 Samuel," in *Global Bible Commentary,* ed. Daniel Patte (Nashville: Abingdon, 2004), 95.

pregnant while her husband is away fighting a war), Bathsheba is the agent whose words compel the king to do something.

David acts, again, as a king at the height of his power by sending for a servant: Joab, his right hand commander, who is to send for Uriah and bring him before the king. (Note again how adept and accustomed David is to "sending" for others.) The ostensible reason for this summons is for the king to hear about the course of the war. Then, in a suggestion that both betrays David's defiance of the law and his own distance from those who are fighting on his behalf, he tells Uriah to go down to his house and wash his feet, a euphemism for having sex with Bathsheba. The suggestion is doubly offensive from Uriah's perspective: it violates the command for soldiers to refrain from sexual intercourse during battle (cf. Deut. 23:9–14), and it places Uriah outside solidarity with his fellow soldiers. (How can Uriah indulge himself when his comrades are restraining themselves?) In direct rejection of the king's command and as a symbol of his own uprightness regarding the law, Uriah refuses to enter his house and instead sleeps at the entrance of David's (vv. 6–9). The implication of the story is clear: a Hittite is stronger in upholding the law than the king of Israel. The one who is seemingly less bound to the law, indeed, shows greater adherence than the one who is to be the example to all Israel. The judgment is obvious: the king has been revealed for who he is by one who is an "outsider" to the covenant. David finds out that Uriah has not followed through on his suggestion/command and tries to cajole his servant again, claiming that Uriah needs to rest after a journey. The suggestion is for Uriah to become more like David: one who rests while others labor and risk their lives for his behalf. This time, however, Uriah resists the king's words in speech: he cannot eat and drink and lie with his wife while the ark is in a booth and the servants of the king are camping in the open. Embedded in these remarks is criticism of the king's isolation from his army and the lack of a house for the ark. Again, the Hittite is more pious than the Israelite king. Finally, in desperation, David tries to get Uriah drunk, thinking that he will surely renege on his piety in a compromised state (vv. 10–13). But again the ploy fails. Even when drunk, Uriah outperforms the king in piety and purity.

11:14–27
David Orders Uriah Killed

Sin, according, to many theologians in the Reformed tradition, twists the soul so much that it becomes unable to distinguish good from evil. The Second Helvetic Confession describes sin as "that innate corruption of man . . . by which we, immersed in perverse desires and averse to all good, are inclined to all evil. Full of all wickedness, distrust, contempt and hatred of God, we are unable to do or even to think anything good of ourselves."[21] The more we incline away from God, the more we become accustomed to it. Sin provides its own conditioning: we become used to it and trapped within it, even when we try to escape from it. Seeking to remedy what we have done, we can wind up even more mired in the morass. This is precisely what happens in David's case, where in an attempt to cover up his action, he kills an innocent person.

After David's cover-up fails, he composes a letter to Joab and sends it by Uriah's hand. David knows his servant's loyalty: he knows Joab will follow whatever order David gives, and he knows that Uriah will not look at a letter composed for another person. By sending a letter to Joab via Uriah, moreover, David has Uriah carry his own death warrant. The letter to Joab is direct; it does not disguise the king's murderous intent: place Uriah where the fighting is heaviest and then draw back from him "so that he may be struck down and die" (v. 15). It is not only foolish military strategy but also an unmerited death sentence. Leaders throughout history have required right-hand men like Joab, willing to carry out reprehensible commands that allow leaders to keep their hands unsullied.

> Sin is a very cruel and powerful tyrant over all men throughout the world, a tyrant who cannot be overthrown and expelled by the power of any creatures, whether angels or men.
>
> Martin Luther, *Lectures on Galatians, Chapters 1–4, Luther's Works*, vol. 26, ed. Jaroslav Pelikan (St. Louis: Concordia, 1963), 33.

---

21. The Second Helvetic Confession, in *Constitution of the Presbyterian Church (U.S.A.)*, Part I, *Book of Confessions*, (Louisville, KY: Office of the General Assembly, Presbyterian Church (U.S.A.), 1996), 5.037.

Reagan had Oliver North; Obama has remote pilots of drone aircraft in Pakistan. They carry out commands unquestioningly, giving credit to the king and taking blame when plans fail miserably. Joab carries out the king's command. The battle is narrated tersely, but the objective is accomplished: Uriah is dead (vv. 16–17).

If Joab executes the king's command without question, his return message to David conveys distance and judgment. Joab sends a messenger to report on news from the front lines. His instructions to this messenger are elaborate: after reporting news of the battle, if the king's anger is kindled, and if he recalls the death of Abimelech (Judg. 9:50–55), then the messenger should report Uriah's death as well (vv. 19–21). But if Joab's means of presenting this information to the messenger is roundabout, the intent is clear: David simply wants to know if Uriah is dead. Indeed, the messenger can see through this rather elaborate ruse. Instead of waiting for the king's anger or his question, he simply reports on the battle and Uriah's death, saving the crucial detail for last (vv. 22–24). By reporting the matter to the king in this way, the messenger also reveals his own judgment on the king, and the king cannot claim innocence or ignorance.

Instead, David sends the messenger back to Joab with words of hollow absolution: "Do not let this matter trouble you" (v. 25). These words, of course, are a lie. The deed has troubled Joab, and it will trouble David for the rest of his life. They are connected not only to the rape of an innocent woman and the death of an innocent man but also to a subsequent rape in David's household, rebellion in the ranks of his family, and a loss of power and honor. The words that David sends back to Joab are not so much an absolution, but further evidence of one transgression leading to others. Without pious condescension, the narrator makes one thing clear: David is guilty of murder.

Bathsheba provides narrative closure to this haunting episode. Faced with indescribable loss, she laments Uriah's death. When her period of mourning is over, David undertakes his duty to become the husband to the woman who bears his child. Again, David "sends" and "brings" Bathsheba to his house. If this entire saga is filled with judgment against the king, it also bears traces of hope: Bathsheba will eventually give birth to Solomon, who will build YHWH a house. Even in desperation and loss, there are traces of divine redemption, reminders that no place is ever devoid of hope. But the blessings of that future child are yet to come. The final word at this point is stark judgment in words rare for the Deuteronomist: "But the thing that David had done displeased the LORD" (v. 27). Other translations make it even more emphatic: what David did was evil in God's sight. The aftereffects of this evil, moreover, will haunt David and his house for a long time.

12:1–15a
Nathan Admonishes David

David's actions have not gone unnoticed. In this section, readers learn how YHWH and YHWH's prophet, Nathan, call David to take responsibility for the evil he has committed. The episode offers a further window on the unique relationship between the king and the prophet. As this narrative shows, David listens even more closely when the words Nathan utters are painful ones for the king. This relatively short interchange between the two men contains words of condemnation as well as hope, judgment as well as grace, death as well as life. It is hard to overestimate their significance. Polzin describes this section as "the hermeneutic center of the entire royal history,"[22] the fulfillment of the Deuteronomist's warning about kingship. They further illustrate the extent to which David stands under authorities and promises much larger than himself, even when he is prone to ignore them.

If David has been the one who "sends" in the previous chapter, here YHWH sends Nathan to the king. In the king's presence, Nathan speaks the first word: a parable, which offers a contrast between a rich and a poor man. Often the story of David and Bathsheba gets interpreted as a sexual story of uncontrollable lust. But at a deeper level, as Nathan's parable makes clear, it is about the greed of a wealthy man whose covetousness cannot be stopped, who grabs whatever he can. What makes the story of David and Bathsheba so

22. Polzin, *David*, 120.

unforgettable is that it combines greed, power, and sex in a toxic mix. The story that Nathan tells, therefore, is a story also about class and the abuse of power. The rich man has many flocks; the poor man has only one lamb whom he cherishes as a daughter. When the rich man entertains a traveler, he takes not one of his flock but the only lamb the poor man has (vv. 1–4). The recurrence of the verb "take" recalls Samuel's earlier warning against kingship (1 Sam. 8:11–18), where Israel is warned that its kings will take sons, daughters, fields, vineyards, cattle, and flocks. In Nathan's story the rich man is insatiable; his greed causes him to take from the poor. He is an apt personification of the cardinal sin of avarice, which winds up consuming the person trapped in greed. Dante's description of hell contains this remark about souls consumed by avarice: "Not all the gold beneath the moon's bright face, or that ever was, could bring rest to as much as one of the weary spirits in this place."[23] In the end, nothing can satisfy greed.

David is outraged by Nathan's story. His words are swift, driven by righteous indignation: the man deserves to die and should restore what he has stolen fourfold (vv. 5–6). His reaction illustrates how much easier it is to diagnose sickness in someone other than oneself, to be able to see the speck in someone else's eye rather than the log in one's own (Matt. 7:3–5). David is unaware that he is pronouncing judgment upon himself until Nathan makes his own declaration: "You are the man!" (v. 7). The meaning of his statement is multivalent. Polzin notes,

> When Nathan says to David, "You are *the man* (of my story)," he means many things at once: David *was* the wayfarer, "the one who comes," insofar as his past dealings with God are concerned (12:7–8); he *is* the rich man when his present crimes are brought into the picture (12:9–10); and he *will be* the poor man when God's punishing future for him and his house arrives (12:11–12).[24]

Here is a subject of the king admonishing the king, effectively agreeing with the king's pronouncement of his own death sentence.

---

23. Dante Alighieri, *Inferno*, trans. Michael Palma (New York: W. W. Norton & Company, 2002), 75.
24. Polzin, *David*, 126.

Here is not a portrait of royal power run amok but of royal power that permits itself to be chastened and corrected. And Nathan says more. Before David ever responds, Nathan enumerates God's consistent acts of graciousness toward David. YHWH has anointed, rescued, and given David a house and wives. And God would have given David even more (v. 8). Some textual issues emerge here, such as Nathan's claim that God has given David his "master's wives," indicating that David marries the spouses of Saul. Other than a possible identity between David's wife Ahinoam and Saul's wife of the same name, however, there is no textual evidence in the cycle of David stories for such a claim. Nathan's message to David, however, is clear: YHWH has made the king what he is, and in response the king has "despised the word of the Lord, to do what is evil in his sight." In response to YHWH's ceaseless generosity to David, David has chosen to take what has not been given to him. He has spurned God's gift by stealing from one who has comparatively little. If David thought he was disguising murder, Nathan sees it for what it is: "You have struck down Uriah the Hittite with the sword" (v. 9). Because David has spurned God's gifts and violently seized what does not belong to him, he can expect violence and division in his own house. If David has "taken" what does not belong to him, God, too, will take away David's wives: not in secret as David has done, but before all Israel (vv. 10–11). Nathan's words to the king are direct, but there is a striking absence in them. As Exum notes, Nathan interprets David's crime as being against God and against Uriah, but "they are not treated as crimes against Bathsheba, who is defined solely in terms of her relation to Uriah."[25] Even in this word of judgment, the woman's perspective disappears.

These are incriminating words. It is easy to imagine someone justifying themselves in the face of them: defending their actions as misunderstood or inevitable. But David accepts them and takes responsibility for his actions. His words to Nathan are honest and succinct: "I have sinned against the LORD" (v. 13). There is no evasion here, only a simple and direct accounting of one's own guilt. David has sinned against God and neighbor. The nature of his words,

25. Exum, *Fragmented Women*, 184.

of course, raises questions about the practice of confession. Several things are noteworthy here: First, David speaks without embellishment. His words do not attempt to describe why he acted in the way he did; they simply admit his sin. Secondly, David's confession occurs in the presence of another person, adding a public dimension to his words. Though confessing one's sin alone before God has a place of honor and integrity in the church's history, there is something about owning up to our sin in the company of another that calls us to greater accountability. In an age where talk is cheap (whether in the form of advertising jingles or political promises), laying bare one's sin in the company of another can spur us to accept responsibility for our behavior and ask for assistance (from God and others) in turning away from sin. Allan Cole writes, "Confession made to other Christians fosters the breakthrough of learning to accept responsibility for our transgressions more readily by strengthening our resolve to go forward living differently than before—that is, in a different relationship to the sin or burden."[26] Confession without some public dimension risks becoming cheap words that no one else hears.

Nathan meets David's succinct confession with words of absolution: "Now the Lord has put away your sin; you shall not die" (v. 13). He pronounces words of grace to David, God's beloved. These words point to the hope of transformation, even in the midst of the most violent and tragic instance recorded in David's life. But David's actions will also bear consequences that he cannot stop. Death, when it is orchestrated, can redound to further destruction and loss. Nathan claims that the child born to Bathsheba will die. Is this divine "punishment," returning the tit of David's sin with the tat of taking away life from David's family? Or is it further testimony of the insidious scope of sin, of how it gives

> If we say that we have no sin, we deceive ourselves, and the truth is not in us. If we confess our sins, he who is faithful and just will forgive us our sins and cleanse us from all unrighteousness.
>
> 1 John 1:8–9

---

26. Allan Hugh Cole Jr., "The Need to Confess," *Insights: The Faculty Journal of Austin Seminary* 125, no. 2 (Spring 2010): 8.

birth to unanticipated consequences. Violence begets more violence when there is no practice of forgiveness or reconciliation. Greed tends toward more rapacious acts of greed when devoid of accountability or confession. When David orders others killed, death redounds on other sides, eventually enveloping his own household. The words are enough. The consequences of David's behavior are real. The prophet goes home, leaving David to further consider the consequences of his own actions (vv. 14–15). If David is contrite, his piety does not exempt him from the tragedy that is yet to come.

12:15b–23
The Death of a Child

Losing a child is a parent's worst nightmare. Each child's death reneges the future, ripping a hole in a parent's life, leaving a hollowness that cannot be filled. Nicholas Wolterstorff, reflecting on his own son's death, writes: "It's the *neverness* that is so painful. *Never again* to be here with us—never to sit with us at table, never to travel with us, never to laugh with us, never to cry with us, never to embrace us as he leaves for school, never to see his brothers and sister marry. All the rest of our lives we must live without him. Only our death can stop the pain of his death."[27] The child in this episode, perhaps as testament to the life that is lost and the future that will not be, does not have a name. The narrator does not even identify the child's gender, though David subsequently refers to the child as "he," indicating a son. Something about this death compromises the future, even to the point that the child's name is lost to history. In its mission statement, Manchester University, a school affiliated with the Church of the Brethren, "respects the infinite worth of every individual,"[28] attesting to each life as given by God, entrusted to God. Something about a person's infinite worth is conveyed in this story and the unspeakable loss of a child's untimely death.

God acts directly in this episode, striking David's child with

---

27. Nicholas Wolterstorff, *Lament for a Son* (Grand Rapids: Eerdmans, 1987), 15.
28. http://www.manchester.edu/Common/AboutManchester/Mission.htm.

illness. Bathsheba is still identified as Uriah's wife, even though she and David are now married. If there was any hint that the judgment against David has subsided, that is dispelled. David is still named as someone who has taken another's wife. But the narrator, intriguingly, does not identify the child's illness as David's "punishment." History, for the Deuteronomist, has meaning and purpose because it is directly connected to God's will and purpose. Even this tragic illness is connected mysteriously to God's providence. David, however, does not blithely accept what has occurred as God's will. Instead, he tries to influence and affect the course of events, displaying piety and desperation. He pleads with God for the child, fasts, and lies "all night on the ground," indicating a posture of genuflection and self-abasement (v. 16). His mourning and pleading run against the advice of his elders, who urge him to rise and eat. But what parent cannot understand his actions? What parent would not utter protest or try anything to see a child live? What is comprehensible to parents seems excessive in the eyes of the elders. Indeed, they are afraid to tell David the news that his son has died. They are concerned about his stability and emotional state, worried that the king may hurt himself. If parents can understand this father's pleas, there is also a sense that his pleas are all out of proportion. David seems to have forgotten everything; for him there is nothing other than him and his ill son. Grief can isolate those who grieve. We can become so consumed by it that we are unable to receive others' gestures of empathy and comfort: In grief and despondence we can even become dangers to ourselves. If the elders seek to protect David by not telling him the news, their whispers give the news away: the child is dead (vv. 17–19).

The narrative raises several questions. Is David's pleading an instance of genuine piety or piety run amok? On the one hand, David's capacity to grieve is a witness to a parent's capacity for love. Grief is most anguished for those we love the most intensely. To love is to become vulnerable and to open oneself up to loss, a loss that David experiences rather acutely. On the other hand, David's lamentation isolates him from the elders and from Bathsheba (whose voice is not heard in this episode). David is alone in his grief and seems to have lost himself. John Chrysostom claims that David became "stupefied with that affliction."[29] His pleading, moreover, may also be construed as an attempt to change something that cannot be changed. Nathan had previously informed him of the loss of his child (v. 13), which David brought on himself when he seized Bathsheba and ordered Uriah to be killed. His lamentation, in the most jaundiced light, may also be one last desperate attempt to undo his sin and avoid responsibility for it. Perhaps the fairest interpretation of his behavior in this story is that it contains a mixture of all these elements: a parent's desperation and an unwillingness to face the consequences of one's behavior, as well as the intensity of parental love and an earnest plea for God to rescue one's child. David both accepts what God brings about and wrestles with it. His piety is struggle and his struggle is piety.

The episode also causes the reader to ask about the efficacy of prayer. For, if David prays for his son's deliverance from illness, that prayer fails. Again, there are no easy answers here. The efficacy of prayer, at least according to this narrative, does not correspond to the intensity of effort. Indeed, it is hard to imagine prayers more intense and focused than David's. The broad scope of 1 and 2 Samuel offers examples of answered prayers (such as Hannah's) and anguished entreaties that go unanswered. God, however, is present in both of them, in the anguish and the answer; in the resolution and the silence. People who pray can both express thanksgiving and God-forsakenness. Indeed, Jesus' last earthly prayer, according to Mark, reflects the latter more than the former: "My God, my God, why have you forsaken me?" (Mark 15:34). Success stories do not make for a faithful life of prayer; instead, the struggle of prayer marks the course of a faithful life. C. S. Lewis reflects on grief and unanswered prayer: "Where is God? . . . Go to Him when your need is desperate, when all other help is in vain, and what do you find? A door slammed in your face, and a sound of bolting and double bolting on the inside. After that, silence. You may as well turn away. The longer you wait, the more emphatic the silence will

29. John Chrysostom, "Homilies on 2 Corinthians 4:6," in John R. Franke, ed., *Ancient Christian Commentary on Scripture. Old Testament IV: Joshua, Judges, Ruth, 1–2 Samuel* (Downers Grove, IL: InterVarsity, 2005), 365.

become."[30] In David, there is both struggle with God's silence and acceptance of God's will.

After David hears the news, he rises from the ground, washes, anoints, and prepares for worship. There is a textual anachronism here suggesting that David goes into the house of the Lord (v. 20) when the temple has not yet been built. After he worships, he eats. The most intense mourning, one would expect, would occur after one's child has died, once the loss is final. David reverses standard behavior here: mourning before death, praising God afterward. The story has evoked multiple responses. Ambrose says we should emulate it: "David wept for his son who was about to die; he did not grieve for him when dead. He wept that he might not be snatched from him, but he ceased to weep when he was snatched away, for he knew that he was with Christ."[31] Johanna van Wijk-Bos finds in David's unexpected behavior a king who "faces his own mortality through the death of a child and speaks of it in a bleakly realistic tone, stripped of all deception and blandishments. For the moment, the deceitful, violent, manipulative David has disappeared."[32] On the one hand, David seems to be finally accepting the extent of his actions. His praise of God is testament to his trust in YHWH. He is past arguing with God over his past actions and their consequences. But on the other hand, there is something of grief that is truncated here, of "moving on" in the recognition that he cannot bring his son back again (v. 23). Psychologists inform us that there are stages of grief. David seems to have moved through them rather quickly, bypassing necessary stages in coming to grips with catastrophic loss. But even in this possible denial of grief's stages, he does voice a hope: that he shall "go to him." This is a difficult text to decipher, but it bears witness to a relationship that is not severed even in death. It is, perhaps, what every parent hopes for: a love as strong as death, so that not even death will make a loved one lost forever. Even here, amid the most agonizing loss a parent can imagine, death does not hold the final word.

30. C. S. Lewis, *A Grief Observed* (New York: Seabury, 1961), 9.
31. Ambrose, "Consolation on the Death of Emperor Valentinian," in *Ancient Christian Commentary*, ed. John R. Franke (Downers Grove, IL: InterVarsity Press, 2005), 367.
32. Wijk-Bos, *Reading Samuel*, 199.

12:24–25
Solomon's Birth

If David's lament has cut him off from others, his praise of God now directs his attention to others. He consoles Bathsheba, who has been experiencing the tragedy as acutely as David, if not more than him. David's shift here from a person struggling with God, trying to undo his prior deeds, to one accepting the consequences of his actions brings comfort to the afflicted. There is death that cannot be denied, but out of this death, God also brings new life. Bathsheba bears a son, Solomon (meaning "his replacement"), who will be the heir to David's throne. The one whose kingdom will outshine even his father's comes from the marriage that begins with a rape and leads to murder, and eventually the loss of a child. Nothing here is beyond hope, and the result of hope sometimes is more bounteous than could be imagined.

> When we teach our children to be good, to be gentle, to be forgiving (all these are attributes of God), to be generous, to love their fellow men, to regard this present age as nothing, we instill virtue in their souls, and reveal the image of God within them.
>
> John Chrysostom, *On Marriage and Family Life*, trans. Catherine P. Roth and David Anderson (Crestwood, NY: St. Vladimir's Seminary Press, 1986), 44.

YHWH is also partial toward this son, who is also named Jedidiah ("beloved of the Lord"), a name that is found nowhere else in Scripture. A new chapter is about to begin, one that brings even greater tragedy and tumult to the house of David, but it is preceded by the birth of a child who heralds the hope of a king and the hopes of a people.

12:26–31
War against the Ammonites Continues

David's sin and its aftereffects take place against the backdrop of war against the Ammonites, as narrated in chapters 10–11. The narrative resumes here as it describes the resolution to these skirmishes.

Joab acts decisively, attacking the city of Rabbah and sending word to David of his progress. Joab uses his siege of the royal city to his advantage: His message to David is an assertion of his own power and rings as a disguised threat: send more people to assist or I will name the city for myself (vv. 26–28). Joab has already proved himself indispensable to David's kingdom: he is loyal, he does what he is told by the king, and his military campaigns have succeeded almost without exception. David needs Joab to strengthen his hand, and Joab knows it. Joab's words to the king resemble Pentagon demands. It is rare that the military asks for less than it is provided; more, the assumption goes, is always better. In this exchange between Joab and David, readers sense the delicate balance between civilian and military rule and how it teeters out of balance at times. Here, Joab is ordering the king rather than the other way around.

David accedes to Joab's demand: he gathers "all the people together," goes to Rabbah, and seizes it (v. 29). David has now become the primary actor, even if he is following Joab's command. If Joab is exerting power behind the scenes, David again acts as king. As he captures the city, David takes the crown of Milcom, an enormous crown most likely used to adorn a statue of the Ammonite god (cf. 1 Kgs. 11:5, 33). By placing it on his head, David vanquishes enemies and exposes the foreign deity as powerless. But it is also the first treasure in the great spoil of the city that Israel now claims. In a final act of victory, David takes the Ammonite people and puts them to work with picks and saws and axes (vv. 30–31). Israel, who remembers its own enslavement in Egypt, now enslaves others. The reach of the kingdom is now at a high point: lands far to the north and the east now fall under David's rule. The army is formidable. A royal city gleams. Foreign powers have made alliances with the new king. David, even in his transgression, is at the height of his power, even if he must contend with a military leader who knows how indispensable he is. If God has expressed anger at the evil David has committed, this does not renege God's promise to David: that his kingdom shall last forever. At both high and low points, David remains God's beloved. But if God's promises to David abide, there is much trouble within David's own house. Those troubles will occupy the next several chapters of Israel's story.

2 Samuel 13:1-20:22

Revolt and Restoration

Just as David's consolidation of the kingdom seems complete, the walls of his own house start to crumble. What begins as unrest within his family, moreover, spills out into the affairs of the nation. It begins with the unspeakable, horrific crime of a son raping his half-sister. The crime leads to bloodshed, and eventually David's son Absalom's seizure of the kingdom. The boundaries between the personal and the political become blurred: there are no rigid distinctions between a private family matter and an issue of vital public importance. David's inability to negotiate the tense, conflicted, and violent elements of his own household, moreover, translates into his inability to lead Israel effectively. Rebellion and revolt are the tragic result, with his own son offering an alternative to what he perceives as his father's failed leadership.

The events chronicled in these several chapters fulfill Nathan's parable in chapter 12. If David eventually is restored to the throne, the kingdom that he regains is forever changed. The rest of his reign will not be quite the same, as it has lost much of its luster. But even if the kingdom that David regains has changed, the king is still upheld by God's irrevocable promise. The king who returns to the throne is chagrined but also wiser. He has lost much, but in the midst of catastrophic loss, David does not lose faith in the living God. That is perhaps the most striking part of this story: David's confidence in God's provenance even in the midst of unspeakable tragedy.

13:1–22

Amnon Rapes Tamar

The first story in this cycle is a text of terror. But it begins with a seemingly innocuous sentence: "Some time passed" (v. 1). Some periods of time are more eventful than others. Drama accompanies David's accession to the throne: war with the house of Saul, foreign military endeavors, the establishment of Jerusalem as a royal city, the procession of the ark, and an illicit liaison that leads to the birth of a future king. But some periods of time the Deuteronomist skips over. This is such a case, where a gap in the story leads readers to surmise what happened in the gap. Typically, the placid and relatively uneventful times receive the lightest treatment in historical or mythical narratives. It is reasonable to assume that the time between the conquest of Rabbah and the rape of Tamar was a time like this: of a king at the height of his power, at the inauguration of a small Israelite empire, and the relative prosperity of a people. But whatever placidness the people experience, it soon comes to a violent end. The story of Amnon's rape of Tamar is an instance of family horror that presages the national tumult that will soon commence.

Three of David's children play key roles in the ensuing drama: Absalom and Tamar, children of David's wife Macah, and Amnon, who is their half-brother. The Deuteronomist notes Tamar's beauty, which has captivated Amnon, who falls in love with her. Amnon is so "tormented" by this love "that he made himself ill" (v. 2). His torment, no doubt, is because he knows his love of Tamar to be illicit. This is not familial love but sexual desire. Since incest is forbidden by Israelite law (Lev. 18:9, 11), his torment is all the more foreboding. The object of his lust is a blood relative and a virgin. To touch her is doubly forbidden, but Amnon seems to have nothing but her on his mind. The language of the narrator is revealing: he finds it "impossible . . . to do anything to her" (v. 2). In Amnon's mind, Tamar is nothing more than an object of his lust; she is not a person, not a sister, but something to be had and done with. His attitude is indicative of attitudes that cultivate rape and hostility toward women. For rape to occur, a woman must be objectified and treated as someone without a will, without desire. Indeed the rape has already begun in Amnon's mind, in his attitude toward his half-sister. Rape is fostered in a culture that silences and objectifies women. And though the headline-grabbing news today often focuses on non-Western cultures that silence women (such the Pakistani Taliban, who as I write these words has jubilantly celebrated the shooting of fourteen-year-old Malala Yousufzai, who advocated girls' education), the lens can also be turned closer to home, where popular culture (from music to advertising) sexualizes girls at increasingly younger ages, where men's magazines consider women primarily as objects of the male gaze, where legal defenses of rapists still seek to exonerate the accused because the woman was dressing provocatively. Rape, in short, is enabled by culture. It has been for millennia.

Another contributor to Amnon's rape of Tamar is a cousin, Jonadab. The narrator describes him as a "very crafty man" (v. 3), not exactly a compliment and more suggestive of a wily schemer. He notices Amnon's tormented condition and inquires of its cause. Amnon speaks of his "love" for Tamar, which is a lie, since what follows can hardly be described as the result of love. Indeed, it is the furthest thing from love. Jonadab, the crafty one, concocts the plot that will cure Amnon of his supposed lovesickness: for Amnon to feign illness and tell David to send for Tamar, so that she might feed Amnon with food she has prepared. Amnon readily agrees to this plan, and David agrees to Amnon's request (vv. 4–7). David thus plays a pivotal role in Tamar's rape, as he is easily duped. David asks no questions of Amnon's rather odd request for Tamar alone. Gerald West notes how "each of the male characters—whether it be David, Amnon, Jonadab, the servants, or Absalom—plays a role in the rape of Tamar, though their roles are different. This is how many men it takes to rape a woman!"[1] The crime that ensues, in other words, is not only Amnon's; it is abetted by a chorus of other male members of the household.

Once Tamar arrives at Amnon's house, she prepares food in his sight, but Amnon still does not eat. In order to carry out his crime, Amnon must dismiss all others. When they leave, he makes the revolting request to eat from Tamar's hand in his chamber. These are

---

1. Gerald West, "1 and 2 Samuel," in *Global Bible Commentary*, ed. Daniel Patte (Nashville: Abingdon Press, 2004), 98.

gestures typically reserved for lovers, as they mingle taste and touch in the bedroom. John Milbank and Catherine Pickstock have noted how taste is "a more intimate mode of touch."[2] Eating from another's hand is a whisper of sexual intimacy. The connection becomes clear—and forced—as Amnon seizes Tamar and tells his sister to lie with him (vv. 8–11). By calling Tamar his sister, he names his own crime.

Tamar's response to Amnon shows striking resolve and resistance. On the threshold of a horrific crime, she exhibits remarkable strength in her efforts to stop the unspeakable. Her words to her half-brother are direct: "such a thing is not done in Israel; do not do anything so vile!" (v. 12). West notes how Tamar defends herself clearly and carefully: she says "no," she reminds Amnon of their family relationship, their cultural heritage that forbids his request, and she describes his request as evil.[3] She even urges Amnon to speak to David, suggesting that "he will not withhold me from you" (v. 13). This suggestion is somewhat puzzling: it is either Tamar's further attempt to buy time and escape, or it may indicate a practice that the royal family was exempt from the commandment against incest during this period of time in Israel's history.[4] All of these suggestions and protests, however, fall on deaf ears; the words mean nothing to Amnon, as he seizes Tamar and forces her to lay with him (v. 14).

As soon as he acts on his desire, however, Amnon's attitude toward Tamar changes radically. This shift represents a disturbing pattern common in sexual crimes: of perpetrators blaming the victim of their crime and loathing the object of his desire. His response is a compelling psychological study: confronted with his own crime, the self-loathing that Amnon likely experiences quickly gets directed elsewhere. He tries to escape responsibility for his action by blaming Tamar, being consumed with a loathing "even greater than the lust he had felt for her" (v. 15), and orders her to leave. Amnon compounds the humiliation and violence he has heaped on Tamar and himself by banishing Tamar from his sight. Even in the aftermath of this act of violent rape, Tamar retains a strong voice. She again argues

2. John Milbank and Catherine Pickstock, *Truth in Aquinas* (New York: Routledge, 2001), 71.

3. West, "1 and 2 Samuel," in Patte, ed., *Global Bible Commentary*, 97.

4. P. Kyle McCarter Jr., "2 Samuel," textual notes in *The HarperCollins Study Bible*, ed. Wayne A. Meeks (New York: HarperCollins, 1993), 486.

with Amnon, urging him not to commit a greater offense by sending her away. Covenantal law stipulates that if a man rapes a virgin, he is to take the victim of his crime as his wife, thus ensuring that the woman would not be bereft of a future family (cf. Deut. 22:28–29). But Amnon ignores this requirement of law, thus compounding his violation of it. He has his servant throw Tamar out and bolt the door behind her, referring to her with the pronoun "*zot*," meaning "this one" or someone without an identity (vv. 16–17).[5]

Tamar tears the clothing she wore to Amnon's chambers that designated her virginity and turns to mourning. She does not keep secret what has happened to her. When the men that surround her encourage her to be silent (including her brother Absalom), she makes her condition public. She refuses to have the violence committed against her render her powerless. But the result of her public outcry does not make the ending a happy one, for she remains a "desolate woman" in Absalom's house (v. 20). David further contributes to the conspiracy of silence that surrounds this crime: he becomes angry, but refuses to punish Amnon "because he loved him, for he was his firstborn" (v. 21). David's attachment to his eldest son makes him incapable of providing the discipline necessary to address the crime. His love, in short, flies in the face of justice. In the end, Tamar is surrounded by men who abet, commit, and cover up the act of violence against her, all in the name of family ties. In the end, family is betrayed by men who seek to uphold family name and honor, even if it winds up silencing a woman, leaving her bereft of a future.

Absalom, meanwhile, broods, harboring hatred for his brother Amnon. Though he is the male character who recognizes the gravity of the crime committed against his sister, he, too, contributes to the silencing of Tamar by refusing to speak to his brother Amnon or confront him with his crime.

> The Spirit gives us courage to pray without ceasing, to witness among all peoples to Christ as Lord and Savior, to unmask idolatries in Church and culture, to hear the voices of peoples long silenced, and to work with others for justice, freedom, and peace.
>
> "A Brief Statement of Faith," Presbyterian Church (U.S.A.).

5. Johanna W. H. van Wijk-Bos, *Reading Samuel: A Literary and Theological Commentary* (Macon, GA: Smyth & Helwys Publishing, Inc., 2011), 205.

13:23–39
Absalom Orders Amnon Killed

Two years pass, a long time to harbor anger. There is no narration of events that occur in the intervening years, but the impact of Amnon's crime lingers. Indeed, time has made its effects even more acutely felt. If the rape has ebbed from Amnon's and David's consciousness, it is living history for Absalom. Each of these men, who played a role in the rape of Tamar, now reappear. Absalom has sheepshearers at Baal-hazor, to the north of Jerusalem. At a time of customary celebration, he invites all the king's sons to take part. He relays his invitation to David, whom he addresses in the most formal way: not as son to his father, but as loyal servant to his king. David, however, addresses Absalom as his son and declines the invitation, ostensibly so that the king and his sons will not pose a burden for Absalom. The decline of invitation sounds flimsy, however, and Absalom urges David to reconsider it. Again the king declines but provides his blessing on Absalom (vv. 23–25).

Absalom tries another tack and requests Amnon instead of the king and all his sons. Whereas David immediately acceded to Amnon's request of Tamar without question, David is suspicious of Absalom's invitation. The protective instincts that should have been in place in relation to Tamar are now manifested for Amnon. The partiality of a parent to one child can often result in greater misery for the whole family, as children jockey for a parent's attention. David's family is no exception. In his case, it leads to rape and murder. Apparently, Absalom's continued pressing of the king proves effective: not only will Amnon take part in the sheep shearing festival, so will all of David's sons, where they will feast like kings (vv. 26–27).

Absalom's ruse is now set. He commands his servants to kill Amnon once he has had enough wine, when his defenses are down and the killing will be easy. Absalom's words to his servants to be "courageous and valiant" (v. 28) sound hollow. This is not an act of courage but of revenge, carried out far from Jerusalem and the king, under false hospitality. The servants do as commanded; Amnon is dead, and his brothers flee. The report that travels back to David is exaggerated in its claim that all David's sons have died.

When David hears word that he has lost his heirs, he tears his garments and lies on the ground, followed by servants who do likewise. But the false report is corrected by none other than Jonadab, the orchestrator of Tamar's rape. He tells the king that only Amnon has been killed, a fate that had been sealed ever since his rape of Tamar. The mordant irony is that the man who set the tragic wheels of crime in motion becomes the consoler of the king. But Jonadab's words also ring hollow and disingenuous, as if only one child's death could soothe a father's heart (vv. 29–33).

While the king's sons return to Jerusalem, Absalom flees. Jonadab announces the arrival of David's sons, accompanied by weeping and lamentation. There is no consolation here. One son has killed another and David's entire house mourns. Absalom, meanwhile, seeks refuge in the Transjordan with his maternal grandfather, Talmai in Geshur, in the area of the kingdom that historically gave the strongest support to Saul. Ironies thus compound, as the son of David finds safe haven in the land that was most partisan toward Saul. There Absalom stays for three years (vv. 34–38). David, however, does not seek revenge for the killing of Amnon. Once the mourning for Amnon has subsided, the king yearns for Absalom. The narration of this is staggering: "the heart of the king went out" (v. 39) as if the passion of his life were extinguished. David, the king, is now not only a man who cannot maintain order in his own household. He has lost the fire that sustains him. Bereft of a son, yearning for another, he is the picture of a tragic man. It is a foreboding scene, indeed, a foretaste of more that David will lose.

14:1–24

Absalom Returns

There is a saying that time heals all wounds. But as the previous episode has indicated, that saying is often far from the truth. Martin Luther King Jr., in his "Letter from Birmingham City Jail," writes of

> the strangely irrational notion that there is something in the very flow of time that will inevitably cure all ills. Actually time is neutral. It can be used either destructively or constructively.

... We must come to see that human progress never rolls in on wheels of inevitability. It comes through the tireless efforts and persistent work of men willing to be co-workers with God, and without this hard word time itself becomes an ally of the forces of social stagnation.[6]

Time can make wounds of injustice fester. Three years have passed without any contact or reconciliation between David and Absalom, yet Absalom is continually on David's mind. Joab knows that division in the king's house cannot be good for the kingdom. He orchestrates a plan that will put David in a position where he *has* to welcome Absalom home. Joab appears to have the best interest of the kingdom in mind, but his actions also reveal that he is capable of manipulating others in order to get what he deems best. Here, he is not the soldier who receives orders from the king but the schemer who pulls strings behind the scene. Once again, the relationship between David and Joab is complex, as David's response to the story Joab concocts reveals how hard it is to say "no" to the military that protects the regime. In this instance, Joab is the one issuing orders.

To achieve his aims, Joab enlists the help of a "wise woman" from Tekoa (v. 2), a town south of Jerusalem. She is never named in the story but proves instrumental in changing David's mind. She is a woman skilled in rhetoric, whom Joab instructs to behave as a mother in mourning. The words that she speaks, moreover, Joab puts "into her mouth" (v. 3). She appears before the king and pays proper obeisance, asking for the king's help. When David asks her what her trouble is, she relays the story that Joab placed on her lips: her two sons were in a field, got into an argument, and one killed the other. Her extended family is now clamoring for the surviving son to pay the requisite bloodguilt with his own life. But if that is done, the woman will be left with nothing (vv. 4–7).

David initially does not promise the woman anything but tells her to return to her house where he "will give orders concerning you" (v. 8). Revealing both her skill as a rhetorician and her strong personality, however, the woman does not immediately accede to

6. Martin Luther King Jr., "Letter from Birmingham City Jail," in *A Testament of Hope: The Essential Writings and Speeches of Martin Luther King, Jr.,* ed. James M. Washington (San Francisco: HarperCollins, 1986), 296.

the king's command. Instead, she increases her appeal to David by taking any of the guilt of David's pardon of her son upon herself and her father's house. The strength of her rhetoric is hard to overestimate: she will not leave until she has accomplished the aim that Joab has set before her. Apparently, David is convinced by her: "If anyone says anything to you, bring him to me, and he shall never touch you again" (v. 10). David now seems inclined not only to pardon the woman's remaining son but to safeguard her life. But again, this is not quite enough. She asks for one final thing: for David to swear an oath, to "keep the Lord your God in mind," so that her remaining son will not be killed. Even if the words have been put in her mouth, this woman is the picture of determination, unrelenting until the promise to her is made in blood. Because of her persistence, David agrees: "As the Lord lives, not one hair of your son shall fall to the ground" (v. 11).

Having accomplished her initial aim, the woman approaches David boldly again: "Please let your servant speak a word to my lord the king" (v. 12). Though she follows the protocol for speech in front of the king, her words to David are a reprimand. She contrasts the king's mercy in her case with his stubbornness in the case of Absalom, asserting that his refusal to welcome Absalom home is against Israel. She also stresses the ephemeral nature of human life, how it, like water when spilled on the ground, cannot be gathered up again. With these words, the woman places David's continued banishment of Absalom in direct opposition to God's sustenance of him. After admonishing David, however, the woman also makes use of flattery, how David's word will set her at rest, how it is like an angel of God, how the king can discern good and evil (vv. 13–17). Her final speech before the king mixes admonition with high praise. She is a skilled rhetorician indeed. Joab has chosen her well.

But now it is David's turn to speak and make requests. He inverts their previous conversation by asking the woman not to withhold anything from him. David suspects that his commander is the orchestrator of the episode, and he asks the woman directly about Joab's involvement. The woman answers affirmatively but also with further words of flattery for the king: Joab has put the words in her mouth "in order to change the course of affairs," but the king is the one who has wisdom unparalleled, akin to an angel of God's (vv. 18–20). The truth has now been revealed: both David's failure to act as a reconciler in his own family and Joab's scheme to bring the banished son back home. The king cannot go back on his word to the woman.

As the woman disappears from the scene, David's attention turns to Joab. His command to Joab is brief: to bring back Absalom. But in his command, David also distances himself from his son, as Absalom is referred to not in family terms but as a "young man." The order comes not as a relief to David, of one being reunited with family, but as a concession to Joab, to the man to whom his reign owes much. It is more a reluctant agreement with a military advisor than the pardon of a parent. Joab adheres to protocol tightly: showing obeisance, professing his allegiance to David, expressing thanksgiving that the king has granted his request. Joab retrieves Absalom from his exile, but the son does not return with fanfare or to a father's open arms. Instead, David orders Absalom sent to his own house. He is not even to come into the presence of his father (vv. 21–24). The homecoming thus appears worse than exile. Joab's request has been granted, but the rift in David's household has not been mended. Because it continues to fester, the state of the nation is at risk. David, furthermore, refuses to discipline Absalom, just as he refused to discipline Amnon. As a result, a rape and a murder both go unaddressed. Turning his head from the violence of his own family, David also imperils the nation.

14:25–33

Reconciliation, of Sorts

Time passes on. Reconciliation between father and son does not occur, but the nation notices the beauty of the son. Indeed, it is reminiscent of the father's (cf. 1 Sam. 16:12). But Absalom now has surpassed David in appearance: throughout Israel there is no one like him. Beauty, in the pages of 1 and 2 Samuel, is often a mixed blessing. It does not guarantee the integrity of the one possessing beauty. Absalom's hair is particularly captivating, tresses that he cuts once a year, locks that eventually contribute to his downfall (18:9). The nation is struck by this handsome, returning son, who has a family. His daughter, Tamar, is named in honor of her aunt, further testimony that Absalom has not forgotten the unspeakable crime. Two years pass without Absalom seeing his father (vv. 25–28). Wounds continue to fester.

> Cheap grace means grace as bargain—basement goods, cut-rate forgiveness, cut-rate comfort, cut-rate sacrament; grace as the church's inexhaustible pantry, from which it is doled out by careless hands without hesitation or limit. It is grace without a price, without costs.
>
> Dietrich Bonhoeffer, *Discipleship*, ed. Geffrey B. Kelly and John D. Godsey (Minneapolis: Fortress, 2001), 43.

Absalom seeks reconciliation with David by asking for Joab. It is Joab, after all, who orchestrated his homecoming. But Joab does not respond to Absalom's repeated requests. In desperation, Absalom forces Joab's hand by commanding his servants to burn Joab's field. When Joab confronts Absalom about the damage, the king's son claims it would have been better to remain in Geshur and entreats Joab to grant him access to the king, even if it means death. Joab grants the request, but the reconciliation is accomplished without words between father and son. They perform the ritual: Absalom prostrates himself before David and David kisses his son (vv. 29–33). It appears like reconciliation, but gestures can easily be misinterpreted. Judas betrayed Jesus with a kiss. Persons can genuflect before the king and plot against the king at the same time. The rift still remains.

15:1–12

Absalom Seizes the Throne

Any supposed reconciliation between father and son is quickly dispelled by Absalom's public behavior. His first act is to ride a chariot with fifty men running in advance, a regal mode of transport. By itself, the scene is comical, akin to someone other than the president traversing the nation on *Air Force One*. But by acquiring men, Absalom is also accumulating an army that will bolster his subsequent claim to the throne. His strategy is manipulative: to stand at the gate to the city and address every person who comes with a suit before the king. Before they get the chance to petition David, Absalom asks where they are from, flatters the petitioners that their claims are just, and laments that there is no one designated by the king to hear them. He also turns the attention on himself: if only Absalom were judge in the land, he would execute justice. The tactics work, and those who come to the city gates treat Absalom more and more like a king: they do obeisance to him, and Absalom kisses them (vv. 1–5). All of this happens without much initial knowledge on David's part. As time goes by, however, it is hard to imagine how David could not know about the actions of his son, especially as the narrator notes how Absalom "stole the hearts of the people of Israel" (v. 6). Absalom is stealing the people's loyalty to David and claiming it for himself.

Four years pass before Absalom approaches the king to make a request. Since his return, this is the one occasion where he speaks directly to David. Absalom claims that he wants to fulfill a vow he made while in exile: to worship the Lord in Hebron if he ever returned to Jerusalem. Now the time has come for him to fulfill that vow. But Absalom's ostensible reasons for worship disguise his intent of launching a rebellion in Hebron, the historical seat of Judahite power. Absalom's move is strategic: he has already stolen the hearts of the Israelites; he will now mount a challenge to the king by claiming the kingdom for himself, buoyed by troops that will assist him from this ancient seat of power. In some regards, Absalom's choice of Hebron is a nostalgic move, reflecting the old guard of Judah rather than the new royal city of David. It suggests David as the imposter to the throne, while Absalom represents the old tradition. As Absalom travels to Hebron, he also sends a secret message: at the trumpet's blast, the people will know that Absalom is king in Hebron (vv. 7–10). But the journey also involves persons unaware of his usurpation of the throne: two hundred from Jerusalem who know "nothing of the matter" (v. 11). Absalom's strategy of claiming the throne for himself thus involves willing conspirators and those stuck in the wrong place at the wrong time. One of the pivotal conspirators, however, Absalom gains from David's inner circle: Ahithophel, David's counselor, who becomes one of Absalom's chief advisors. This, too, will make the conspiracy stronger, as the numbers of people aligned with Absalom keep increasing (v. 12).

15:13–31
David Flees

David receives word of events summed up in the messenger's report that the hearts of the people have "gone after Absalom" (v. 13). That word compels David to leave Jerusalem, revealing the king's protective instincts and concern for the royal city. He wants to spare himself and his party from Absalom's sword, but he also does not want Jerusalem to suffer. The officials, accordingly, are willing to do whatever David commands. The evacuation appears somewhat hasty, encompassing David's entire household with the exception of ten concubines who will watch over the house. This detail is telling, as it presages Absalom's seizure of the women David leaves behind (16:21–22), the final affront to David's kingship. A somber parade passes by the king as David bestows thanks upon all. Those who depart include many foreigners: Cherethites, Pelethites, and Gittites who have been loyal to David ever since his sojourn in Philistine territory. David, legitimately concerned for their welfare, offers them an out, to return to their places of origin. His question to them is moving, "You came only yesterday and shall I today make you wander about with us, while I go wherever I can?" (v. 20). This dismissal of the foreign parties also shows David's willingness to forgo protection (since they number among David's bodyguards). But they ignore David's suggestion, captured by Ittai the Gittite's claim that wherever the king will be, there will he be too, in life and in death (vv. 14–21).

Scripture is filled with instances such as this: of "outsiders" who are not obliged to show faithfulness to "insiders" but who choose to ally themselves with peoples from other places, to follow a person who is not of their tribe.

Ruth follows Naomi (Ruth 1:16–22), and the Ethiopian eunuch becomes a follower of the Way (Acts 8: 26–40). One further detail of these "outsiders" is significant: The group that travels with David is not simply a company of soldiers but also includes children who will

slow the pace of flight. If Absalom
seizes the throne for himself, David
is concerned for the well-being
of his followers, whether they be
young or old. The party crosses the
Wadi Kidron, the eastern boundary
of Jerusalem, and heads toward the
wilderness (v. 22–23). It is a scene
of mourning, as weeping accompanies the travelers, but there is also a

> **The family of Christ includes not only the "stranger" but even the criminal—the one who stands convicted of wrongdoing.**
>
> Lisa Sowle Cahill, *Family: A Christian Social Perspective* (Minneapolis: Fortress, 2000), 130.

glimmer of hope. The wilderness, after all, is the place where David
found strength in flight from Saul. Perhaps this pattern will repeat
itself as David flees from his son.

The priest Zadok and the Levites also appear ready to depart
with the king. They set down the ark, which the people pass by as
they leave the city. But David tells Zadok to bring the ark back into
Jerusalem, confirming that the ark is not his personal totem. It is
the presence of God for the people of God and ought to remain in
the space consecrated for it. If David finds favor with God, he will
see the ark again; if not, then David is content with whatever seems
good to God. David stakes his future not with a religious object that
will protect him but with the living God who will provide for him.
If David's leadership of his family has failed recently, his present
actions reveal a consummate leader, concerned with the well-being
of his people and whether his conduct accords with God's wisdom.
David's instincts of self-preservation, indeed, seem secondary. David
tells Zadok to return to Jerusalem with Abiathar, along with their
sons Ahimaaz and Jonathan, while David will wait in the wilderness
for a message from Zadok (vv. 24–29). While the king is in flight,
worship of the Lord will still take place at the appointed place in
Jerusalem. It is not quite business as usual, but David's gesture indicates that proper worship takes precedence over the king's legacy.

Nonetheless, the journey from Jerusalem is tragic, with unmistakable marks of mourning. The rift in David's family has now
resulted in a fractured nation. When David finds out that his counsel
Ahithophel is among the conspirators, it increases David's misery.
In response to this news, David utters one of his more distinctive

prayers, for God to turn Ahithophel's counsel of Absalom into folly (vv. 30–31), indirectly praying for Absalom's downfall. Even David, who entrusts to God the future—whether he will see the ark again or not—prays for God to intervene favorably on his behalf. Trust in God, again, is portrayed here not as passive acceptance of the status quo. David both trusts God to provide for the future and acts in the creation of that future, even if it means praying for the conspirators' foolishness.

15:32–37

Hushai's Task

David arrives at the peak of the Mount of Olives, outside Jerusalem, "where God was worshiped" (v. 32), an odd description since this place is not identified with worship anywhere else in the Hebrew Bible. Hushai, an Archite from the tribe of Benjamin, comes to the king in the appearance of mourning. David claims that Hushai will be a burden if he travels with the exiles. Why this trusted servant would constitute a burden, however, is difficult to surmise. David may be using a rhetorical ploy to convince Hushai to undertake a risky endeavor: to infiltrate Absalom's court and foil the counsel of David's betrayer, Ahithophel. The plot rings with intrigue and counter-intrigue: Hushai is to offer his services to Absalom so that he may listen in on affairs in the king's house and relay what he hears to the priests Zadok and Abiathar. David's enlisting of the chief priests shows that they are not only in Jerusalem for ceremonial purposes; they will play a primary role in the counterrebellion by relaying critical information to David in exile. The layers of deception here are deep: a counsel to Absalom who really works for David, priests who remain in Jerusalem to conduct proper worship who also serve as intelligence officers. The entire arrangement is built on lies and deception. Indeed, the plan raises interesting questions about lying and whether it is ever legitimate.

David encourages lying in the face of a breakdown in civil order: the usurpation of the throne and betrayal by one of his own children. He encourages one of his trusted servants not only to lie once to

Absalom but to live a continual lie by serving in Absalom's court. Hushai's task conflicts with the blanket prohibition against lying in Immanuel Kant's categorical imperative: *"Act only on that maxim whereby thou canst at the same time will that it should become a universal law."*[7] In Kant's view, lying is always wrong because if lying were tolerated (as becoming a universal law), then one could no longer rely on anyone else to be truthful. Hushai, however, acts differently from this maxim: he enters Jerusalem just as Absalom arrives, ready to lie for the sake of the deposed king (vv. 33–37).

16:1–4

David and Ziba

As Hushai returns to Jerusalem, David and his party journey into the wilderness. On the way, David encounters Ziba, who has donkeys saddled for a journey, substantial provisions, and wine for the fleeing party. These gifts are offerings of hospitality and also pledges of allegiance. When David inquires about Mephibosheth, Ziba claims that his master has remained in the city to celebrate David's departure. More than that, Ziba reports that Mephibosheth believes he will sit on the throne to regain Saul's kingdom. Ziba thus implicates Mephibosheth in a further conspiracy: it is not only Absalom who endangers the Davidic kingdom; it is also Saul's grandson who wants the kingdom for himself. The charge is a serious one, which Mephibosheth denies when David returns to Jerusalem and is restored to the throne (cf. 19:24–27). It further testifies that Mephibosheth has spurned David's kindness to him (9:1–13). Again, this episode raises questions about lying, since either Ziba lies to curry favor with David by slandering Mephibosheth or Mephibosheth lies to save his face once his aspirations to the throne have gone up in smoke. David's response to Ziba implies that he takes Ziba at his word, as he transfers Mephibosheth's possessions to the servant. For the moment, this accomplishes Ziba's intent: he pays David obeisance and pledges his loyalty, a loyalty that apparently has

---

7. Immanuel Kant, *Fundamental Principles of the Metaphysics of Morals*, trans. Thomas K. Abbott (New York: Macmillan, 1949), 38.

benefits (vv. 1–4). For the moment, however, it is difficult to discern who David can trust, for Ziba does not remain with David.

16:5–14
Shimei's Curse

The narrative moves from the east to the north, to Bahurim, a Benjaminite town outside Jerusalem. Shimei, from the house of Saul, approaches David's with curses, behavior that indicates the rivalries between David's and Saul's houses are far from over. Even the Deuteronomist's concern for establishing the legitimacy of David's reign cannot paste over alternative claims to the throne. Adding to the insult, Shimei throws stones at David and his servants, even though David is surrounded by military guards. Shimei's speech is a combination of exaggeration and prophetic truth: he calls David a murderer for killing members of Saul's house, and for this bloodguilt, the Lord has given the kingdom to Absalom (vv. 5–8). No doubt Shimei has in mind Saul's sons whose execution David had ordered (cf. 21:5–9), but perhaps also Saul and Jonathan, who die battling David's troops. The reader, however, also has in mind others whose deaths are related to David's action or inaction, such as Uriah and Amnon. If David is a "man of blood," as Shimei claims, it may be for the deaths of those other than the ones Shimei mentions.

Abishai, Joab's brother, immediately perceives the insult to David by countering with his own insult. Shimei is a "dead dog" who is an affront to the king. Abishai volunteers to behead Shimei to avenge the insult, but David exercises restraint.

> But I say to you that listen, Love your enemies, do good to those who hate you, bless those who curse you, pray for those who abuse you.
>
> Luke 6:27–28

Remarkably, he takes Shimei's words to heart by asking whether they are from the Lord. He instructs his party to leave Shimei alone, exonerating the king from further bloodshed and distancing him from his more impulsive servants. David's response models patient acceptance in the midst of adversity; it even suggests that suffering insult may be a mark of faithfulness. In this regard, David's behavior is akin to the counsel of 1 Peter: "If you endure when you do right and suffer for it, you have God's approval" (1 Pet. 2:20b). For 1 Peter, the suffering of the faithful is directly connected to Jesus' suffering, which the Savior did not avenge by inflicting further suffering. For David, his endurance of Shimei's insults is impetus from God for deeper self-examination and discernment of God's work in human life. God may repay the insult of today with good tomorrow (vv. 9–12).

The boundary between patience in adversity and self-abnegation, however, is often delicate. Indeed, 1 Peter singles out slaves in developing virtue: "Slaves, accept the authority of your masters with all deference, not only those who are kind and gentle but also those who are harsh. For it is a credit to you if, being aware of God, you endure pain while suffering unjustly" (1 Pet. 2:18–19). Such counsel seems to preclude just resistance to unjust arrangements of power. Indeed, the Christian church has often sanctioned quiescence in the face of injustice and abuse. As James Evans notes, "From about 1772 until 1850 the Bible was the primary source of authority and legitimation for the enslavement of Africans. Slaveholders turned to the Scriptures to prove that slavery was in no way contrary to the will of God."[8] The pattern for developing patience in adversity and submission to God can become a veneer that covers unjust and demonic powers.

> **For of all slaveholders with whom I have ever met, religious slaveholders are the worst.**
>
> Frederick Douglass, "Slaveholding Religion and the Christianity of Christ," in *Afro-American Religious History: A Documentary Witness*, ed. Milton C. Sernett (Durham: Duke University Press, 1985), 101.

Historically, those who have been encouraged most to "submit" have been those outside the corridors of power: women, the poor, resident aliens. But such submission can serve to mask and perpetuate structural sin. Gustavo Gutiérrez describes sin "as the fundamental alienation, the root of a situation of injustice and exploitation."[9]

8. James H. Evans Jr., *We Have Been Believers: An African-American Systematic Theology* (Minneapolis: Fortress Press, 1992), 35.
9. Gustavo Gutiérrez, *A Theology of Liberation*, rev. ed., trans. Caridad Inda and John Eagleson

Submission to adversity, in other words, can perpetuate the sin and injustice we are called to resist. David's patience, however, is not for the sake of self-abnegation. Rather, it is for the sake of life: that he might grow in faithfulness and service to both God and others. Self-abnegation sees submission as an end in itself; patience in adversity sees present suffering for the sake of a more abundant life in the future. Throughout the Deuteronomistic History, God is inviting God's people into the fullness of life: God's continued promise that life will flourish is not a phantom but a promise that gets realized in history. The people endure so that they might flourish. Here, the king endures the curses of a fierce partisan so that he might better serve as king at some point in the future. And this too is for the sake of the people Israel. The boundary between unnecessary suffering that must be resisted and the patient endurance of faith that accepts suffering often can be discerned by asking these questions: Is the suffering of the present for the sake of life? Does the endurance of suffering invite us into a fuller understanding of God's abundant life given to the world? David endures Shimei's curse, as his party travels beyond Shimei's hometown. The journey is not easy: they arrive at the Jordan weary, ready for the refreshment that the waters and the rest provide (vv. 13–14).

16:15–17:4

Ahithophel Advises Absalom

The narrative returns to Absalom, whom the reader last encountered on the threshold of Jerusalem. His arrival in the royal city is

(Maryknoll, NY: Orbis, 1988), 103. Gutiérrez also describes sin as "a rejection of friendship with God and, in consequence, with other human beings. It is a personal, free act by which we refuse to accept the gift of God's love. . . . As seen in the light of faith, sin thus understood is the root of all social injustice, because sin, like every human act, necessarily has a social dimension." Ibid., 226. Catherine Keller, in a similar vein, questions all forms of submission and self-sacrifice as being somehow normative for Christian life. "The call to agapic self-sacrifice may indeed provide the proper corrective to the hypertrophic masculine ego, which patriarchal society eggs on to inflated forms of ego development. But women sin in the opposite and complementary direction: that of the underdevelopment of the self." Catherine Keller, "Scoop Up the Water and the Moon Is in Your Hands: On Feminist Theology and Dynamic Self-Emptying," in *The Emptying God: A Buddhist-Jewish-Christian Conversation*, ed. John B. Cobb Jr. and Christopher Ives (Maryknoll, NY: Orbis, 1990), 105.

accompanied by multitudes who signify Absalom's popularity. Absalom did not ignite this rebellion in an instant but cultivated it over time: its strength lies, in part, with the collective will of the people. Hushai is among these multitudes, and his address to the king is rich in double-meaning. His words, "Long live the king!" are, in the ears of most who would hear, directed to Absalom, but he does not name Absalom as king. Absalom, however, suspects Hushai's words: "Is this your loyalty to your friend?" (vv. 16–17). Hushai answers Absalom's suspicion with other words that deceive: he will remain with the one chosen by the Lord and the people Israel. In Hushai's mind, this means David, but it can also be heard as a pledge of loyalty to Absalom. Thus far, Hushai does not lie directly to Absalom; he speaks words that are easily interpreted differently from his intent. Only Hushai's final words to Absalom are overt deception: "Just as I have served your father, so I will serve you" (vv. 18–19). The intrigue is deep: double-talk, overt deception, suspicion of words, and acceptance of them. For Absalom, these final words seem enough. He does not question Hushai any longer and solicits his counsel shortly hereafter. Part of Absalom's downfall is thus related to how readily he has come to trust people. Perhaps the multitudes have gone to his head.

Absalom turns to his most trusted counsel, Ahithophel, and asks for advice. Ahithophel urges his master to take the dramatic step of seizing his father's concubines in the sight of all Israel. There is no mistaking this gesture: Absalom will occupy his father's house and act as king by publicly humiliating David and asserting power. Ahithophel claims that this act will strengthen all who are with the new king, but it will also make him "odious" to his father (vv. 20–21). Thus Absalom fulfills Nathan's warning to David, of a neighbor claiming David's wives for himself (12:11); the neighbor, it turns out, is none other than David's son. Johanna van Wijk-Bos interprets Ahithophel's advice, which she correlates with rape, as further demonstration of Absalom's degeneration: "Absalom, although believing himself at the height of his power through taking possession of his father's women, has now sunk a great deal lower than his brother Amnon."[10] Absalom's first act as king in Jerusalem, in other words, is

---

10. Johanna van Wijk-Bos, *Reading Samuel*, 220.

not for the sake of others but for the sake of himself. He does what he does because he can. The advice, moreover, comes from the lips of one whose counsel is regarded as an oracle of God, both by David and Absalom (vv. 22–23).

These high words concerning Ahithophel precede his subsequent counsel for pursuing the fleeing David. Indeed, Ahithophel volunteers to pursue the deposed king this very night. Absalom will not even get his hands dirty in tracking down his father. Ahithophel's counsel does seem sound, at least in military terms, since David is on the run and is weary. Ahithophel promises to strike only the king (17:1–2), thus avoiding unnecessary bloodshed and war. Ahithophel sweetens the proposal by suggesting that the quick disposal of David will result in David's followers rushing back to Jerusalem (and Absalom) "as a bride comes home to her husband" (v. 3). The people, Ahithophel implies, do not want more war; they just want peace. Cutting off the head will spare many lives. It is, Ahithophel claims, only one life and the servant of the king will do it. The elders and Absalom are pleased with the idea (v. 4). It just may be the proposal that strengthens their hand even more.

17:5–14

Hushai's Counter-Advice

Despite the pleasing nature of Ahithophel's advice, Absalom solicits further input by calling Hushai (vv. 5–6). It is surprising that the new king would seek counsel from this new arrival to his camp. Perhaps it portrays Absalom's eagerness to trust others; perhaps it indicates that, since Hushai was with David most recently, he is best able to report on the status of David's flight. Hushai is blunt with Absalom, at least at first: He claims that Ahithophel's counsel is "not good" (v. 7). His further words exaggerate the status of David's ragtag army: they are warriors who are enraged, like bears who have had their cubs taken from them. He extols David as an "expert in war" (v. 8), though the reader has not seen David in the battlefield for quite some time. The appeal to David as a warrior is more nostalgic than anything else. The exaggeration continues: If David's troops have gone into hiding, it is not out of desperation but in order to ensnare Absalom's troops. If even one of Absalom's soldiers is felled, it will ignite rumors of a slaughter. In the face of those words, even Absalom's most valiant warriors will melt in fear (vv. 9–10).

In contrast to Ahithophel, Hushai advises Absalom to take more time, to gather greater numbers of troops so they can overpower David's army with superior force. Absalom, moreover, should not stay in Jerusalem but go into battle himself. This advice accomplishes two aims that Hushai does not express: it gives David more time to prepare for the battle that lies ahead and it puts Absalom in harm's way. Hushai's hyperbole plays on Absalom's growing intoxication with his own power. If Absalom will wait to assemble a massive number of troops, they will be able to overcome David in any situation. If David flees to a city, Absalom's troops will be able to drag the city with ropes into the valley, so that not even a "pebble" will be found where the city once stood (vv. 11–13). The words are convincing enough. Absalom and "all the men of Israel" are convinced that Hushai's counsel is superior to Ahithophel's. But their decision to follow the newcomer's advice is not simply the result of his golden tongue. It is the Lord's doing, who ordained the "defeat of the good counsel of Ahithophel" (v. 14). In this case, superior advice is thwarted by God working through advice that is more spurious but *sounds* wise.

The folly of the newcomer's advice thus becomes the "wisdom" that the new king acts on. This juxtaposition of wise advice that Absalom rejects in favor of unwise advice displays the interweaving of human and divine action. As Song-Mi Suzie Park notes, "Absalom is deceived by God, who has in mind a preordained plan; yet even in God's deception, Absalom's volition in choosing is not lost. The human role is not absent, but neither is God's ordained plan nullified."[11]

> **Absalom, by following what initially appeared and** *sounded* **wise, was really acting unwisely. What sounded wisest was not wise for Absalom and yet was wise from the viewpoint of the deity.**
>
> Song-Mi Suzie Park, "The Frustration of Wisdom: Wisdom, Counsel, and Divine Will in 2 Samuel 17:1–23," *Journal of Biblical Literature* 128, no. 3 (2009): 465, italics in original.

11. Song-Mi Suzie Park, "The Frustration of Wisdom: Wisdom, Counsel, and Divine Will in 2 Samuel 17:1–23," *Journal of Biblical Literature* 128, no. 3 (2009): 466.

17:15–29
Hushai Warns David; David Escapes

As Absalom acts on Hushai's counsel, Hushai summons others to engage in covert operations. In prose reminiscent of a spy novel, the narrator charts movements of several partisans who bring messages to King David. First, Hushai informs the high priests, Zadok and Abiathar, of Absalom's actions. But the high priests will not carry the message to David; that task will be for their sons, Jonathan and Ahimaaz, who are waiting outside the city at En-rogel, a spring of the Wadi Kidron, one of the traditional boundaries of Jerusalem. Because their lives are at risk in this conspiracy, they cannot be seen entering and leaving the city. A boy sees them and tells Absalom, which makes their journey more urgent and hasty, leading them to Bahurim, the town just north of Jerusalem where Shimei lives. David's last brush with this town provoked hostility; now it provides a refuge for Jonathan and Ahimaaz, who are hidden in a well by a woman (vv. 16–19). Indeed, throughout this episode, areas where David had earlier encountered resistance now offer safe harbor.

Absalom's servants arrive at the woman's door and ask where the two men are. She answers with a lie: they have already crossed over. Her lie, in other words, is for the sake of protecting Jonathan and Ahimaaz's lives. Again, her response raises questions about lying and truth-telling. Immanuel Kant considered it a duty to speak the truth even if we were hiding a friend from a murderer. If the murder came to our door and asked whether our fried was in our house, we should tell the murderer the truth: "Truthfulness in statements that one cannot avoid is a human being's duty to everyone, however great the disadvantage to him or to another that may result from it. . . . [A lie] always harms another, even if not another individual, nevertheless humanity generally, inasmuch as it makes the source of right unusable."[12] The woman's words are an eerie echo of Kant's example, but in direct contradiction to Kantian ethics, she misleads the searchers at her door. When their search for the men proves fruitless, the servants of Absalom return to Jerusalem. Jonathan and Ahimaaz emerge from hiding to relay Hushai's message to David,

12. Immanuel Kant, "On a Supposed Right to Lie from Philanthropy," in Kant, *Practical Philosophy*, ed. Mary J. Gregor (New York: Cambridge University Press, 1996), 612.

but they report only Ahithophel's counsel (and not Hushai's). By failing to mention Hushai's advice, the two messengers convey a greater urgency to David's flight. He has to cross the Jordan, lest he be overcome by Absalom's army soon (vv. 20–22). David crosses the Jordan thinking that Absalom's men are fast on his heels. By withholding some information, Jonathan and Ahimaaz thus accomplish Hushai's aim even more quickly.

The narrator interrupts the movement of David's troops by mentioning Ahithophel's fate. Once his counsel is rejected, he goes to his hometown and hangs himself (v. 23). No reason for his suicide is given. Ahithophel may well be experiencing despair over Absalom's unwise action and consternation that his once privileged position as the king's advisor has now been supplanted. Whatever the case, Ahithophel's suicide presages Absalom's own death. Perhaps he already sees the writing on the wall. Before Absalom's troops engage David's army, their defeat is already a foregone conclusion.

In the Transjordan, meanwhile, David finds refuge. One further mark of his kingship of all Israel is that he is able to make friends out of previous enemies. His name as "beloved" is certainly well-deserved. Absalom follows David with the army he has assembled. The overseer of his troops is Amasa, who is related to David's commander, Joab. Absalom manipulates people and positions: It almost seems as if Absalom is mimicking David, that he is chiefly concerned with the *appearance* of a legitimate kingship, and hence he tries to re-create the entourage that surrounds David. The Israelites make camp and prepare for battle. But they are also weary, hungry, and thirsty. Aid, again, comes from unexpected places: from the Ammonite king Shobi as well as Machir and Barzillai (vv. 24–27). David, who had earlier been engaged in war against the Ammonites, now finds sustenance in Ammonite hands. With friends like this, his troops are well-equipped to engage the king's son.

18:1–18

David's Troops Defeat Absalom

Having been replenished in his exile, David prepares the troops for battle. The narrator indicates that this is not a ragtag band but a sizable army, with commanders of "thousands" and "hundreds" (v. 1). Absalom may have stolen the heart of Israel, but he does not have the loyalty of the entire population. The three divisions of David's army are allotted to Joab, Abishai, and Ittai the Gittite. The first two have already figured prominently in the story, distinguished by their impulsiveness and violence. That David entrusts two thirds of his troops to them shows that he is keenly aware that the success of his troops depends on violent men, ready to kill without compunction. The other third of the troops are commanded by Ittai, a foreigner who has chosen to remain at David's side even when the king has offered him an out during a time of danger (15:19–21). His inclusion among the three chief commanders indicates that the battle that is about to commence affects the wider world in some way: neighbors, allies, and foes of Israel also have an interest in the outcome. David wants to engage in combat, but the men (probably the three commanders) warn against it. Their warning accomplishes two things: first, it indicates that David is a marked man for Absalom's forces, a prize worth ten thousand men who would likely be killed if captured. On this level, David's commanders are protecting David's kingship by protecting his life. On another level, their warning to David will distance the king from Absalom's death. Thus, he cannot be directly implicated in the death of his son that follows. David listens to his men's counsel and changes his mind (vv. 2–4). As David surveys the thousands parading into battle, he issues one final order, to "deal gently for my sake with the young man Absalom" (v. 5), words that are heard by all the soldiers gathered. This command further exonerates David from Absalom's death and it also reflects his prior leniency with Absalom and Amnon. Rightly or wrongly, David places family ties over some of the cold realities of military campaigns. Battles, after all, cannot guarantee that any one life will be spared. But David's command to the troops also shows wisdom, in that he knows the nation's affection for Absalom. Sparing Absalom's life not only saves him a son, it also will increase David's stature in the eyes of Israel. The command, in other words, unveils both the fierce bonds of family and political calculation.

David's army goes out "into the field against Israel; and the battle was fought in the forest of Ephraim" (v. 6). It is significant that

Absalom's troops are called "Israel;" they are not chiefly identified as partisans of the upstart king but as people of the nation. This indicates both the extent of Absalom's support among the people and the formidable challenge that awaits David if Absalom's army is defeated. There will be a popular campaign of winning back the people's hearts if the one who stole them is no longer on the throne. Second, this inaugural sentence indicates two arenas of battle: the field and the forest. The latter favors David's troops, who have learned the tactics of surprise in their previous exile on the run from Saul. If Absalom's troops outnumber David's, a battle in the forest could work to David's advantage. Indeed, this is precisely what happens. The narrator may be taking interpretive license in an exaggerated body count, but s/he also clarifies that the forest claims more lives than the sword (vv. 7–8). Hushai's advice to Absalom to wait and gather more troops has come to no avail; in fact, it will lead to his army's destruction.

From a general description of battle, the narration turns to Absalom. He is riding through the forest, regally. As he is passing under an oak, his head catches in the branches. Although the narrator does not specify Absalom's hair, much scholarship has suggested that Absalom's extensive locks snag him. The source of his pride (cf. 14:26) thus becomes his trap, leaving him "hanging between heaven and earth" (v. 9). One of David's soldiers who sees Absalom's vulnerability reports it to Joab, who in turn reprimands the man for not killing Absalom. Joab's desire to see Absalom killed is intensified with his willingness to give away ten pieces of silver and a belt. The life of the usurper is worth much in Joab's eyes. But the soldier, in an ironic reversal of roles, reprimands the commander by reminding Joab of David's command. The soldier further indicates that even if he had killed Absalom, Joab would not have sided with him (vv. 10–13). The soldier exposes Joab as an opportunist more interested in killing Absalom than he is with following orders and only interested in the assassination if he can keep his hands clean of it. Joab's response to this unexpected reprimand is further example of his own impulsiveness and violence. His rebuff is blunt: "I will not waste time like this with you" (v. 14), and, in an excessive display of violence, Joab impales Absalom's heart with three spears as

Joab's ten armor-bearers strike and kill the king's son. The act goes beyond the conventional patterns of battle; it resembles a ritual killing or violence spun out of control, killing a man who is hanging in a tree. In the end, a gang devours the king's son. Absalom's death in the tree furthermore signals how he is cursed (Deut. 21:22–23), "the primary way in which kings are presented as cursed within" Deuteronomistic history.[13] Polzin also suggests that Absalom's fate can be regarded as "an explicit and graphic image of—that is a simile for—the fate of *all Israel*, a nation which should now be seen, the Deuteronomist is telling us, as hanging cursed from the tree just as Absalom was."[14] The violence of kings and their henchmen, in this reading, is also inflicted on the nation.

If Joab's behavior toward Absalom at the end of his life represents a lack of restraint, his subsequent commands to the troops model it. As David's troops emerge victorious, they do not pursue Absalom's. Even Joab seems to know that there is a world of people to win over in the wake of Absalom's death. Further vengeance on his troops will yield nothing. Absalom's burial, however, is decidedly unceremonial. Soldiers throw his body in a large pit in the forest, the site of his defeat. They raise a great heap of stones but offer no words of mourning, no opportunity for David to be present (vv. 16–17). The conclusion to the episode seems to have been written to explain the monument to Absalom. On the details, moreover, there is much discrepancy. The burial site of Absalom is linked to a pillar he had set up for himself during his lifetime, ostensibly because he had "no son to keep my name in remembrance" (v. 18). But earlier the reader has read of Absalom's family, among whom number at least three sons (14:27). The memory of Absalom, in other words, is not simply of a villain. As David returns to the throne, he is a chastened man. Gone are the acts of arrogance and abuse of power that eventually led to rebellion in David's household. Returned is a man more aware of the ambiguities of power and his own kingship. The restoration, in short, cannot simply be celebrated, for there is still much to mourn.

13. Robert Polzin, *David and the Deuteronomist* (Bloomington: Indiana University Press, 1993), 186.
14. Ibid., 190–91.

18:19–32
Two Messengers Bring David News

Word of the battle and of his son's death has not yet reached the king, who has heeded his commanders' advice and remained at the gate. David's trusted messenger, Ahimaaz, volunteers and attributes David's victory to YHWH's deliverance (v. 19). Ahimaaz's theology is sound, and his role seems appropriate, since he has already played a significant role in protecting David (cf. 17:15–22). But Ahimaaz also seems eager just to be the messenger, along with the attention it might bring. (His failure to report Absalom's death in v. 29 indicates further that he only wants to be the bearer of good news.) If Ahimaaz is ignorant of Absalom's death, Joab's words convey the grim news. It is a day for all Israel to mourn. The irony, of course, is that Joab's actions have been the cause of mourning. Joab's words to Ahimaaz thus reverse his role in the previous episode: whereas earlier he disregarded David's command by killing the king's son, at this juncture he heeds protocol. Joab, if nothing else, is shrewd, sliding readily from one role to another. He is aware of the extent of his power and his ability to shape events. Hardly an innocent, he is not above manipulation of affairs so long as they work to his advantage. All the while, however, he remains staunchly loyal to David. But loyalty can wear many faces. In political life, there is rarely such a thing as absolute loyalty. Those close to the center of power also look out for themselves, even when they take hits for their boss.

If Ahimaaz cannot carry word of the defeat of the opposing army and Absalom's death, Joab claims that a foreigner, the Cushite (who is not even named, accentuating his outsider status) can. Most likely a man of African descent, the Cushite is instructed by Joab to tell David everything that he has seen. As the Cushite leaves, Ahimaaz presses his case with Joab, suggesting that Ahimaaz's desire has more to do with himself than relaying the news. A messenger has already been sent; sending another is surely superfluous. But those who wander the corridors of power often jockey for position. Joab questions Ahimaaz's request with words that indicate that Ahimaaz can expect no reward for bearing the news. If Ahimaaz seems ready to accept whatever comes his way because of the news, he is only prepared to tell David half of the truth. By taking another route, he winds up outrunning the Cushite (vv. 21–27).

Before either messenger arrives before David, the sentinel spots both men. David, aware of Ahimaaz's identity as the first runner, is convinced of good news even before he hears it. His words indicate how easy it is to regard the messenger more than the message itself.[15] David's presumption of what tidings Ahimaaz brings are confirmed by Ahimaaz's words and show of obeisance, "All is well!" Ahimaaz even spouts the correct theology, proclaiming God's blessing and deliverance of David from his enemies (v. 28). The words, however, are half-truths, since they fail to report on Absalom's death. The half-truth becomes a lie when Ahimaaz claims ignorance in the face of David's question of whether it is well with Absalom: "I saw a great tumult, but I do not know what it was" (v. 29). Many lies have preceded this one; some have wound up saving lives (cf. 17:20), but this lie can hardly be justified. Indeed, the only explanation is that Ahimaaz wants to be the bearer of good news before the king. David, however, wants to wait until he hears tidings from the next messenger, instructing Ahimaaz to stay near (v. 30).

The Cushite thus becomes the bearer of the fateful news. His initial words are similar to Ahimaaz's, ascribing praise to YHWH for David's deliverance from enemies. But whereas Ahimaaz tells half-truths and lies in response to David's question of whether Absalom is well, the Cushite confirms that David's troops have not dealt with Absalom gently. Indeed, the Cushite seems to think his words will give the king relief, in the hope that all who rise up against the king will meet a similar fate (vv. 31–32). But David hears these words neither as hope nor as good news. Victory is not just tainted; it has turned, in some ways, to defeat.

18:33–19:8a

David Mourns

David is now faced with the challenge of dealing with personal grief and national mourning. As he grapples with his own loss, however,

---

15. Americans now "shop" for news the way they do for any other product. Many of us gravitate toward the networks or media that confirm our sociopolitical outlooks. The messenger, in this sense, becomes more important than the message.

his behavior comes into conflict with his role as leader of a nation. Indeed, his grief even puts his status as king at risk. Here the impetuous Joab also proves a wise counselor to the king, saving him from possible insurrection among David's staunchest loyalists.

David is despondent. He goes to a chamber and weeps, thus disappearing from view. His private grief has trumped his public responsibility as the one who greets his troops as they return from battle. The extent of his grief is captured in his lament that it would have been preferable for David to die rather than Absalom.

Joab hears of the king's grief, which changes the troops' mood. Their return is more a stealth operation covered in shame than it is a victory parade (18:33–19:4). The scene is reminiscent of American soldiers returning from the Vietnam War. For those young men (often from the poorer segments of American society) who risked life and limb, there were no ticker tape parades but shouts of "baby killers" from those who avoided the draft. David's troops steal into the city, avoiding sight of the king. In a scene that has repeated itself throughout centuries, those who have done the risky and dirty work of battle are abandoned by the civilian leader who does not want to be associated with their uglier deeds.

> My lyre is turned to mourning, and my pipe to the voice of those who weep.
>
> Job 30:31

Joab reprimands the king for this behavior. He does not acknowledge David's grief or his own role in it. Joab's words combine his own refusal to acknowledge his disobedience of David's command with sage political advice. Joab is a complicated character: rash, impulsive, and violent but a fiercely loyal partisan of David who often says things that the king needs to hear. David, Joab claims, has covered his soldiers with shame. They are the ones who have saved his life and the lives of his house. His behavior of mourning a recalcitrant son shows hatred toward those who love him. David, in effect, is antagonizing his base. Joab informs the king that he is facing an urgent crisis and that his public display of protocol (or lack of it) will set the stage for either his auspicious return to Jerusalem or an even greater disaster than the one that has recently befallen him (vv. 5–7). David needs to speak to his loyal soldiers lest he lose them. David does not respond to Joab's rebuke with words, but he does take a seat "in the gate" (v. 8), the symbolic position of a judge. For the moment, David must swallow his personal loss in the name of preserving his base and honoring the soldiers who secured his restoration. David silently does what is required of him in the name of the nation and those who support him. For that, he owes thanks to Joab.

19:8b–15

David Returns

David's restoration to the throne is not smooth. Instead, fear, chaos, and disagreement reign as the Israelites dispute the kingship and flee to their homes. On the one hand, memories of David's military triumphs over the Philistines linger. But people also recall how David fled Absalom. Absalom, the one whom the Israelites anointed, is now dead, but the vacancy on the throne has not led to popular acclamation for David's return. The one who won their hearts, apparently, has not let go. Yet some are murmuring that David should return (vv. 8–10).

David rebukes his kin in Judah via a message given to Zadok and Abiathar, the chief priests who have already played critical roles during the revolt. While others in the land appeal for his restoration, Judah has been silent (vv. 11–12). But David's words do not simply express disappointment with his own tribe; they also display an astute political strategy. He appoints Amasa as overseer of the army, the man who served as commander of Absalom's troops (v. 13; cf. 17:25), dismissing Joab as a result. Much lies behind this replacement: (1) David disempowers the man who disobeyed the king's order by killing Absalom; (2) David further distances himself from Absalom's death by making an appointment that effectively exonerates David; (3) David still has to win back the hearts of Judah *and* Israel with this new appointment. David shows continuity with the reign of the usurper and his need for allies from Absalom's camp. One can only imagine Joab's reaction: after maintaining loyalty without question, he is replaced, solely because he killed the one man who represented the greatest threat to the kingdom. But his lot is the lot of many loyal soldiers throughout history who follow orders zealously and then take the blame for the commander in chief. Amasa, meanwhile, wins back the hearts of Judah for David, paving the way for the king's homecoming. It occurs without much fanfare, but it begins with the Judahites who come to Gilgal, a place laden with symbol and history (1 Sam. 10:8). The people bring David over the Jordan, back home again (vv. 14–15).

19:16–23
David Pardons Shimei

When David returns to Jerusalem, he does not immediately right all the wrongs committed against him. He acts not out of revenge but with mercy. His behavior reveals the character of his leadership in this latter period and his continued need to cultivate allies among former adversaries. Shimei hurries to meet the king, along with one thousand Benjaminites and Ziba's household (vv. 16–18). Shimei's haste indicates desperation. He knows his own life is in danger because he has cursed the returning king. His only hope lies in a last-minute appeal. The large number of Benjaminites, moreover, may indicate apprehension among the tribe since they have historically been the least receptive to David's leadership. But their inclusion may also indicate a groundswell of support that David is beginning to receive beyond his own kinsmen.

Shimei approaches the king in a posture of submission, falling down before David, just as the king is about to cross the Jordan. There is some comedy in the scene: an interruption of a ceremonial crossing by a desperate (and, judging by his past behavior, mentally unstable) man. Shimei speaks, moreover, before the king addresses him. But Shimei's words are hardly comedic: he begs for forgiveness, calls what he has done a sin, and claims that he has come "first of the house of Joseph" to meet the king. Though his words are desperate, they are not dissembling. After Shimei's address, David is not the first to speak; that role falls to Abishai, who, in nearly identical posture to his last encounter with Shimei (16:9), urges David to put Shimei to death. But David again distances himself from this rash—if not just—suggestion. Indeed, he claims that Abishai, in suggesting as much, has "become an adversary" to him. The words are striking: by calling Abishai an adversary (Heb. *satan*), David shows that it is not Shimei who is his foe but Abishai, his military commander. The order of friends and foes is suddenly stood on its head. No one, David claims, will be put to death on this day. He responds to Shimei's request swearing an oath that Shimei will not die (vv. 19–23).

This exchange between king and subject raises intriguing questions about the nature of mercy. What is the point of mercy? To forgive and forget? To move past old grudges and grievances? Often mercy is interpreted as a soft gesture: that in the face of injustice or crime, one simply forgives the offender. But mercy in much of the theological tradition bears little resemblance to forgiving and forgetting. Rather, it offers another way of rendering justice. At its most basic level, acts of mercy seek to stop the endless cycles of violence and counterviolence that often parade under the banner of justice. When those who are offended show mercy toward the offenders, they are not showing the desire to forget or move beyond the offense. Rather, they express the desire to start something new out of the violence and injustice of the offense. The quintessential symbol for mercy in Christian tradition is the resurrection—that out of the violence of crucifixion, God gives rise to something new: new life that does not forget the violence of the past but that re-members it in the flesh of the risen Christ (who still bears the scars of the cross). Acts of mercy are truly merciful when they provide opportunities for new life. They do not encourage the offended to acquiesce to the offense; they are occasions for the offender and the offended to envision a living hope. When David pardons Shimei, Shimei gains new life. But David is also freed from harboring resentment against Shimei and the wrong he has committed. Mercy, at least for the moment, has given new life to king and subject. As testament to the incompleteness of this new life, however, mercy will not have the final word in this story: David subsequently instructs his son Solomon to carry out Shimei's execution (1 Kgs. 2:8–9).

19:24–30
David and Mephibosheth, Revisited

Just as the demise of David's kingship began personally, with unrest in his own house, his return to the throne is marked by two personal grievances. In each, the personal becomes political. With Shimei, there is a well-documented offense against the king. With Mephibosheth, there is an *allegation* of an offense against the king, brought by Mephibosheth's servant Ziba (cf. 16:1–4).

Mephibosheth approaches David as a man in mourning. He has not trimmed his beard or washed since the king fled Jerusalem. The narrator also calls attention to Mephibosheth's feet, which Mephibosheth also has not cared for. Though it is difficult to determine the meaning of this remark, it calls further attention to Mephibosheth's physical disability. Yet his appearance fails to convince David that Mephibosheth has not conspired against the king. Instead, David's question conveys immediate suspicion: "Why did you not go with me, Mephibosheth?" (v. 25). At this point, David seems more inclined to believe Ziba than Mephibosheth. Mephibosheth responds by accusing Ziba of slander and deception. But his words are more than an attempt to clear his name, since they are mixed with flattery of the king: David is "like the angel of God," whatever David decides will be good (v. 27). It is impossible to determine who speaks truthfully, Ziba or Mephibosheth. Both could have ulterior motives: Ziba might be seeking the king's favor at the expense of his master; Mephibosheth may have secretly harbored a desire to claim the throne for himself. But both could also have noble motives: Ziba may have wanted to warn the king of betrayal; Mephibosheth may indeed be wrongly accused. Mephibosheth's subsequent memory of David's kindness to him further indicates the debt that he owes the king. He claims that he will accept the king's judgment. Faced with one person's word against another, David decides not to investigate further but to divide Mephibosheth's land in half, giving an equal part to each claimant. This, effectively, is neither a full acceptance of either party's story nor a rejection of either claim. But Mephibosheth, faced with this judgment, claims that Ziba can take it all (vv. 28–30). Depending on how one interprets this response, it is either a full admission of guilt or a consummate show of righteousness. Either the wrongly accused has rendered everything to his vengeful accuser in a display of superior morality or the rightly accused tacitly admits his offense. David is content with the response and does not seek to reverse it.

19:31–43
David, Barzillai, and Chimham

David turns now from dealing with persons who have offended (or allegedly offended) him to one who has befriended him during his exile. Again, personal interactions prove to have important political implications. Barzillai, despite his advanced age, accompanies David to the Jordan: he is very old and very wealthy. He is one of those who offered provision to David's weary army (17:27–28). David has not forgotten these acts of kindness and offers Barzillai a place at the royal court in Jerusalem, where David will provide for him at his side. But Barzillai declines the invitation because of his age, his desire to be buried among his ancestors, and because he does not want to be a burden to the king (vv. 31–37). In response, Barzillai proposes that David take Chimham with him, whom Barzillai refers to as "your servant" (v. 37). Some have speculated that Chimham is Barzillai's son, a designation that is certainly possible. If that is indeed the case, Barzillai offers David much by giving up someone precious to him; David is also thereby honoring Barzillai's family by granting Chimham a place in court. In their interaction, both men give something to the other. Barzillai's original gift of hospitality to David results in greater acts of giving. The circle of hospitality, in other words, does not end but continues to expand as time goes by. David's responds to Barzillai's offer with a promise: "I will do for him whatever seems good to you; and all that you desire of me I will do for you" (v. 38). This promise stands out in the Deuteronomistic History since it is unconditional. These are the kinds of promises that God makes to Israel. But God also invites God's people to make analogous promises to one another, to live out of the divine promise by becoming a promise-making people.

There are echoes here of David's covenant with Jonathan: in words, in David's blessing and kissing of Barzillai (cf. 1 Sam 18:1–4; 20:41–42). Barzillai returns home while Chimham accompanies David across the river to Gilgal. Accompanying them are "all the people of Judah" and "half the people of Israel," an indication of rivalries that are yet to be settled (vv. 39–40).

> When Christians take the name *adopted children* of God, they are saying to those who have been legally and literally adopted: I will add your name to my name so that all of us can be seen to belong together, at home in God's family.
>
> Jeanne Stevenson-Moessner, *The Spirit of Adoption: At Home in God's Family* (Louisville, KY: Westminster John Knox Press, 2003), 100.

The episode ends with a frank acknowledgment of rivalries. The people of Israel accuse the people of Judah (likely referring to armed militias from each tribe[16]) of stealing away the king. The Judahites respond by claiming the king as their kin and that he has done them no special favors (vv. 41–42). Far from settling the matter, this ignites Israel's claim that it called for the restoration of David first, that it has "ten shares in the king" (an allusion to the ten northern tribes), and that Judah has despised the other tribes. David does not address these squabbles and hence they are unresolved. Though the narrator claims that the words of Judah were "fiercer than the words of the people of Israel" (v. 43), rivalries will continue to fester. David may owe his return to the people of Judah. But he is king of all Israel, and a chastened king at that. The remainder of his reign will be occupied with matters that address the ambiguities of his return.

20:1–22

Sheba's Rebellion

Almost as soon as David has crossed the Jordan, the seeds of another rebellion take root. The previous section has given readers a hint of

---

16. McCarter, "2 Samuel," textual notes, in Meeks, ed., *HarperCollins Study Bible*, 498.

this possibility, as it charted the war of words between Judah and Israel. Those words now erupt into outright rebellion in the person of Sheba, whom the narrator dubs a "scoundrel" (v. 1). A Benjaminite, Sheba raises the trumpet (a traditional gesture of gathering troops to battle) to summon comrades to abandon David. As he claims that Israel has no portion in David, he gathers the northern tribes. With little fanfare, Israel follows Sheba while Judah returns with David to Jerusalem (v. 2). The stage is thus set for the eventual split of the kingdom, which will occur after Solomon's death.

Before David can address the rebellion, however, he must address the delicate matter of his own household. He places the ten concubines whom he left in the city to watch over his house under house arrest. David does not go into them and instead places guards around the house (v. 3). There are several explanations for this punishment: First, it can be seen as the result of the concubines' failure to watch over David's house (cf. 15:16). Absalom came, Absalom took, and the concubines did not put up resistance. The most charitable interpretation of David's actions here is that the concubines experience the consequences of their rather swift transfer of allegiance from David to Absalom. But this interpretation is probably too charitable toward David. Indeed, it seems more plausible that David is punishing the wrong people. The concubines had been seized by Absalom in a brazen assertion of royal prerogative; the concubines were not collaborators; they are treated as pawns in the game of kingly power. David's interactions with his sons have been fairly lenient. Here, his leniency with them contrasts with his harshness toward the victims of his son Absalom's crime. In the end, David punishes those who are most vulnerable, those who were left behind as Absalom's army was advancing on the city. David misplaces action here: strictness with the concubines that ought to have been expressed earlier with Absalom (and David's other children, such as Amnon). But the psychology of this interaction is actually quite common: in the aftermath of crime, people are often prone to leap on those nearest at hand to extract judgment. If the perpetrator of crime is not available, then the desire to address the original crime can devolve into blaming the victim: "You shouldn't have been hanging out with those people in the first place." However one interprets this incident, it is clear that the disorder of David's household is far from being calmed. Instead, reminders of that disorder are constantly present at the house surrounded by guards.

Having dealt with one difficulty in his own house, David now addresses the incipient rebellion. He turns to Amasa, the one-time advisor to Absalom, and orders him to gather troops within three days to confront the rebellion. But Amasa takes more time than he is ordered. In his first official duty as commander of the army, Amasa fails. This is hardly auspicious for a servant to the king. If David's appointment of Amasa hinged on political considerations (summoning the loyalty of Absalom partisans), it has hardly been good military strategy. David recognizes this failure as he turns to Abishai with the crux of his concern: Sheba's rebellion may prove even more destructive than Absalom's. Pursue him (vv. 5–6). David entrusts this task to Abishai, knowing full well his violent history. Clearly, the king wants Sheba disposed.

Joab arrives on the scene, along with the Cherethites and Pelethites who have served as David's guardians since his time in Philistia. David now entrusts the two sons of Zeruiah with the tasks that were originally given to Amasa. They may be inserting themselves into roles not allotted to them, but they are roles that David does not explicitly forbid them. As the pursuit of Sheba commences, it is clear who is really in charge of the army. Amasa reappears to meet Joab in Gibeon, just north of Jerusalem. The troops have not traveled far and before they get much farther, Joab wants to deal with the one who seems not fully up to the task. Joab resents Amasa because of his military incompetence and because he has replaced Joab as commander. He approaches Amasa in a gesture of peace, asking him if all is well, even referring to Amasa as his "brother." A gesture of a kiss belies the real intention, and as Joab approaches Amasa in peace, he stabs the man who constitutes a threat to his position, killing him with one swift jab, spilling his entrails on the ground (vv. 7–10). The matter, in typical Joab fashion, is settled swiftly, impulsively, and violently. Joab has made a fateful decision: before the pursuit of Sheba can continue, the internal problem of Amasa's leadership must be squashed.

But even Amasa's death has not settled the matter. Amasa's body

lies on the highway, as a man of Joab announces that the army must
follow Joab. But as they progress, the soldiers keep stopping to view
the carnage in the road. The man then decides to hide the evidence
of Amasa's death by moving him into a field and throwing a garment
over the body. There is no proper burial, no last rites. The corpse is
simply an obstacle to progress in the march northward (vv. 11–13).
It goes without saying that this is not the way to treat the king's commander, but the story is told without passing judgment on the sons
of Zeruiah.

Sheba, meanwhile, has lodged in the far north of the kingdom. He
has moved, symbolically, as far away from Jerusalem (and David) as
he can get and still be among the Israelite tribes. His refuge in Abel
of Beth-maacah, apparently, is not very secure. Joab's troops batter
the city wall to break it down, a siege that provokes negotiation, as
a "wise woman" from the city asks for Joab (vv. 14–16). Her role is
reminiscent of Joab's own use of a wise woman to persuade David
to let Absalom return to Jerusalem (14:1–24). But in this case,
the woman speaks first: she speaks of her faithfulness and that she
comes in peace. She accuses Joab of trying to destroy a city that "is
a mother in Israel," a prominent place. She claims that Joab is swal-
lowing up the heritage of the Lord. Joab's disavowal of these charges
points to the threat that Sheba poses to Israel: Sheba is the one who
has lifted his hand against the king. If the city were to give up Sheba,
Joab would withdraw the siege. The woman answers with a proposal
beyond what even Joab proposes. She outguns even the impulsive
Joab with the promise that Sheba's head will be thrown over the
city wall. It is a symbolic form of killing, vanquishing the rebellion
by decapitating its leader, graphically and gratuitously violent. But,
as Polzin notes, "Those who oppose David are typically subject to
beheading," such as Goliath, Saul, Ishbosheth, and Shimei.[17] The
"wise" plan is executed and the head is tossed over the walls like a
piece of offal. Joab sounds the trumpet as the troops disperse and
Joab returns to the king (vv. 17–22). But the carnage has been substantial: the king's commander has been killed in a sneak attack, his
corpse abandoned along the highway; the rebel has been executed

---

17. Polzin, *David*, 199–200. Polzin claims that "blood flows from the heads of David's enemies
more often than with any other character in the Bible." Ibid., 199.

while his head has been treated as a trophy.

The unrest of David's household, the rebellion of his son, and David's eventual restoration have given rise to further acts of violence. There is much that continues to be unsettled: between northern and southern tribes, between members of David's household as the king faces the remaining years of his reign. Memories of the past will occupy much attention during these years. To those memories—and to David's legacy—the narrative now turns.

> Spears and swords of iron we leave to those who, alas, consider human blood and swine's blood of well nigh equal value.
>
> Menno Simons, "The Writings of Menno Simons," in *Readings in the History of Christian Theology*, vol. 2, ed. William C. Placher, 34 (Philadelphia: Westminster Press, 1988), 34.

2 Samuel 20:23–24:25
Legacy

The high points of the story have already been noted: David has proven to be a formidable king and military commander. A small empire has begun under his reign as David's household has also grown. He has remained a faithful servant of YHWH in times of success and failure. He has united disparate parties within Israel as his own power has increased. He has sinned, attempted to cover up his sin, and shown remorse. He has mismanaged internal family affairs that have led to outright rebellion in the nation. And he has regained the throne a chastened man. These closing chapters are less occupied with describing pivotal moments in Israel's history and more concerned with their legacy for the future. To be sure, critical events still occur: battles with Philistines, David's fateful decision to implement a census, and his purchase of land that eventually becomes the site of the temple. But these concluding chapters mainly offer a series of reflections, and in the middle of them is a king in praise and song. The lasting impression of these chapters, then, is not its exaltation of a king who wields power but a prayer of a king who remains a servant of YHWH. David thus becomes a model for subsequent kings in Israel not because of his virtuosity or because his reign is ideal but because he subjects himself to the living God.

20:23–26
David's Officers

Leaders are only as strong as those that surround and advise them. In David's case, his servants' leadership has been tested thoroughly.

This roster corresponds roughly to an earlier list (8:15–18). After a brief interlude when Amasa held the position, Joab is back as commander of the army. Despite his impulsiveness, Joab still has the king's trust. Benaiah is in charge of the Cherethites and Pelethites, the loyal foreigners who have remained at David's side ever since his exile in Philistia. Their enduring presence is testament to the charisma of David's leadership. Adoram is not listed in the previous roster. A scribal error likely accounts for the discrepancy between "Adoram" in this roster and "Adoniram" in 1 Kings 4:6 and 5:14. He is in charge of "forced labor," a practice that has not received much attention in the story of David. But Adoram's position indicates that David's reign is bolstered by conscripting Israelites for state projects. Israel, which at Passover remembers its own experience as slaves in Egypt, now practices a form of slavery in its own land, where Israelites are forced to labor for the king. Although this practice is mentioned without judgment, it is hard not to sense a reversal of Passover here: Israel remembers its enslavement, yet significant numbers of the Israelites continue to experience it. The king also has a recorder and secretary, those who serve in public relations and document David's reign. There are priests who serve in cultic roles and who assisted in the conspiracy against Absalom. (Intriguingly, the priests listed here are Zadok and Abiathar, not Zadok and Ahimelech, cf. 8:17. Since Abiathar is mentioned in the episodes during Absalom's rebellion, chapter 8 seems to include a scribal error.) Finally, a new position appears: David's personal priest, Ira, who is not of the tribe of Levi. David has looked outside the traditional priestly class when forming his own inner circle.

21:1–14

David Settles Old Scores, Rizpah Responds

Despite the growth of his empire, the closing years of David's reign are not overly prosperous. Instead, desperation comes to the land in a famine that lasts three years. In these days, thousands are struggling for life. David leads the people at this critical stage with what has become a typical posture for him: inquiring of God in prayer.

YHWH answers David directly: the famine has occurred because of bloodguilt in Saul's house "because he put the Gibeonites to death" (v. 1). This killing, however, is never mentioned elsewhere in the Deuteronomistic History, which has led some scholars to suggest the bloodguilt refers to Saul's execution of the priests at Nob. This textual oddity raises several interpretive possibilities: (1) David is acting in response to an incident recorded elsewhere in Israelite lore; (2) Saul's "offense" against the Gibeonites may have been concocted by David's partisans as the excuse for the final decimation of Saul's household; (3) David is responding to other offenses of Saul's household and places the Gibeonites in the position of settling the final score against his house. The Gibeonites, as recorded in Joshua 9, are non-Israelites who saved themselves during the conquest of Canaan through trickery and ingenuity. They are allowed to stay in the land and are granted a special status as "hewers of wood and drawers of water for the congregation and for the altar of the Lord" (Josh. 9:27). In short, they are non-Israelites who hold an important liturgical function in the cultic life of Israel.

David approaches the Gibeonites and asks how he should amend the offense against them. The Gibeonites respond that they do not desire riches, nor is it their prerogative to put others to death in Israel, a surprising claim since soon thereafter, they kill several members of Saul's household. They seem to be asking for David's permission to kill Saul's progeny because of Saul's attempt to destroy them and leave them bereft of the land. Their proposal, indeed, is gruesome: they ask for seven of Saul's sons to be impaled "before the LORD at Gibeon on the mountain of the LORD" (vv. 3–6). The scene indicates a ritual killing at a holy site in the presence of YHWH. The Gibeonites are requesting to commit a murder that demeans the victims and denies them death with dignity. Instead, the corpses will be exposed to the wild beasts. David consents to their shocking proposal without question. Perhaps here is the desperate attempt of a king seeking to end famine in the land; perhaps it is a leader who will resort to anything—even the sacrilegious desecration of corpses of a long-vanquished foe—in order to bring bountiful harvests back to the land.

David's offer of Saul's sons, however, is not without exception, since he spares Mephibosheth, who enters the story one last time as a reminder of the lasting covenant David established with Jonathan. The sons given the Gibeonites, then, are not descendants of Jonathan, but Saul's children with his concubine, Rizpah, and the sons of Saul's daughter, Merab.[1] By handing over this remnant of Saul's already decimated house, David ensures the virtual extinction of Saul's lineage. Rizpah's appearance is significant: she is the concubine that Abner, Saul's military advisor, seized after Saul's death, an event that eventually led to Abner's—and later, Ishbaal's—death (3:6–4:12). Rizpah held a prominent position in Saul's house, but now, as the former concubine of a deposed, dead king, she is an outsider. As David hands over her two sons to the Gibeonites, he takes away what little she has left. Their death by impaling is humiliating and occurs, oddly, at the beginning of harvest (vv. 7–9). Thus, gratuitously violent deaths are juxtaposed with the bounty of the land (perhaps indicating an end to famine).

If the interactions between David and the Gibeonites represent a long-harbored attempt to right past wrongs (on the Gibeonite side) or the desperate desire to avert further starvation in the land (on David's side), Rizpah's subsequent behavior is a protest against the theology of death and bloodguilt that each of them represent. Instead of acquiescing to her sons' and relatives' deaths, she provides a shred of dignity for the men who were killed so mercilessly. Deprived a proper burial, they are attended by Rizpah as she protects them from birds by day and wild animals by night (v. 10). As Gerald West notes, Rizpah's actions are a "political act of protest. She was caring for the dead because men with power do not care for the living." Her basic acts of decency suggest "women's resistance to dominant ideologies and theologies."[2] Indeed, she lodges protest against several characters: clearly against David and the Gibeonites, who consent to a killing that will avenge past deaths. But her

---

1. Some ancient manuscripts have "Michal" instead of "Merab." Exum notes how either reading demonstrates a drive to silence Michal in the text: "Depriving her of children is a symbolic way of killing Michal." If the sons in question are Merab's, "Michal's suppression and humiliation become complete: she loses her name to a variant. . . . The narrative gives her children only to take them away again." J. Cheryl Exum, *Tragedy and Biblical Narrative: Arrows of the Almighty* (Cambridge: Cambridge University Press, 1992), 90–91.
2. Gerald West, "1 and 2 Samuel," in *Global Bible Commentary*, ed. Daniel Patte (Nashville: Abingdon Press, 2004), 103.

acts also serve as protest against the Deuteronomistic framework of interpreting God in history.

If the Deuteronomist interprets history as the result of God's will, Rizpah's actions cry out against interpreting *everything* as the result of God's will. The episode begins with YHWH claiming there is a bloodguilt on Saul's house. Even if God does not offer the solution of killing Saul's seven sons to address the bloodguilt (that solution comes from the Gibeonites), God does not discourage the ritual killings from happening. In this story, men in power resort to further death to avenge the living, a cycle that breeds further death and eventually neglects the living. If this is the case, her actions are a warning against carrying Deuteronomistic theology too far. Everything that happens is not the result of an inexorable divine will; much of what happens is the result of violent men bent on death and is hence *not* God's will. Perhaps her actions protest against God as well, for the logic of bloodguilt rarely results in healing.

> The exaltation as Messiah and Lord of one who suffered, was bruised and wounded, and lay dead and buried in company with the powerless and tearful, with the exiled and executed of the world, is God's final affirmation that victory rests not with the earth's victors but with its victims, not with humanity's mighty few but with its impotent many.
>
> Alan E. Lewis, *Between Cross and Resurrection: A Theology of Holy Saturday* (Grand Rapids: Eerdmans, 2001), 64–65.

Rizpah's protest, furthermore, invites the church to reconsider how it interprets the quintessential death of its own tradition, the crucifixion of Jesus. Some historical traditions, such as Anselm's, emphasize the importance of an atoning, sacrificial death of a sinless Christ because the debt incurred by human sin is infinitely great: "The debt was so great that, while man alone owed it, only God could pay it, so that the same person must be both man and God.... The life of this Man was so sublime, so precious, that it can suffice to pay what is owing for the sins of the whole world, and infinitely more."[3] Others, such as Schleiermacher, resist making the crucifix-

---

3. Anselm, "Why God Became Man," in *A Scholastic Miscellany: Anselm to Ockham,* ed. Eugene R. Fairweather (Philadelphia: Westminster, 1956), 176.

ion the pivot of soteriology. The cross, in this view, is significant only within the wider context of Jesus' life and resurrection.

It is not just Jesus' death that saves humanity but Christ's incarnation, teaching, death, and resurrection: "Least of all is it proper to ascribe such a special reconciling value to [Christ's] physical sufferings. . . . These sufferings in themselves have only the loosest connexion with His reaction against sin."[4] The danger of Anselm's perspective is that it valorizes death and risks perpetuating cycles of death. Rita Nakashima Brock likens this version of atonement theory to divine child abuse:

> No suffering which is not bound up with the redemptive activity of Christ can be regarded as belonging to reconciliation. . . .
>
> Friedrich Schleiermacher, *The Christian Faith*, ed. H. R. Mackintosh and J. S. Stewart (Edinburgh: T & T Clark, 1989), 437.

"The father allows, or even inflicts, the death of his only perfect son. The emphasis is on the goodness and power of the father and the unworthiness and powerlessness of his children, so that the father's punishment is just, and the children are to blame."[5] On the other hand, the danger of Schleiermacher's perspective is that it can minimize God's solidarity with the suffering and dying. The challenge for the contemporary church is to uphold Christ's incarnation, death, and resurrection in ways that affirm human life. To claim that Christ has died does not automatically lead us to valorize death; instead, to claim that Christ dies shows that he takes the world's sin as his own, incorporating the world's suffering in the new resurrection life given through him. The One who dies is also risen from the dead.

Rizpah's actions have an effect on the king who contributed to the cycle of death. Hearing of Rizpah's acts, David is moved to provide the final acts of dignity for Saul and Jonathan: He takes the bones and gives them proper burial in the land of Benjamin (vv. 11–14). Saul and Jonathan receive a final homecoming. Rizpah's behavior has changed the mind of a king. Only after that burial does God heed

4. Friedrich Schleiermacher, *The Christian Faith*, ed. H. R. Mackintosh and J. S. Stewart (Edinburgh: T. & T. Clark, 1989), 437.
5. Rita Nakashima Brock, *Journeys By Heart: A Christology of Erotic Power* (New York: Crossroad, 1988), 56.

the "supplications for the land" (v. 14). Perhaps Rizpah has changed YHWH's mind as well.

21:15–22
Further Battles against the Philistines

The Philistines, who have disappeared from the narrative for a time, now return. But in reality they have never really left the story, since reminders of their threat and their military echo throughout Deuteronomistic history. Their appearance at this point in the story allows David to return to the place of many successes: the battlefield. In the context of his former glory, David goes into battle with his troops but grows weary. This is a detail readers have not heard before in earlier campaigns. Perhaps the fighting is particularly arduous, perhaps the king is no longer the warrior he once was. The Philistine Ishbi-benob, who is described in exaggerated form (as a descendant of the giants, with massive armor and the finest weapons), takes aim to kill David. David is only saved by one of his impulsive men who has caused him trouble in the past, Abishai, who attacks the Philistine giant, kills him, and tells David not to battle with the troops any longer (vv. 15–17). If David's last stint on the battlefield has brought success, it is not because of his combat skills. No longer will the king engage in war; others will fight for him. David the warrior is already becoming a distant memory.

A subsequent battle with the Philistines takes place at Gob, a location only mentioned here in Scripture. Again, the Philistine warriors are formidable and legendary: giants armed with sizable weapons, one who possesses more fingers and toes than ordinary humans (vv. 18–20). But, as in times past, David's troops are up to the task before them. Verse 19 contains an independent account of the slaying of Goliath, not by David but by another Bethlehemite, Elhanan. But as in the earlier accounts of campaigns against the Philistines, whatever taunts and technological superiority the Philistines possess are answered by Israelite competence on the battlefield. The formidable opponents are vanquished, as the descendants of the giants "fell by the hands of David and his servants" (v. 22). Even as he is away from the battlefield, the victory comes from David's hands. The king may not be present in battle, but the results are the same as they always were with him in command, as the Philistines disappear from the narrative.

22:1–51

David Gives Thanks

David's exploits as a warrior have occupied several episodes in 1 and 2 Samuel. But as this narrative draws to a close, readers encounter David in a role that has also appeared at critical junctures but is generally less developed than David the soldier or David the king: David as poet and musician. Yet this role is perhaps most cherished in Israel's collective memory of David. For David, according to tradition, is the author of the Psalms, which constitute one of the central pieces of Israel's corporate worship and liturgical life. Here, David prays and sings. According to the introduction, David sang this psalm when God had delivered him from his enemies and Saul (v. 1). Its placement at this later point in the narrative, therefore, turns the reader's attention to the past. But as it does this, the psalm also directs the reader's attention to God's continually sustaining grace. As a whole, the psalm does not merely recall past glory but centers those who hear it (and sing it) in the God who comes near to creation and blesses it as God's own, in a God who hears the cries of the persecuted and pursued and rescues them and a God who takes a man from the tribe of Judah and makes him a herald of God's reign over the nations. The song, which occurs similarly in Psalm 18, contains three sections: (1) a section that emphasizes God's rescue of David in the shaking of heaven and earth (vv. 2–20); (2) a transition that echoes Deuteronomistic themes of God's steadfastness with the righteous and judgment of the wicked (vv. 21–28); and (3) a conclusion that emphasizes God's strengthening of David in battle. Together, the sections express a king in personal devotion and the hopes of a people for the world. The psalm, in other words, combines the personal, the political, and the cosmic and names each as sites of God's intervention and sustaining grace.

David refers first to God as a rock and a fortress.

In an age such as ours where disputes over God language can become quite heated, it is important to recall the expansive biblical heritage. Here is some of the depth and breadth of that heritage: a God who is a rock and fortress that provide refuge for those under siege. The images connote steadfastness, reliability in the midst of turmoil, a place of safety when all seems lost. Military images abound: God is a shield and a stronghold, a savior who rescues from violence.

> A mighty fortress is our God, / a bulwark never failing; / Our helper he, amid the flood / of mortal ills prevailing.
>
> Martin Luther, "A Mighty Fortress Is Our God," in *Glory to God* (Louisville, KY: Westminster John Knox Press, 2013), #275.

The military images found in the psalm, however, are not offensive weapons (such as spears and swords) but instruments of defense. The God who saves David does not blast the enemy to smithereens but protects the vulnerable from violence in the hope that violence will end (vv. 2–4).

In verses 5 and 6, David is surrounded by death as water threatens to drown and engulf him. Here, and subsequently, God's presence and salvation is felt amid the elements of nature. God will hear the one who calls on the Lord in distress as God has heard David. The allusion to YHWH's temple in verse 7 is not to the physical site in Jerusalem but to God's celestial home. Yet the language of temple here also foreshadows the construction of the temple in Jerusalem, a project that David wanted to undertake himself.

God's response to David's plea summons heaven and earth. Several verses outline the consequences of God's anger, which is felt in the rocking of the earth and the trembling of the heavens. The anthropomorphisms are significant here, with smoke issuing from God's nostrils and fire extending from the Lord's mouth (vv. 8–9), ending with a blast of rebuke from God's nostrils that lays the earth bare (v. 16). This depiction of YHWH raises several questions. First, what is the character of God's anger? Though the effects of God's anger are felt throughout creation, it arises from the death that surrounds God's anointed. The anger, most likely, is directed against the forces of death that threaten David's life. God's anger, in short, is for the sake of life. Indeed, the course of that anger (revealed in thunderstorms and the quaking of earth) shows that God's power is stronger than death. The anger of YHWH is not simply to avenge, but to promote life. Secondly, the depiction of God in these verses points to the close connection between natural phenomena and God's agency. The God that David sings to is not a God who remains remote from creation but who reveals God's very self in thunderstorms and clouds, in darkness and in blazing light, in waters and earth.

This is a God who comes near, who speaks through weather and landscapes, in wind and rain. He rides on a cherub (v. 11) and is seen in the coursing of the wind. Twenty-first-century Christians in the West tend to desacralize the cosmos. Weather can be described by jet streams, ocean currents, and colliding air masses. Landscapes are not the footprint of God but are formed by erosion and continental uplift. Lightning is caused by electrical fields in the atmosphere. Of course this desacralization has its merit. Earthquakes do not happen because God has pronounced judgment on some corner of the world (whatever Pat Robertson says to the contrary[6]). Some coastal towns are spared hurricanes, but not because they are more righteous than their neighbors. But the evacuation of the cosmos of divine presence also has its consequences: it strips mystery from the landscape; it can foster attitudes that treat nature as a thing to be used (or used up) rather than revered and preserved. Throughout the world, we are experiencing ecological crises caused, in part, by desacralization.

> The implications of the model of the world as God's body are, first, that we must know our world and where we fit into it; second, that we must acknowledge God as the only source of life, love, truth, and goodness; and third, that we realize that while God is in charge of the world, so are we.
>
> Sallie McFague, "Is God in Charge?" in *Essentials of Christian Theology*, ed. William C. Placher (Louisville, KY: Westminster John Knox press, 2003), 111.

6. In the aftermath of the catastrophic Haiti earthquake of January 2010, Pat Robertson attributed the devastation to a pact with the devil. The founders of Haiti, according to Robertson, "were under the heel of the French. . . . And they got together and swore a pact to the devil. They said, 'We will serve you if you will get us free from the French.' True story. And so, the devil said, 'OK, it's a deal.'" http://articles.cnn.com/2010-01-13/us/haiti.pat.robertson_1_pat-robertson-disasters-and-terrorist-attacks-devil?_s=PM:US.

What is most important about the depiction of God in these verses is God's *nearness* to creation. This is a God who comes close to us, who takes and blesses all creation as God's own, and who invites us to consider God's presence in all things. If we listen to the psalmist here, we are encouraged to pay attention to creation anew. If we do, we also attend to God.

From this soaring cosmic vision, the psalmist turns to the personal. The God who speaks through thunder and lighting is the God who rescues David from waters and those who despise him. The God who is angry at the destruction and death that surround God's anointed is also a God who delights in him (vv. 17–20). This theme of delight is significant, since it indicates that God takes pleasure in creation and loves it intensely. The God who labors for the sake of life does so because the life of creation brings pleasure to the Lord. God works on David's behalf not out of compulsion or an overwrought sense of duty but out of delight. To claim as much has obvious consequences for our own labors as creatures in God's image. We work best not when we are controlled by an obligatory sense of duty or burdened by an excessive sense of attachment to the products of labor. Work is good when it takes its shape from God's delight for the world. And, as James Francis notes, "almost every trade and craft is used in the imagery of [biblical] theism e.g. the refiner's fire, the metal worker's forge, irrigation, bleaching, building, pottery, forestry and threshing."[7] God takes our work and blesses it. Good work is not a monotonous drag but a source of pleasure because it brings something of life to the world and to others, drawing life from God's work for the world.

The song transitions as it echoes major themes of Deuteronomistic history. Here David correlates rescue with his adherence to the ways of God. Those who keep the law can also expect God's recompense and reward (vv. 21–25). God's action to the righteous is consistent and reliable: "With the loyal you show yourself loyal; with the blameless you show yourself blameless; . . . and with the crooked you show yourself perverse" (vv. 26–27). But God's activity is not

---

7. James Francis, "God as Worker: A Metaphor from Daily Life in Biblical Perspective," in *Metaphor, Canon and Community: Jewish, Christian and Islamic Approaches*, ed. Ralph Bisschops and James Francis (New York: Peter Lang, 1999), 16.

simply a tit for tat exchange; nor is it a legitimization of the status quo, as if one's position on the social scale is the result of faithfulness or unfaithfulness. That kind of status quo theology, indeed, is precisely what the God of Israel rejects by uplifting those who are laid low by the forces of death, destruction, and dehumanization and bringing low those who benefit from the poverty of others: "You deliver a humble people, but your eyes are upon the haughty to bring them down" (v. 28). The God whom David praises is also a God of great reversals, who lays bare the inequities and travesties of human life, working consistently on behalf of the oppressed.

> Humanity's meaning is found in the oppressed people's fight for freedom, for in the fight for liberation God joins them and grants them the vision to see beyond the present to the future. Faith is thus God's gift to those in trouble.
>
> James Cone, *God of the Oppressed* (Maryknoll, NY: Orbis Books, 1997), 178.

After this transitional section, the song concludes by connecting David's success in battle to divine providence. God is the one who brings light into darkness and enables David to accomplish great military feats. God provides the sure defense of a shield and equips David for combat: girding the king with strength, opening a path, making his feet swift, and training hands for battle "so that my arms can bend a bow of bronze" (vv. 29–35). This combination of military imagery with God's activity strengthens David in battle but also turns attention ultimately away from battle. True salvation lies not in assured military victory but in the God who saves and will not let us go.

Where David calls on the Lord and finds strength, moreover, his enemies find no salvation: "They cried to the LORD, but he did not answer them" (v. 42). The marked contrast between David's petitions, which are answered, and those of the enemies, which are not, raises a host of difficult questions. Why does God answer some prayers and not others? Does God play favorites, especially with God's beloved, David? Resorting to the Deuteronomistic view of history (that God rewards the righteous and punishes the unrighteous) both answers and exacerbates these questions. If the introduction to this psalm is correct, the "enemies" that David refers to are Saul's partisans. They are not foreigners who worship other gods but devotees of YHWH. The psalmist here does not tell us *why* the prayers of David's enemies go unanswered. But unanswered they remain. For the psalmist, this recognition is not a dilemma to be solved but a mystery to be considered. But perhaps it also suggests that the power of prayer is not so much how it changes God but how it changes *us* by bringing us closer to God's intentions. If that is the case, even when prayers go unanswered, we encounter a God who will not let us go.

God's initiative with David extends not just to Israel but to all nations: "You kept me as the head of the nations; people whom I had not known served me" (v. 44). This verse recalls foreigners' willing allegiance to David (such as the Cherethites and Pelethites) and the growth of empire to include other lands. But it also suggests something more than the addition of lands and people; it claims that God is doing something in David that is also good news for the world, that what is happening in him brings light to the world. For Christians, the climax of this movement is the incarnation of Jesus, who is of the house and lineage of David (Luke 2:4). What begins in the anointing of a servant to the Lord culminates in the gift of God's own son for the sake of the world. Here and elsewhere the God of Israel invites the whole world to partake in fullness so that all nations may find a home in God.

It is this hope, in part, that is expressed in the emphatic declaration "The LORD lives!" (v. 47). God has brought life out of death. Whatever David does is subject to the law that God has given, and whatever he does rightly directs Israel back to the living God. The song concludes by recollecting God's promise to the house of David, God's steadfast love to that house forever (vv. 50–51). That David owes his position to YHWH is an understatement: YHWH's covenant is the pulse of his life and the life of the people Israel.

23:1–7

David's "Last Words"

David's life is not yet over, but the narrator includes these "last words" at this juncture. This poem considers David's personal history and also lists traits of a just ruler. It also appears before another pivotal misstep in David's reign: his ordering of a census. Though chronologically they are not David's last words in the story (he has much more to say before he dies in 1 Kings 2:10), they read as an act of thanksgiving to YHWH and of hope for the future of David's house.

The poem begins with several names for David: He is Jesse's son and also the man God anointed and exalted, but most conspicuously, David is "the favorite of the Strong One of Israel" (v. 1). Many episodes attest to David as God's beloved: he is favored by God, sometimes in ways that defy logic. It is no exaggeration to claim him as the favorite son. "Strong One" can also be translated as "stronghold" or "fortress," connoting the refuge that David finds in God time and again. David's first words in the poem refer to the Spirit of the Lord, which speaks through him (v. 2). These words capture much of David's story. As God's beloved, he is blessed by God's spirit, which guides his speech and sustains his life. In the life of David, we see how the Spirit of the Lord does not hover above history but enters into human life. As Eugene Rogers notes, "The Spirit rests on material bodies in the economy, because she rests on the Son in the Trinity."[8] God's spirit gets expressed through tongues and touch, in the concrete histories of peoples and cultures. The Spirit is not opposed to the flesh but needs flesh for its full revelation. We see Spirit's expression in the life of David, a life claimed by God, given for the people Israel.

The poem then turns to characteristics of a just ruler, who rules "in the fear of God." This ruler is like the bright, warm sun that brings fertility to the land on a cloudless morning (vv. 3–4). David then asks a rhetorical question, whether his house is "like this with God." Of course, the answer to his question is ambiguous. If David has aspired to a just rule, some incidents within his reign have been decidedly unjust (including the forthcoming census). But the justice of David's rule, in the end, depends less on the person of the king and more on the covenant that God has established with David's house, the everlasting covenant that will secure David's house.

8. Eugene F. Rogers Jr., *After the Spirit: A Constructive Pneumatology from Resources outside the Modern West* (Grand Rapids: Eerdmans, 2005), 62.

> Injustice anywhere is a threat to justice everywhere. We are caught in an
> inescapable network of mutuality, tied in a single garment of destiny.
> Whatever affects one directly affects all indirectly.
>
> Martin Luther King Jr., "Letter from a Birmingham City Jail," in *A Testament of Hope: The Essential
> Writings and Speeches of Martin Luther King, Jr.*, ed. James M. Washington (San Francisco: HarperCol-
> lins, 1986), 290.

The song concludes by contrasting God's relentless hold on
David's house with the state of the godless, those who pay no heed
to the law. Unlike David, they will not be held fast but "thrown away"
like thorns. Unlike the covenant, which is everlasting, the lifespan of
the godless is limited: they will be consumed "in fire on the spot"
(vv. 5–7). Where David is touched and embraced by God's spirit, so
that his house will endure forever, the godless experience the touch
of God (and the governance of the just ruler) as a fire that destroys.
As God's spirit rests on the body, it is experienced by the just and
unjust in different ways: in ways of blessing and ways of judgment.

FURTHER REFLECTIONS
Election

The themes of covenant, blessing, and judgment contained in
David's song of thanksgiving provoke further questions about election: God's initiative in choosing a people for relationship. Few doc-
trines have provoked as much debate within the church as this one.
Election, however, is deeply rooted in Deuteronomistic theology:
"For you are a people holy to the LORD your God; the LORD your God
has chosen you out of all the peoples on earth to be his people, his
treasured possession" (Deut. 7:6). One cornerstone to Israel's identity is that it has been chosen by God for covenant, a relationship
that is to be a light for the nations (Isa. 42:6). In this framework, election is a statement first and foremost about God and second about
a corporate people and only derivatively about individuals.

Much of the struggle over Christian appropriation of this theme
is related to the church's tendency, over time, to narrow the theo-
centric and corporate focus on election to individuals, to the

question of who is "inside" and "outside" God's electing grace. Election (and its correlate, predestination) are significant for Augustine's dispute with Pelagius. Whereas Pelagius argued that human beings were free to sin or not to sin, Augustine stressed our bondage to sin and need for grace: "Free choice alone, if the way of truth is hidden, avails for nothing but sin."[9] Election, for Augustine, is a corollary to salvation by grace. Though the Augustinian parameters of election echo throughout the Middle Ages, John Calvin (and the subsequent Reformed tradition) emphasize the full-blown logic of election. God does not only elect some for salvation, God also withholds salvation from others: "God is said to have ordained from eternity those whom he wills to embrace in love, and those upon whom he wills to vent his wrath. Yet he announces salvation to all men indiscriminately."[10] For Calvin, however, election does not elevate one class of persons over another; election, rather, summons us to serve others and the common good: "God's electing of us was in order to call us to holiness of life."[11] Over time, however, the doctrine of double predestination became a prominent marker of Reformed orthodoxy, reaching its apogee in the Westminster Confession: "By the decree of God, for the manifestation of his glory, some men and angels are predestinated unto everlasting life, and others fore-ordained to everlasting death."[12] At times, this doctrine fostered an obsessive concern over who was "within" the community of the elect and who stood "outside" it. As Amy Plantinga Pauw notes,

> The temptation to construe election as an exclusive privilege afflicts both Israel and the Christian community throughout their histories. . . . But the heart of the doctrine of election is grace, not privilege or exclusion: God works through the particular for the sake of the universal. . . . The election of a

9. Augustine, "The Spirit and the Letter," in John Burnaby, trans., *Augustine: Later Works* (Philadelphia: Westminster, 1955), 197.

10. John Calvin, *Institutes of the Christian Religion* 3.24.17; ed. John T. McNeill, trans. Ford Lewis Battles, LCC (Philadelphia: Westminster Press, 1960), 2:985.

11. Calvin, "Election Is to Service," in *Reformed Reader: A Sourcebook in Christian Theology*, vol. 1, ed. William Stacy Johnson and John H. Leith (Louisville, KY: Westminster/John Knox Press, 1993), 94.

12. The Westminster Confession of Faith, in *The Constitution of the Presbyterian Church (U.S.A.)*, Part I, *Book of Confessions* (Louisville, KY: Office of the General Assembly, Presbyterian Church (U.S.A.), 1996), 6.016.

particular group is a blessing from God that enables them to become a sign of God's faithfulness and a source of blessing to others.[13]

More recent attempts to wrestle with the doctrine of election have resulted in different emphases. Karl Barth focuses not on particular communities but instead claims Jesus Christ as the One eternally elected for the sake of all humanity: "In Jesus Christ God in His free grace determines Himself for sinful man and sinful man for Himself. He therefore takes upon Himself the rejection of man with all its consequences, and elects man to participation in His own glory."[14] Christ is chosen and rejected for our sake, and thereby all humanity is included in God's electing grace. Liberation theologians often emphasize another trajectory, by claiming the poor as God's elect: the very ones whom society rejects and despises are those within God's "preferential option." By choosing the poor, God shows solidarity with the lowly, those outside the privilege of the world. For Gutiérrez, "the very term *preference* obviously precludes any exclusivity; it simply points to who ought to be the first—not the only—objects of our solidarity. . . . The poor are preferred not because they are necessarily better than others from a moral or religious standpoint, but because God is God."[15] Finally, some feminist theologians have recovered the doctrine of election as a way of affirming the diversity of creation, effectively thwarting tendencies within the tradition that focus on who is "inside" electing grace. Margit Ernst-Habib writes,

> In Christ, God has elected humanity in all its diversity. . . . We can no longer see others as 'others,' as those whose souls we have to save from damnation; we can only see them as fellow elected and witness to them our understanding of what

---

13. Amy Plantinga Pauw, "Election" in *The Cambridge Dictionary of Christian Theology*, ed. Ian McFarland et al. (New York: Cambridge University Press, 2011), 160.

14. Karl Barth, *Church Dogmatics* II.2, ed. G. W. Bromiley and T. F. Torrance (New York: T. & T. Clark, 1957), 94.

15. Gustavo Gutiérrez, "Option for the Poor," in *Mysterium Liberationis: Fundamental Concepts of Liberation Theology*, ed. Ignacio Ellacuría and Jon Sobrino (Maryknoll, NY: Orbis Books, 1993), 239–41.

election means. At the same time, we remain radically open to what God may be teaching us through them.[16]

The doctrine of election will no doubt provoke continued disputes within the Christian church. However it gets debated, one important consequence of the doctrine is its emphasis that God will not rest until *all* creation takes part in God's abundance. If we take this consequence into account, David's "last words" express God's judgment of the godless in the context of God's desire for the nations: that they, too, might come to know and experience the fullness of God's wisdom and grace in due time.

23:8–39

David's Warriors

Like the poem that precedes it, this list of David's soldiers is retrospective, as it recalls pivotal battles and figures that have enabled David's military success. If the previous poem depicts the king as musician and poet on bended knee, this section recalls another side of David: the consummate warrior, who owes his success to his soldiers. This roster contains four parts: (1) memories of three major warriors (vv. 8–12); (2) a recollection of David's actions during battle with the Philistines (vv. 13–17); (3) memories of Abishai and Benaiah's exploits (vv. 18–23); and (4) a listing of thirty other significant soldiers at David's side.

The exploits of the Three are recounted in legendary fashion. Josheb-basshebeth is ferocious and insurmountable, killing eight hundred with a spear at one time. This unbelievable account is contrasted slightly with Eleazar, who is not indefatigable but fights Philistines until he grows weary. Nonetheless, he clings to his sword. If Josheb-basshebeth is ferocious, Eleazar is tenacious and unwilling to surrender. Both kinds of warriors serve the king well. But the narrator also notes that their victory in battle is due to the Lord who brings it. Third in this roster is Shammah, who defends Lehi as the

---

16. Margit Ernst-Habib, "'Chosen by Grace': Reconsidering the Doctrine of Predestination," in *Feminist and Womanist Essays in Reformed Dogmatics*, ed. Amy Plantinga Pauw and Serene Jones (Louisville, KY: Westminster John Knox Press, 2006), 93.

Israelite army flees from the Philistines. Standing in the middle of
a field of lentils (symbolizing the riches and fertility of the land),
Shammah takes his stand against the invaders alone. In the face of
overwhelming odds, he succeeds (vv. 8–12). Again, the narrator
claims this miraculous victory comes from the hand of YHWH
(recalling Samson's earlier defense of Lehi from the Philistines in
Judg. 15:9–19).

From these exploits, the narrative briefly considers David's
behavior as commander of troops. The episode seems to have
occurred during David's time of exile, on the run from Saul, since
it occurs when David is at the stronghold of Adullam. While he
is there, David hears of the Philistines garrisoned in Bethlehem,
his hometown (vv. 13–14). David's words to his men express his
mourning for Bethlehem and his thirst: "O that someone would
give me water to drink from the well of Bethlehem that is by the
gate!" (v. 15). His troops hear the literal sense of his words, and
loyal to their commander, three of them break through the Philistine ranks and draw water from the well. But David will not
drink the water they bring to him, comparing it to drinking the
blood of men who risked their lives on the errand. Instead, David
pours the water out to the Lord (vv. 16–17). His actions reveal
both his devotional piety and his unwillingness to put his troops
at unnecessary risk. He is the shrewd commander who is also a
devout king.

The third section of the roster remembers Abishai and Benaiah.
Abishai is remembered for his impetuous and violent streak. Though
his exploits are legendary (killing three hundred men with a spear),
he is the foremost of the Thirty but does not gain a place among the
Three (vv. 18–19). Benaiah is also noted for heroic exploits, including killing a lion and a "handsome" Egyptian, whom he kills with
the spear he has taken from the man's hand (v. 21). These descriptions, however, are more than legends; they also remind readers
that David's position is secured, in part, by soldiers who undertake
dangerous missions on his behalf. God has anointed, chosen, and
blessed David. But his kingship is also made possible because of the
violence of his troops, both in self-defense and in raids against the
surrounding powers. There is no sugarcoating of David's reign here,

for violence is never far from the scene. David rewards Benaiah by putting him in charge of his bodyguard (v. 23).

The section concludes by enumerating other soldiers who are key to David's reign. The list begins and ends with pivotal figures: The first person noted is Asahel, the brother of Joab and Abishai, whose relentless pursuit of Abner, Saul's commander, leads to his own death at Abner's hand (2:18–23). The last soldier is a loyal warrior who becomes David's victim: Uriah the Hittite (v. 39). His presence at the end of this roster reminds readers that despite David's unprecedented military success, his actions as king have not always lived up to the ideals of justice outlined in his "last words." If Asahel is killed because of his ferocity of devotion to his commander, Uriah is killed by a commander who betrays him. Uriah's presence at the end of this list is a haunting reminder of ways in which David falls short. In between these two warriors are many others, most of them Israelites but some of them from other lands (vv. 24–39). The net effect of the song of David's "last words" and this roster of warriors leaves readers with the sense that David owes his very position to others. He is hardly a "self-made man," but a shepherd anointed by God to be king, sustained by God's spirit, surrounded by soldiers and servants willing to undertake dangerous missions on the king's behalf.

24:1–9

Census

Memories of David's warriors fade into the background as David makes a fateful decision in these closing years of his reign. The narrator prefaces his decision with provocative language, noting how God's anger has been "kindled against Israel" and how God "incited David against them" (v. 1). Consistent with the Deuteronomistic perspective on history, these

> **The God of Israel cannot be God of either past or future unless He is still God of the present.**
>
> Emil L. Fackenheim, *God's Presence in History: Jewish Affirmations and Philosophical Reflections* (New York: Harper & Row, 1970), 31.

descriptions point to a God who works behind the scenes, using people to accomplish God's purposes.

No reason is given as the cause of God's anger, but David becomes the instrument of this anger as David is told to conduct a census of Israel and Judah. This incitement of David causes interpretive difficulties, especially since the census is considered sinful (v. 10). If God's anger is the prime instigator of the census, divine anger clearly runs against the divine command. Some have suggested that God's anger functions independently of YHWH in this passage.[17] Exum claims that here readers encounter once again "the dangerous, demonic side of God."[18] The Chronicler, obviously aware of these interpretive difficulties, rephrases this episode by claiming that Satan incites David to conduct the census (1 Chr. 21:1). But for the Deuteronomist, it is consistent to claim that *nothing* happens apart from God's involvement, that no sphere of human activity is bracketed apart from God's activity. Here the narrator makes no attempt to reconcile God's incitement of David to conduct a census with God's judgment of the census as sin. Rather, God is mysteriously and palpably present through it all. Though this theological perspective of God's activity is not the only one present in Scripture, it is emphatic in naming God's pervasive, inescapable presence. ("Where can I go from your spirit? Or where can I flee from your presence? If I ascend to heaven, you are there; if I make my bed in Sheol, you are there" [Ps. 139:7–8].) There are potential dangers, however, to this perspective. When pushed to its extreme it attributes every tragedy and injustice to God's will, rendering God an indifferent autocrat. Richard Mourdock, candidate for U.S. Senate in Indiana, claimed in October 2012 that "even when life begins in that horrible situation of rape, that is something that God intended to happen."[19] It is faithful to argue against this theological position, to protest against the extremes of it, in the name of the God who desires the flourishing of creation. Nonetheless, the Deuteronomist takes a long view of

17. P. Kyle McCarter Jr., "2 Samuel," textual notes in *The HarperCollins Study Bible,* ed. Wayne A. Meeks (New York: HarperCollins, 1993), 506.
18. Exum, *Tragedy,* 119.
19. See http://abcnews.go.com/Politics/OTUS/richard-mourdock-rape-comment-puts-romney -defense/story?id=17552263.

history, as the ill-conceived census yields to a contrite confession and a purchase of land that leads to building the temple. These acts become possible, in part, because of David's sin in conducting the census.

If God's anger incites David, the king takes the task quickly as his own by instructing Joab and the army commanders to count the members of the tribes. David gives no indication of God's incitement and instead assumes the census as his military responsibility: David wants to know how many soldiers are potentially available for future campaigns.[20] He knows that the size of the army (and of the nation) matters. The reader also detects in this command more than a hint of pride, as if numbers provide validation of his accomplishments. Torah stipulates rules for census-taking: In Exodus, those who are registered in a census "shall give a ransom for their lives to the LORD, so that no plague may come upon them for being registered" (Exod. 30:12b). Conducting a census without the proper ritual, in other words, endangers the entire nation. Joab, aware of these risks, attempts to dissuade David, but his counsel proves to no avail, as the king's word prevails. Loyal to the end, Joab follows through on an order that he disagrees with (vv. 2–4).

Census-takers circumnavigate the kingdom, stretching from its southern to northern boundaries. Lasting nine months and twenty days, the census yields a vast number, which Joab reports to David: eight hundred thousand soldiers in Israel; five hundred thousand in Judah (vv. 5–9). Though these numbers are surely exaggerated for rhetorical effect, the numbers duly impress. The kingdom has grown in land and people. David is back at the height of power and has minions at his potential command. It is enough to make any king content, even proud. But, as Polzin argues, the census (and its aftermath) illustrate for Israel that there "is little safety in numbers."[21]

20. David's conducting of the census may not be only an expression of military leadership. Park interprets David's sin in ordering a count as "mimicking God's creative act by counting, and thus impinging on Yahweh's sovereignty and power." Song-Mi Suzie Park, "Census and Censure: Sacred Threshing Floors and Counting Taboos in 2 Samuel 24," *Horizons in Biblical Theology* 35, no. 1 (2013): 32.
21. Robert Polzin, *David and the Deuteronomist* (Bloomington: Indiana University Press, 1993), 214.

24:10–17
Plague

As soon as David receives word of the results, however, he is stricken
with remorse. His guilt in calling for the census is clear. This makes
him, as Exum notes, different from the character of Saul (whose
guilt is often not as clear). And unlike the case of Saul, "God does
not abandon" David, even in the abyss.[22] David's remorse yields to
the honest confession that he has sinned greatly and a prayer that
God will take away his guilt. He offers no excuses, no qualifications
of his actions, just a succinct confession and the desire to be transformed. Here, as in his confession after the killing of Uriah (2 Sam.
12:13), David shows penitence, a willingness to be corrected, and
the hope of transformation. David's relationship with the prophet
Gad is key to this confession. Like Nathan before him, Gad can say
things to David that are impossible for others. Gad offers David a
choice. God will judge David's sin, but David has a choice in the consequences: (1) three years of famine (all of the people and land suffering for a long period of time); (2) three months of David fleeing
before his foes (affecting David primarily but also his soldiers and
subjects in Israel); or (3) three days' pestilence in the land (affecting all of the people in the land for a relatively brief time, though the
deaths may be great). The three choices are offered in descending
order of duration, but some affect the king more directly than others
(vv. 10–13). None of them are good options, though it is possible
that the second option would have less effect on the people than the
other options. In the end, David is faced with a choice of how long
the consequences should last and who, primarily, will bear the brunt
of them. His answer to Gad both reveals his trust in the Lord and
also his own fear. He does not choose an option directly but instead
expresses the desire that Israel fall into "the hand of the LORD, for his
mercy is great" (v. 14). In the end, he leaves the option to God and
trusts God, whatever might come. But his concluding words also
reveal a fear of the second option, as his expression of not falling
into human hands can be interpreted as wanting to spare his own

22. Exum, *Tragedy*, 120–21.

life and reign. His response reveals both trust in the Lord and some degree of self-preservation. Perhaps both are necessary for kingship.

The pestilence comes, lasting the shortest span of time, but with devastating effects: seventy thousand deaths throughout the kingdom (v. 15). As the angel of pestilence verges on Jerusalem, however, there is an abrupt change: God relents "concerning the evil" (v. 16) and instructs the angel to spare the royal city. God modifies even this third option by changing God's mind. This abrupt transition indicates how mercy prevails over judgment *and* how mercy and justice are bound together. Indeed, the very place where the angel stops the pestilence is Araunah's threshing floor, the location that ultimately becomes the site of the temple. Here, where Israel will celebrate the central rites of its cultic practice, where the symbols of the covenant are enshrined, where God makes a home among mortals, is also the place where God's mercy is revealed. The events have clear effects on the king: witnessing the chaos and the carnage, David prays to God that he alone has sinned, that the people who are dying are innocent, that God's hand should not be against them but against David and his father's house (v. 17). Here is conversion from a king concerned with his legacy (as shown in conducting the census) to a king willing to experience the full consequences of his sin, a king who desires to spare his people senseless destruction. Even in this tragic instance, David embodies traits of a just ruler.

24:18–25

A Gesture of Hope

David's final actions in this cycle of stories cast the entire narrative in the context of hope. Amid the ashes of David's sin and its tragic consequences, he makes a critical purchase that results in the central symbol of Israel's cultic life: the temple. This decision is instigated, appropriately, by the prophet Gad, who tells David to erect an altar on the threshing floor of Araunah. As a Jebusite, Araunah descends from the occupants of Jerusalem whom the Judahites could not drive out of the land (Josh. 15:63). David follows Gad's instructions and approaches Araunah, who prostrates himself before the king.

When David discloses his intent to buy Araunah's threshing floor, Araunah offers up oxen to perform the sacrifice. He wants to give the king the first offerings for sacrifice as well as wood to build the fire (vv. 18–22). These actions make a non-Israelite a central player in perhaps the most significant cultic practice in Israel. Here once again the lines between "insider" and "outsider" become blurred. Indeed, Araunah even names God: "May the LORD your God respond favorably to you" (v. 23). David, however, wants the offering and the altar to come at a price (for him) and not gratis. He cannot offer sacrifices that cost him nothing (v. 24), and thus David buys the oxen and threshing floor, builds an altar, and makes appropriate offerings. The transaction between king and subject ends with God's resolution for the nation: "So the LORD answered his supplication for the land, and the plague was averted from Israel" (v. 25). This is more than a happy ending to a devastating chapter of Israel's history.

It directs the reader's (and Israel's) attention to the future. The last verse of 2 Samuel is not a retrospective glance at the glories of the Davidic kingdom, not memories of a king's acts of valor, but a glance forward. The narrative ends with a place: a former threshing floor that now is the site of an altar, an altar that will eventually become the temple of the Lord. These majestic stories end with a hope: that God will have a home among God's people, that all will be well with the land and the people whom God has chosen as God's own. The last verse of this long saga, in other words, ends not with David but with God's affection for the people Israel and the promise that God will not let God's people go.

> Our story of God and with God is ongoing and has no end. . . . Who God is and who we are continue to be revealed in and through our faithful embrace of life. As long as the God of life is with us, time's tale continues. . . . And hope abides.
>
> Flora A Keshgegian, *A Time for Hope: Practices for Living in Today's World* (New York: Continuum, 2006), 222.

Afterword

Writing this biblical commentary has been difficult work. I have spent more time on this writing project than any other in my vocation as a theologian, and I needed the span of a sabbatical to finally finish it. In the process, the stories of 1 and 2 Samuel became a part of my life, more than I had expected. I have wrestled with them, argued with them, been haunted by them, dreamed about them, and been surprised by them over and over again.

The theology of 1 and 2 Samuel has presented difficulties for me as an author. The God of these stories shows partiality toward people and characters who do not seem to deserve it. I have wondered why Saul loses divine favor (no matter what *he* does) and David cannot seem to lose it (no matter what *he* does). Though I am part of a theological tradition that has emphasized God's sovereignty and salvation by grace, I have been surprised how often I have resisted that theology in these stories. So much of the air that I breathe stresses benefits and favor for those who have earned it. So much of American piety stresses blessing to those who are faithful. The stories of 1 and 2 Samuel have exposed how potent these cultural winds have been in my thinking and living. The stories, indeed, question much in our culture and church practice, perhaps especially when we resist the stories.

The Deuteronomist is confident that God's will is achieved on earth. The authors and editors of these stories do not glibly claim that *everything* in history happens according to a preordained divine plan (that would be fate), but they are convinced that God's is the guiding hand of history, present even amid the horrors and anguish of personal and corporate tragedy. The way that God chooses and the way that God is present amid tragedy (even as tragedy's cause) has also caused me to struggle. There is much over the course of human history that I do not want to claim as God's will. As I have continued to read these stories, I have also sensed struggle within Deuteronomistic history over these questions. Questions about God's activity in history, no doubt, are as old as biblical faith. The stories of 1 and 2 Samuel do not resolve every question about God's cause or will, but they do point to a divine presence that cannot be avoided, ignored, or shaken. Wherever Israel finds itself, God is already there.

The God of 1 and 2 Samuel chooses surprising people to accomplish God's purposes in history. David is a surprising choice for king. In these stories God makes choices that defy logic. How can it make sense that God would make an "everlasting" covenant with a king who displays such flawed character? Reading these stories has caused me to ask questions about this God (and the doctrine of election) all over again. Those questions are far from being resolved. But I have also learned from these stories that it is precisely in God's partiality, in God's choosing, that God shows God's solidarity with all creation. The God of these stories, the God of Israel, the God of the Christian church, is not a God who hovers above history and chooses creation or humanity in general. Rather, this God sinks an anchor in history, pledging God's very self to particular people (regardless of their flaws) and thereby showing God's love for all creation. Election and partiality are not the opposite of God's universal love; rather, they are the way God's universal love is made concrete—and even vulnerable—in history. What happens in God's covenant with Israel, in God's pledge of faithfulness to David, also happens in the incarnation of Jesus Christ: a scandalously particular (and partial) outpouring of divine love, not for the sake of exclusion, but for enfolding the world in the divine embrace. The universal needs the particular to become real, to become a living truth.

The word that best captures my experience with these stories over the past years is *struggle*. The commentary has been a struggle to write, the stories have posed theological struggles, the characters of the stories are engaged in all kinds of struggles. Sometimes I have felt the weight of my own tradition in ways that attempt to overcome struggle. One of the legacies of the Reformed tradition, with its insistence on the authority of Scripture alone, has been the sometimes noble and sometimes flawed attempts to arrive at *the* meaning of particular texts. The statement "the text means . . ." has sometimes lurked in the background of my writing. This drive is notoriously resistant to multiple readings of biblical texts. If the Bible is authoritative, how can it say two or three things about one topic? How can a story provoke multiple readings and meanings? But I have found in these texts multiple readings, as readers are invited to view the stories through the angles of different characters (and not just one), to accept the Deuteronomistic reading of history *and* to raise questions of it. The stories, in other words, invite theological imagination and the posing of alternative interpretations. After struggling with these stories, I am convinced that the Jewish tradition of midrash, of imaginative and playful readings of texts, makes consummate sense, especially with these stories. The stories simply cannot be exhausted by merely one interpretation or reading. They are stories, in short, that demand to be struggled with. They have showed me that faith itself is a form of struggle. Faith is not simply trust, not simply receiving truths or even the grace of Jesus Christ. Rather, faith represents a lifetime of struggle with the stories of faith and the presence of Christ that continue to claim our lives.

Finally, writing on 1 and 2 Samuel has made me reflect on the significance of story in Christian faith. For all the church's diversity, one thing that unites Christians across cultures is the shared stories of the Bible. Many things can be said about the Bible: it is an ancient book, a dangerous book, a revolutionary book, the church's book, a book of God's word, a book that orients its readers in the world. But perhaps at its most basic level, the Bible is a book of stories. It is not so much a book of propositions, timeless truths, or laws. Of course the Bible contains some propositions and plenty of laws. But what gives these laws and truths their roots are the stories underneath them, the stories that have become a part of so many cultures across time: of Noah and the flood, of God's covenant with Abraham, of David and Goliath, of Jesus in the wilderness and his ministry, trial, death, and resurrection. The stories of Scripture make the church a people of stories. These stories seep into our bones and stay there even when we find ourselves so disillusioned by the church or the faith that we leave it. We are formed by stories, bound together by stories, and have hope in the grandest story of all: the homecoming of all creation to the new life of God's reign. As we are shaped by and struggle with the stories of biblical faith, we are invited to find our own stories within them. What makes Christian faith compelling, in the end, is not its rational arguments, not its proofs, not its propositions, and not even its best theologies. What keeps us coming back to faith is its stories: stories that tell the truth about the human condition, our shared corporate life, and the life God gives to the world. First and Second Samuel contain plenty of stories like these. That is why we return to them again and again. They are stories worth a lifetime of telling.

Selected Bibliography

Aquinas, Thomas. *Summa Theologica*. Vols. 1–5. Translated by the Fathers of the English Dominican Province. Notre Dame, IN: Ave Maria, 1981.

Barth, Karl. *Church Dogmatics*. Vols. I–IV. Edited by G.W. Bromiley and T.F. Torrance. Edinburgh: T & T Clark.

Brock, Rita Nakashima. *Journeys by Heart: A Christology of Erotic Power*. New York: Crossroad, 1988.

Brueggemann, Walter. *First and Second Samuel*. Louisville, KY: John Knox Press, 1990.

Calvin, John. *Institutes of the Christian Religion*. Edited by John T. McNeill. Translated by Ford Lewis Battles. LCC 20–21. Philadelphia: Westminster Press, 1960.

De La Torre, Miguel A. *Handbook of U.S. Theologies of Liberation*. St. Louis: Chalice, 2004.

Exum, J. Cheryl. *Fragmented Women: Feminist (Sub)versions of Biblical Narratives*. Valley Forge, PA: Trinity Press International, 1993.

_____. *Tragedy and Biblical Narrative: Arrows of the Almighty*. Cambridge: Cambridge University Press, 1992.

Franke, John R., ed. *Ancient Christian Commentary on Scripture: Old Testament IV, Joshua, Judges, Ruth, 1–2 Samuel*. Downers Grove, IL: InterVarsity, 2005.

Green, Barbara. *King Saul's Asking*. Collegeville, MN: Liturgical Press, 2003.

Gutiérrez, Gustavo. *A Theology of Liberation.* Translated and edited by Caridad Inda and John Eagleson. Maryknoll, NY: Orbis, 1988.

Hertzberg, Hans Wilhelm. *I & II Samuel.* Translated by J. S. Bowden. Philadelphia: Westminster Press, 1964.

Keller, Catherine. *On the Mystery: Discerning God in Process.* Minneapolis: Fortress, 2008.

King, Martin Luther Jr. *A Testament of Hope: The Essential Writings and Speeches of Martin Luther King, Jr.* Edited by James M. Washington. San Francisco: HarperCollins, 1986.

Park, Andrew Sung. *The Wounded Heart of God: The Asian Concept of Han and the Christian Doctrine of Sin.* Nashville: Abingdon, 1993.

Polzin, Robert. *David and the Deuteronomist.* Bloomington: Indiana University Press, 1993.

_____. *Samuel and the Deuteronomist.* San Francisco: Harper & Row, 1989.

Schleiermacher, Friedrich. *The Christian Faith.* Edited by H. R. Mackintosh and J. S. Stewart. Reprint, Edinburgh: T. & T. Clark, 1989.

Steussy, Marti J. *Samuel and His God.* Columbia: The University of South Carolina Press, 2010.

van Wijk-Bos, Johanna W. H. *Reading Samuel: A Literary and Theological Commentary.* Macon, GA: Smyth & Helwys, 2012.

Index of Scripture

Index of Subjects

Nabal, 149–52

Nahash, 73–74, 211–12

Naioth, 125–26

nakedness, 125–26, 130, 146, 199, 212

Naomi, 242

narrative, significance in Christian faith, 297

Nathan, 226, 292
  admonishing David, 220–24
  oracle of, 187, 201–5
  parable of, 220, 230

nations, 2, 5–7, 59–60, 80, 95

Nazi regime, 163, 168, 207

nazirites, 20

necromancy, 157

Niebuhr, Reinhold, 159

Noah, 112, 297

Nob, 35, 133–34, 140, 272

Obed-edom the Gittite, 197–98

obedience to God, 36, 92

officers, David's, 271–76

oppression, 2, 11, 19–20, 26, 49, 68, 73–74, 90, 116, 139, 281. *See also* injustice

oracle
  David's "last words," 282–84, 287
  and house of Eli, 141
  Nathan's, 187, 201–5

order, 136

outsiders, 6–7, 26, 137, 161, 165, 197, 217, 242, 257, 273, 294

pacifism, 93–95

Paltiel, 181–82

parable, Nathan's, 220, 230

Paran, wilderness of, 149

Park, Andrew Sung, 19

Park, Song-Mi Suzie, 251, 291n20

Passover, 66, 271

patriarchy, 2, 16, 19, 26, 28, 117, 150, 200, 248n9

patriotism, 159

Paul, 62, 109

Paulsell, Stephanie, 216

Pauw, Amy Plantinga, 106, 285

peace, 22–23, 49, 68, 107, 123, 130,

  150–51, 162, 213, 234, 250, 267–68

pacifism, 93–95

Pelagius, 285

Pelethites, 242, 267, 271, 282

Peninnah, 17, 19–20

personhood, 2–5
  infinite worth of each, 224
  the personal, theme of, 15
  reason and, 192
  the self, 42n32, 159

petitionary prayer, 20–21, 25

Philistia, 43, 47, 50, 80, 111–12, 115, 135, 142, 156, 158, 162, 164, 174, 194–95, 197–98, 267, 271

Philistines, 156, 187
  ark as captured by, 42–49
  battles with, 42–46, 79–86, 91, 142–43, 167–69, 194–95, 206, 276–77
  David as dismissed by army of, 161–64
  David conquering, 206
  David's refuge among, 155–57
  defeating Israel, 167–69
  god of, 47–48
  Jonathan and defeat of, 84–86
  Samuel and defeat of, 52–57
  technology of, 111
  as threat to Israel, 43
  as uncircumcised, 114, 167, 169, 174
  See also individual names, e.g., Goliath; *specific locations,* e.g., Gath; Keilah

Phinehas, 43, 45–46. *See also* Eli: sons of

Pickstock, Catherine, 233

piety, 15, 17, 58, 159, 177, 187, 217, 224–26, 288
  American, 295
  anger and, 197
  appearance of, 96
  patriotism and, 159
  politics and, 86–90, 92, 159, 177
  public, 58, 92, 99

place, 43, 55–57, 201–3, 294
  and displacement, 57
  See also home; land

www.ingramcontent.com/pod-product-compliance
Lightning Source LLC
Chambersburg PA
CBHW021958090426
42811CB00001B/79